ABORIGINAL PEOPLES IN CANADIAN CITIES

Indigenous Studies Series

The Indigenous Studies Series builds on the successes of the past and is inspired by recent critical conversations about Indigenous epistemological frameworks. Recognizing the need to encourage burgeoning scholarship, the series welcomes manuscripts drawing upon Indigenous intellectual traditions and philosophies, particularly in discussions situated within the Humanities.

Series Editor:
Dr. Deanna Reder (Métis), Assistant Professor, First Nations Studies and English, Simon Fraser University

Advisory Board:
Dr. Jo-ann Archibald (Sto:lo), Associate Dean, Indigenous Education, University of British Columbia

Dr. Kristina Fagan (Labrador-Métis), Associate Professor, English, University of Saskatchewan

Dr. Daniel Heath Justice (Cherokee), Associate Professor, Indigenous Studies and English, University of Toronto

Dr. Eldon Yellowhorn (Piikani), Associate Professor, Archaeology, Director of First Nations Studies, Simon Fraser University

For more information, please contact:
Lisa Quinn
Acquisitions Editor
Wilfrid Laurier University Press
75 University Avenue West
Waterloo, ON   N2L 3C5
Canada
Phone: 519-884-0710 ext. 2843
Fax: 519-725-1399
Email: quinn@press.wlu.ca

ABORIGINAL PEOPLES IN CANADIAN CITIES

Transformations and Continuities

Heather A. Howard and Craig Proulx, editors

WILFRID LAURIER
UNIVERSITY PRESS

Wilfrid Laurier University Press acknowledges the financial support of the Government of Canada through its Canada Book Fund for its publishing activities.

Library and Archives Canada Cataloguing in Publication

Aboriginal peoples in Canadian cities : transformations and continuities / Heather A. Howard and Craig Proulx, editors.

(Indigenous studies)
Includes bibliographical references and index.
Also issued in electronic format.
ISBN 978-1-55458-260-0

1. Native peoples—Urban residence—Canada. 2. Native peoples—Canada—Social conditions. 3. Community development—Canada. I. Howard, Heather A., 1966– II. Proulx, Craig, 1955– III. Series: Indigenous studies series

E78.C2A1485 2011   305.897'071   C2010-907864-0

Electronic formats.
ISBN 978-1-55458-314-0 (PDF), ISBN 978-1-55458-345-4 (EPUB)

1. Native peoples—Urban residence—Canada. 2. Native peoples—Canada—Social conditions. 3. Community development—Canada. I. Howard, Heather A., 1966– II. Proulx, Craig, 1955– III. Series: Indigenous studies series (Online)

E78.C2A1485 2011b   305.897'071   C2010-907865-9

Cover design by David Drummond. Cover image by Rosary Spence. Text design by Angela Booth Malleau.

This book is printed on FSC recycled paper and is certified Ecologo. It is made from 100% post-consumer fibre, processed chlorine free, and manufactured using biogas energy.

Printed in Canada.

RECYCLED
Paper made from
recycled material
FSC
www.fsc.org   FSC® C103567

For Susan Applegate Krouse,
friend, colleague, mentor,
Heather

and for Dianne Garrett, the love of my life
Craig

Contents

1

Transformations and Continuities
An Introduction

Heather A. Howard and Craig Proulx

Since the 1970s, more Aboriginal peoples have lived in Canadian cities than on reserves and in rural areas combined. Between 1981 and 2001, urban Aboriginal populations have doubled and, in some cases, tripled (Statistics Canada 2005).[1] Aboriginal rural to urban migration, the flow back and forth between cities and reserves, and the development of urban Aboriginal communities represent some of the most significant shifts in the histories and cultures of Aboriginal people in Canada. Nonetheless, the topic has been largely neglected in Aboriginal studies across disciplines, or much of the existing literature is outdated or policy-oriented rather than scholarly in approach.

The studies of urban Aboriginal community and identity presented in this volume offer innovative perspectives on cultural transformation and continuity. They demonstrate how comparative examinations of the diversity within and across urban Aboriginal experiences contribute to broader understandings of the relationship between Aboriginal people and the Canadian state, and to theoretical debates about power dynamics in the production of community and in processes of identity formation, with consideration of factors such as class, gender, and resistance to colonial structures.

The contributors to this volume present an interdisciplinary range of perspectives from academics and community practitioners, junior and senior researchers, and Aboriginal and non-Aboriginal scholars in dialogue. The authors discuss existing and emerging key themes in transformed and transforming urban Aboriginal contexts. Most of the authors in this volume are directly engaged in urban Aboriginal communities and contribute narratives of unique experiences and aspects of urban Aboriginal life based on this engagement. We demonstrate the wide variety of individual, community, and cultural experiences that make up life in cities for many Aboriginal peoples. This volume provides a much-needed view of Aboriginal life in Canadian cities, in contrast and comparison to the existing American literature on this topic.

Many non-Native people in Canada know very little about Aboriginal peoples, their history, and current life beyond the simplistic and often stereotypical portrayals provided by mainstream media and culturally ignorant education systems (Harding 2006; Silver et al. 2002). This ignorance is magnified in urban contexts through misconceptions about where Aboriginal peoples can or should live (Wilson and Peters 2005, 398–400; Peters 1996, 2002, 2004) and the relative invisibility of Aboriginal peoples to the gaze of non-Aboriginal urban dwellers (Culhane 2003, 593; Proulx 2003). As elaborated below, a continuing misconception is that there is one homogeneous Aboriginal culture in Canada, when in fact there are many. As a result, the large numbers and wide diversity of Aboriginal peoples and cultures existing in cities today are largely invisible. The chapters in this volume attest to the cultural diversity of Aboriginal city dwellers; for example, Anishinaabe, Haudensaunee, Cree, Nis'ga and other Northwest coast peoples, Dakota, Blackfoot, Blood, and Métis lifeworlds and world views populate the cities discussed herein. Moreover, how Aboriginal people discover themselves as Aboriginal, how individuals live and exploit the options presented to them within the economic, institutional, educational, and recreational urban contexts we survey indicates the diversity of Aboriginal city experiences beyond cultural determinants. A key aim of this volume is to correct the myopia in broader Canadian society to the wide diversity of Aboriginal peoples and experiences within cities.

Anthropologist Laura Nader (1997, 712) discusses the transformative nature of central ideas emanating from institutions that operate as dynamic components of power. Calling them "controlling processes," she emphasizes how they work to "construct and institutionalize culture" (2004, 711–12). It is impossible to discuss Aboriginal life in cities without referring to the controlling processes involved in the historic, multi-sited, multi-purposed, and continuing colonial projects in what is now called Canada. Ideas such as the reputed primitiveness of Aboriginal peoples versus the civilized nature of non-Aboriginal peoples, that Aboriginal peoples live only in rural spaces close to the natural world and not in cities, the inability of Aboriginal peoples to effectively cope with industrialized urban life, and that Aboriginal peoples must be benevolently managed by paternalistic non-Aboriginal actors continue to have negative symbolic and material effects on Aboriginal peoples living in cities (Andersen and Denis 2003; Wilson and Peters 2005; Peters 1996, 2004; Furniss 1992).

Ongoing colonial-based stereotypes of Aboriginal peoples as dysfunctional, addicted, incapable, and violent promoted in the media and in the popular imagination also structure how Aboriginal individuals, families, and cultures are perceived as well as their access to the "good life" in cities (Lawrence 2004; Proulx 2003; Sanderson and Howard-Bobiwash 1997). Discourse that so-called "race-based" affirmative action to correct the above misconceptions and practices offends against equality also negatively affects Aboriginal peoples in cities (Curry 2006, A8). Continuing boundary battles between the federal and provincial governments over who has responsibility for Aboriginal peoples in cities, deriving from the Constitutional Act subsection 91(24), are pivotal controlling processes whose capillary power constrains current and potential urban Aboriginal lifeworlds.

These contexts combine to mediate and control Aboriginal and non-Aboriginal relations in cities and beyond. We are in agreement with Chris Andersen and Claude Denis's (2003) assertion that "we need to start thinking about urban communities as legitimate communities, rather than depositories of poverty and pathology. Urban Native communities are real, they endure, they are growing, and it is long past the time when we can make the mistake of perceiving them as vestiges or missives of some more legitimate land-based community.... They are the source of new forms of culture, association and self-perception—both individual and collective—about what it means to be Aboriginal" (385).

Discourses of tradition, kinship, self-identification, social identification, spirituality, community, and authenticity are further controlling processes strategically and tactically, mobilized by Aboriginal peoples across a host of urban domains. How one is socially perceived in terms of kinship, for example, or adherence to particular cultural traditions mediates life in cities. Individual and social positioning and access to resources are arbitrated by one's familial and cultural relations and how effectively this relationality is deployed. Discourses are mobilized by agency elites within Aboriginal social action agencies and have significant individual and social consequences (Howard 2004; Proulx 2003). Reclamation and decolonization of these processes are woven through many urban lives and provide contexts for each of the discussions in this book.

Identities

Issues of identity and its reclamation and retention, both individually and collectively, have been and continue to be a central issue for Aboriginal peoples generally (RCAP 1993, 1996; Sinclair 1994; Lobo 2001). Aboriginal peoples in cities have many of the same identity concerns as Aboriginal people living on reserves and in rural communities, and they utilize many of the same identity processes and markers. Cultural origin stories told as part of oral traditions, kinship, status, and blood quantums are very much a part of common sense objective identification and solidarity in both rural and urban contexts (Proulx 2003, 2006; Garroutte 2003; Lobo and Peters 2001, Jackson 2002).

Aboriginal lands and spirituality also continue to have traditional resonance and promote particular forms of identity, agency, and solidarity (Howard 2004, 65; Wilson and Peters 2005; Rice 2004); however, although Aboriginal land is a predominate resource used in the construction of reserve-based Aboriginal identities, connections to land can be complex in urban settings. On the surface, cities have not retained the qualities of the land that sustain Aboriginal cultural practices and therefore are not suitable places of, or resources for, Aboriginal identification (Rice 2004, 2); however, the discussion of alienation from the land as a factor in the special circumstances affecting Aboriginal people in cities is perhaps overly entrenched in dichotomies that oppose Aboriginal and urban, which is critiqued throughout this volume.

Although there may be some truth to the idea that cities are rootless, temporary constructions disconnected from the natural world it does not necessarily follow that Aboriginal people are particularly powerless and alienated in the urban context. Instead, Aboriginal people in cities actively make the urban place their space. To suggest that that these urban Aboriginal spaces are somehow artificial because they are constructed reifies the problematic idea that Aboriginal people are more natural than cultural beings, and bolsters counterproductive posturing about the authenticity of urban Aboriginal peoples' practices of culture. These perspectives uncritically accept a hierarchical arrangement of Aboriginal culture on a rural to urban lineal decline. Perceptions of Aboriginal culture as static and uniform are particularly troubling in discussions of "culture loss" or "between-two-worlds syndrome," which claim that constant interaction with non-Aboriginal culture and lack of access to land, elders, Aboriginal languages, and ceremonies are assumed characteristics of Aboriginal urban existence.

Instead, Aboriginal peoples in cities anchor themselves to an abstract, largely symbolic, sense of the land thereby linking themselves to traditions and place despite the fact that they "may occupy materially 'deterritorialized' zones" (Buddle 2005, 9). As Wilson and Peters have shown, one way this occurs is through the creation of "small places of cultural safety in urban areas to express their physical and spiritual relationship to the land... [or] participation in pan-Indian ceremonies and beliefs in the sanctity of Mother Earth [which] are ways of sustaining spiritual and symbolic links to the land" (Wilson and Peters 2005, 403). Alternatively, Howard has documented how Aboriginal community-based programs aimed at re-historicizing the city from Aboriginal perspectives represent urban landscapes as transformed but no less connected to Aboriginal identity (Howard 2004, 229–42). In these ways the land is re-territorialized within the city thereby challenging "hegemonic constructions of place and identity" that restrict Aboriginal peoples to land outside of urban spaces (Wilson and Peters 2005, 405). The active memory of land and efforts to revive it and sustain it, therefore, grounds Aboriginal peoples in cities differently, but actively, despite lived dislocations and disjunctures (Clifford 2001, 481).

Aboriginal peoples in cities may self-identify as Aboriginal if they are unable to embed themselves within or use the above common sense identity markers. They may choose from a variety of resources to construct identities (Proulx 2006); for example, they may identify through a particular cultural tradition after an investigation revealed that their heritage derived from that tradition. Alternatively, those who have some knowledge of personal Aboriginal heritage but no verifiable historical or kinship links to a specific culture may utilize pan-Aboriginal spiritual teachings to build an identity and gain social acceptance (Proulx 2006, 408; Howard 2004, 206–22; Wilson and Peters 2005, 403, 407–08). In contexts of culture/identity loss due to colonial projects such as residential schools, forced adoptions, and Indian Act marriage rules, self identification may be the only route for individuals to satisfy their desire to establish or reclaim Aboriginal identity in cities (Proulx 2003, 2006; Garroutte 2003). The nature of these self-identifications may vary over time and space under the influence of desire, material needs, the application of political and legal power, and Aboriginal community membership standards (Proulx 2006, 408; Howard 2004, 206–22).

On the other hand, identities/subject positions may be formed within and through historically constituted discursive practices that largely limit personal agency in identity construction. Precisely because identities are constructed within, not outside, discourse they should be understood as produced in specific historical and institutional sites within specific discursive formations and practices. Moreover, they emerge within the modalities of power and thus are more the product of the marking of difference and exclusion than they are the sign of an identical, naturally constituted unity (Hall 1996, 4; Proulx 2006). Lawrence (2003, 2004) points to the long-term discursive power of Indian Act legislation to exclude Aboriginal people not meeting its legislated identity criteria as a central force in shaping Aboriginal identification in both reserve and urban contexts. Moreover, mixed-blood Aboriginal peoples in cities daily confront their white families' often negative assumptions about identity reclamation based on various discourses about what "nativenness is or is not" (Lawrence 2004, 135; Proulx 2006). The discourse, for example, that "'real' Indians have vanished (or that the few that exist must manifest absolute authenticity—on white terms—to be believable) functions as a constant discipline on urban mixed-bloods, continuously proclaiming to them that urban mixed-blood indigeneity is meaningless and that the indianness of their families has been irrevocably lost" (Lawrence 2004, 135).

Throughout this volume contributors focus on identification as a process of construction continually affected by the contingencies of personal agency and/or one's subject position determined by the discursive, material, and symbolic resources and the power of the constitutive outside (Hall 1996). Rather than seeing Aboriginal identity as one-size-fits-all, we see Aboriginal identity in cities as multilayered (Weaver 2001, 243), situational, and contingent on social networks, roles, class, gender, and the application of power within and across these domains (Proulx 2006; Krouse and Howard 2009; Lobo and Peters 2001).

In one way or another all of the chapters in this volume discuss processes of identity construction, reconstruction, and reclamation in reaction to various colonial and neo-colonial oppressions. Stereotypes continue to mediate identification across a host of domains. Through an analysis of newspaper representations of Aboriginal peoples in cities, Proulx outlines the social context of discursive domination that Aboriginal city dwellers must contend with in their everyday relations with non-Aboriginal peoples. Flynn shows how individual healing of colonially based ills leads to community healing and identification in Vancouver and beyond. Reacting to processes of domination and dispossession also take place at the political and collective level, as Miller illustrates in her discussion of Papaschase identity reclamation as a nation within the confines of the city of Edmonton boundaries.

In the context of education options for Aboriginal peoples in cities, Donovan shows that Aboriginal social action agencies and institutions are also potent sites of, and sources for, processes of collective and individual identification. State processes overlap with local cultural and social practices to shape social institutions, networks, and communities in new dynamic ways, as Patrick and her co-authors effectively demonstrate in their discussion of Inuit identity in Ottawa. Howard's historical perspective on the Friendship Centre highlights aspects of urban Aboriginal community organizing in relation to the dialogical character of local and national Aboriginal issues as they impact Aboriginal people who live in cities. Newhouse also tackles the politics of local and national representation in Aboriginal organizations from a personal experience that challenges the limits of Aboriginal urban identity expectations. Buddle illustrates how and why traditional socializing and identification structures such as the family can take a back seat to structures such as gangs, in which Aboriginal youth create alternative cultural codes and new spaces of fellowship in the city—at once tactically seizing a place for themselves and defying exclusion by "others."

The back and forth movement between reserves and cities provides contexts for the discussion of diasporic and transnational identification processes, forcing us to consider the implications for performing Nativeness in reserve, rural community, and city, as chapters from Ignace, Flynn, Darnell, and Patrick and colleagues explore in contrasting ways. Although these articles deal with being Aboriginal in cities, more importantly, they foreground the multiple pathways to becoming Aboriginal in specifically urban ways. Learning of and performing identities through Aboriginal youth appropriation of hip-hop music and evolving graffiti-based art forms described by Ignace illustrate the hybrid, lived, processes of becoming. Darnell is critical of the term "urban Indian" because it reifies the residence of individuals and families whose actual affiliations to space/place and kindred are multiple and alternating. The term also masks the agency of people who attempt to maximize their resources and choose their futures in the back and forth continuum of reserve to urban to reserve and so on. The "urban Indian" does not take into account this diversity of experience and, therefore, fails to stand as a monolithic category according to Darnell. Flynn, on the other hand, retains and capitalizes the "Urban" in Urban Indian to reflect the significance of urban as an identity marker and as defined by the people themselves. Both of these views provide nuance to a highly politicized domain.

Traditions and Modernities

The city, with its thorough transformation of the landscape and complete erasure or control of nature, epitomizes settler colonialism in its reliance on not only the physical but social displacement of Aboriginal peoples, who are in turn positioned by dominant discourses within the untamed world of nature (Peters 1996). As stereotypically "natural" beings, Aboriginal peoples have historically had no place within urban society unless destroyed or utterly transformed. Aboriginal people in Canada have resisted this paradigm in many forms, including within urban contexts where they have rejected being defined in diametric opposition to all things urban.

The processes that maintain the misconception that Aboriginal peoples and traditions are incompatible with city life are structural in origin, labelled "democratic racism" by Henry and Tator (2000, 294; Proulx 2003), and are reflective of the overall perspective of the bulk of the existing scholarly literature about urbanization and Aboriginal peoples produced during the 1960s and 1970s. This body of work focused primarily on problem-centred issues such as alcoholism, homelessness, assimilation, and other elements of Aboriginal "(mal)adjustment" to city life and revolved around measuring the "failure" of Aboriginal people to adapt to city life, success being gauged in terms of assimilation. Aboriginal urbanization was viewed as a process of transition from "simple" to "complex" society. "Failure" was more often attributed to an incompatibility between Native culture and the culture of modernity than in relation to institutional or systemic causation such as racism and the goals of the dominant society to assimilate Aboriginal people at all costs (Howard 2004, 28–93).

A major flaw in this body of literature is the naturalized opposition assumed between the concepts of "Nativeness" and urban. The conditions of urban living, it is claimed, challenge the possibilities of generating and sustaining "authentic" Native cultural communities in the city. While cities are recognized in this earlier literature as complex and rapidly changing spaces, they also tend to be uniformly and universally represented as round holes into which Native square pegs struggle to fit themselves. Inevitably, it is only by chipping away at their edges (cultural, spiritual, emotional, political, mental, etc.) that Native people find "their place" within the urban setting (Howard 2004, 28–93).

As a counterpoint to this perspective Sol Tax, described by Alfonzo Ortiz as "one of the more unconventional minds in the field of American Indian studies," argued in 1980 that generalizations about "the Urban Indian" are in fact not possible, and that the study of Native urbanization needed to be culturally and socio-economically historicized (Tax 1980). The 1980s marked a transition in the approach of Canadian research literature away from presenting Native people as passive victims of urbanization toward practical studies aimed primarily at assisting Native organizations in planning and development (which were also thin on critical analysis) or a focus on how Native people actively construct viable cultural communities. The latter provides insights on urban Native networks, notions of community, and the multi-layered dimensions of class and gender identities (Howard 2004; 2009). More recently, research has moved away from the failure-to-assimilate model and refuted analysis of Native urbanization modelled on the immigrant experience (Peters and Starchenko 2005). In this volume, David Newhouse effectively draws together the evolution of theories about urban Native experience through his own personal account, best described in his own words as culminating in a "refutation of the notion that the urban is inconsistent with the idea of Aboriginal." As he affirms, "My life in the city has not made me less of an Aboriginal person. It has made me a different Aboriginal person."

Another misconception about Aboriginal cultural practices is that non-Aboriginals believe that it is past customs from colonial times that are being revived without reference to historical and cultural change (Proulx 2003, 28). Rather, it is "tradition, the appeal to values and actions that sustain customs and provide continuity to a social group over time" (Warry 1998, 174) that is being revived in new contexts after years of oppression. Tradition is contingent on the particular culture and the history of change that the culture has undergone. Flynn's chapter, which describes the "Plains-style" Arrows To Freedom Drum group in Vancouver, demonstrates the incorporation of inter-tribal traditions of cultural healing within processes of constructing new social and spiritual "spaces" as part of an ongoing phenomenon of sobriety and a healing movement that stretches across Canada. There is not one tradition but many across "Indian country" in North America (Proulx 2003, 28).

In this volume, we are less concerned with judging the authenticity of "invented" traditions, the use of essentialist resources in those inventions, and largely elite intellectual debates about spurious Indigenous claims to cultural distinctiveness. As Sahlins makes clear, "These people have not organized their existence in answer to what has been troubling us lately. They do not live either for us or as us" (1999, 406). Our focus is on the present states and alternative futures Aboriginal peoples in cities are constructing for themselves through the creative use, reshaping, recontextualizing, recombining, and mobilizing of traditional values and actions.

We are interested in how Aboriginal peoples are indigenizing modernity not in terms of invention of tradition but rather as the "inventiveness" of tradition (Sahlins 1999, 410; Proulx 2006, 426n5).

Many of the chapters emphasize that change is grounded in continuity. Darnell focuses on how resource exploitation strategies that derived from traditional hunting and gathering (nomadic legacies) affect contemporary decision-making strategies. She describes a sense of the world—as an abundant source of resources to be exploited on a temporary but recurrent basis—that has stood the test of time and is thus available for application to new domains such as education, employment and access to medical or social services. These examples illustrate for Aboriginal city dwellers and migrants what James Clifford (2001) describes as the process by which "past in the future [empowers a] changing base of political and cultural operations" (Clifford 2001, 482).

Elsewhere Proulx has described Anishinaabe tradition as a dominant model of cultural practice in Toronto (Proulx 2003). Howard has also noted, however, that the multiculturalism of urban Aboriginal communities can present particular forms of resistance or challenges to the dominance of particular traditions. In the Toronto example, practices of "tradition" may be heavily scrutinized from within the community as positions of leadership among Aboriginal people are legitimized through the mobiliza-tion of ideas about Aboriginal identity presented in diametrical opposition to "whiteness" (Howard 2004, 2009). While the Plains/Anishinaabe big drum may be central at large community ceremonial gatherings, diversity is also gently nudged by Haudensaunee, Cree, Inuit, Mig'Maq, and North-west Coast folks, among others, who contribute to urban ceremonial prac-tice with hand drums, dressing in their own traditional outfits, and by sharing stories, teachings, and songs.

In this volume, Patrick and colleagues outline how, by consciously mak-ing the northern customs (e.g., throat singing) part of one's everyday urban life, urban Inuit may seek to belong to an emotional collective 'ter-ritory' that entitles them to fully state that they are Inuit. Indeed, Northern practices and knowledge are desired forms of cultural capital that validate identity claims. Flynn illustrates how the diffusion of Plains-way culture in Vancouver, as opposed to "other ways" such as Iroquoian or Northwest coast ways, structures significant elements of Aboriginal life and has become a central force in the production of alternatively modern Aboriginal cul-ture in Vancouver. Ignace provides a moving analysis of how Aboriginal youth recreate the traditional practice of leaving marks and messages in the caves and rock faces of natural landscapes of the Interior Plateau, by leaving them on the urban and suburban walls of the city and the local reserve. The new tag messages represent clues to the travels and experiences of their producers just as the old cave marks and messages did. Hence, tradition is central to processes of becoming "alternatively modern" (Knauft 2002) for Aboriginal peoples in cities. Perceptions of the past are themselves an important dynamic in emerging identities.

Traditions are subject to the creative, tactical, and strategic ways in which Aboriginal cultures are being produced in cities. Some Aboriginal people bring a relatively complete form of specific cultural knowledge and practice with them when they move to cities. This culture-specific knowledge and practice is then disseminated through urban elders or through the pragmatic actions of Aboriginal social action agencies, as has occurred in Toronto (Proulx 2003). Howard argues that the particularities of the experience of Native urbanization, combined with the socio-political context of Native and non-Native relations in Canada, provide for a unique and intriguing evolution of Native social movements in relation to urban Native community cultural production. Her chapter in this collection describes the history of the Native Canadian Centre of Toronto in terms of its key roles in local Native community building, in power relations surrounding the mobilization and delineation of Aboriginal culture, tradition, and identity, and in national organizing around urban Aboriginal issues. The centre's transformation from a focus on social service delivery to "cultural service" delivery is especially revealing of the mobilization of Aboriginal culture as a resource in collective action. The centre operates in response to social problems, but it is also a nexus of community production through processes of assertion of its authority on Aboriginal culture. The Native Canadian Centre draws upon its long-standing history in the community, which situates its status differently from other agencies as a "sacred" place and space. Here, programs serve more than to address social problems. They create and set models for the "culture" and "traditions" utilized (and challenged) by programs and other Native organizations in the city.

Tradition produces new modes of living in cities, offering a "way of living nicely together" (Monture-Angus 1994, 140) for long-term city dwellers and for new arrivals. This praxis can be appropriated by those who have "a hole in their heart" (Jackson 2002) in terms of their cultural identities thereby becoming a source for pan-Aboriginal cultural production in a particular locale. Hence, traditional knowledge and practice produce cultures in cities and is spread through the incorporation of an "intentionally selective version of a shaping past and a pre-shaped present

[which mediates] the process of social and cultural definition and identification" (Williams 1981, 115). As many of this volume's contributors illustrate, the incorporation of traditional knowledge and practice becomes a
mode for personal transformation and source of belonging for Aboriginal
people encapsulated by and interacting with other urban cultures.

Related to misconceptions about the place and role of tradition in cities
is the settler refusal to accept Aboriginal modernities (Buddle 2005, 36).
Power struggles over the determination of Aboriginal authenticity are
entangled with stereotypical expectations and compounded by a lack of
awareness of the wide scope of modern Aboriginal occupations, new
modes of agency, and community in cities. Aboriginal legal, business,
artistic, and academic professionals are a growing class whose actions
shape Aboriginal life in cities in novel ways. There are many alternative
Aboriginal modernities in cities.

Several of the authors in this volume present Native urban communities
as examples of loss of power and authority in the processes of colonization
and "modernization" and as illustrations of how assimilationist structures
can be manoeuvred to provide spaces for access to power and for its restoration. The book thus adds to more recent studies on urban Aboriginal people that elaborate the idea of community as a source of empowerment and
cultural generation by documenting community building through the
incorporation of local Native historicity and the integration of local identity discourse shaped by resistance to dominant forces.

This process takes place not only within Native communities encapsulated by states but also in terms of the reconfiguration of the state itself,
or at least its historical representations of itself. As Manitowabi describes,
Casino Rama, located on the Mnjikaning First Nation near Orillia,
Ontario, was lauded as an "Aboriginal" solution to Aboriginal poverty
within the framework of neoliberal reform led by Ontario in the 1990s.
Manitowabi challenges this history by demonstrating that as a consequence of latent colonial membership structures and of disparities and
social divisions generated by the casino, many Aboriginal casino workers
have taken up residence in the city of Orillia, where their urban experience
is conditioned by the interactions of Aboriginal symbolic capital and
neoliberalism.

Given the historical relationship between Aboriginal people and the
Canadian state, Aboriginal voices raised in the urban context have not
only advanced the causes of Native people but have done so by calling
into question the very legitimacy of the nation-state, highlighted by the
exposure of the brutal erasure of Native people from the landscape in his-

torically important places. Donovan's chapter examines the Wiingashk Alternative Secondary School in the city of London, Ontario, and its efforts to challenge the history of urban Aboriginal educational jurisdictional politics and factors that have impeded urban Aboriginal student success, including the various "risk" factors attributed to them by policy-makers and administrators. As she describes, Wiingashk uses holistic educational strategies, and culturally sensitive staff who value and validate the experiences of their students, to reverse damage caused to Aboriginal students by mainstream systems.

Ignace shows how Aboriginal youth appropriate hip-hop culture and music and weave the functions and messages of hip-hop music as art of resistance into very localized messages shaped by their particular histories, meanings, languages, and experiences thereby producing new forms of cultural communication. This book touches on how older ways blend to produce individual and collective approaches to modern Aboriginal cultures.

Communities

During the 1990s and into the early twenty-first century, some policy analysis of urban Aboriginal community furthered the misconception that there are no real, functioning Aboriginal communities in cities; there are only dysfunctional or marginalized Aboriginal individuals who, if they are linked at all, are caught up in the same type of class system that binds non-Aboriginal peoples (LaPrairie 1994). In a discussion of the need for Aboriginal involvement in creating policies for urban Aboriginal peoples and how urban as opposed to land-based Aboriginal peoples "have little organizational cohesion," Hanselmann stated, "there really is no such thing as an urban Aboriginal community" (Hanselmann 2001, 20). This myopia is coupled with the continued involvement of the general public and the media in the disciplinary discourse of stereotypes. It denies that Aboriginal peoples have the ability to integrate into a community (Proulx 2003).

The difficulties in delineating forms of Aboriginal community in cities are complicated by late-twentieth-century anthropological theorizing on space and place and their relation to identity and community in response to musings about the artificiality and permeability of boundaries and borders (Gupta and Ferguson 1992). Moreover, the focus on deterritorialization in the context of globalization, which focuses on how production, communities, politics (Appadurai 1991), and identities become detached from local places, and where the displacement of identities, persons, and meanings are endemic to the postmodern world system (Deleuze and Guattari 1986; Kaplan 1987), have further detracted from the processes of production and "practice of community" in local contexts, which are so important to Aboriginal peoples and other communities within cities (Howard 2004; Halperin 1998).

Rather than a literal entity that is impermeable, and territorially and/or ethnically defined, community is seen as imagined or remembered or affected by and connected to global political and economic forces (Gupta and Ferguson 1992, 10–11). Amit (2002, 3) argues that community is now understood less as an "actualized social form" than as "an idea or quality of sociality" and that this turn toward "community as ideation has been associated with a translation of community as a collective identity rather than an interaction" (see also Amit-Talai and Lustiger-Thaler 1994, 123–24). These perspectives pose significant cautionary questions when it comes to examining Aboriginal community production in urban contexts; for example, what are urban Aboriginal peoples' organizational responses to this condition of flux and spatial ambiguity, and what are Aboriginal peoples in cities actually doing to constitute community? (Proulx 2003, 130).

Recent work with Aboriginal peoples in cities in both the United States and Canada provides some answers and points to new directions for analysis. One strain analyzes community constitution interactively and relationally rather than merely in terms of a bounded spatial location. This strain of community analysis locates one nexus of community in social service agencies built by and for Aboriginal city dwellers (Howard 2004; Proulx 2003; Weibel-Orlando 1999). In this regard, community action structures community both in the address to social problems but also through community centres' roles in the assertion of their "authority on Native culture" (Howard chapter 6, this volume). Another strain focuses on the continuing power of kinship, the family, and the home reserve to structure community in cities. The back and forth movement from rural/reserve to urban or "churn" (Norris and Clatworthy 2003) to visit family, hunt, consult elders, or simply to be on the land affects whom is considered a member of an urban community. Moreover, as Ramirez (2007) maintains, this form of "commuting" aids in generating and maintaining pan-Aboriginal culture wherein many different cultural representatives can be part of the urban community.

A further strain of thought useful for understanding urban Aboriginal community constitution is through Aboriginal mediascapes, a concept devised by Arjun Appadurai and effectively applied by Buddle to

Aboriginal radio, films, and television. She describes this process as providing city dwellers with opportunities to learn and/or re-learn Aboriginal traditions, to embed themselves within real or virtual community relations and to participate in cultural production (Buddle 2005, 23–26). Aboriginal peoples, therefore, relationally combine ideational and practical/social action resources across spatial, interactional, and epistemological boundaries to build and maintain community in cities.

Contributors to this book point to a number of ways to conceptualize Aboriginal community in cities. As Darnell notes, it is important to take into account the movement of Aboriginal people to the city from the reserve and back and forth. This can mean that the same individuals are sometimes "urban Indians" and sometimes not so that community does not necessarily involve geographical contiguity. In his discussion of community for the Aboriginal labour migrants in Orillia, Manitowabi, too, moves away from a community defined by physical places of social and cultural activity such as a Friendship Centre. In that instance, community is defined through social networks that have been established at the workplace (Casino Rama), but employment experiences differentiated by relations of power exert a potent structuring force as individuals move in and out of casino work by choice or otherwise. Hence, for the individual, the community is temporary, but the space is permanent, as though a space has been "reserved" for Aboriginals at Casino Rama and correspondingly in Orillia.

Patrick and colleagues point out how "community" cannot be assumed to be an unproblematic or fixed entity, but may be conceptualized abstractly by members who are part of the social networks, cultural practices, and the institutional landscapes that form this non-geographically bounded community. Hence, they emphasize the diversity and complexity of transnational, diasporic, and local processes that constitute and re-constitute Inuit identities and communities in the Ottawa context but also show how the fluid nature of the urban Inuit community in Ottawa has made it difficult to map it in a definitive sense.

Miller discusses the complex processes of coming to know oneself, one's people, and one's place in a space or collective and how this causes us to rethink our ideas of what an Aboriginal community is and can be. She outlines how Papaschase Band identity has been asserted and community built through the Rossdale/Fort Edmonton Reburial Project. Community is reclaimed through asserting the historical existence of the Papaschase Band and its members as the living descendents of the people that lived and died at this site through a land claim. But it is also lived daily through fighting for the respect of those buried at Fort Edmonton, governing the affairs of the Band, and contacting descendents who have been scattered by the policies and actions of a colonial government. Miller introduces into our discussion the concept of hybridity in terms of personal identities, which are always formed and reformed from unique recombinations of heritage and experience. Miller is critical of the normalization of government-created and imposed identity categories while highlighting examples of the persistence of identity despite the aggressiveness of colonial and assimilative measures imposed precisely through racialized categories.

Buddle discusses how traditional views of spatialized community as places of socialization and belonging have less meaning for recent arrivals to cities. She describes how this crisis of place and belonging gets worked out in Aboriginal gangs in Winnipeg. Gangs provide ways to understand new urban territories, and those who are without connections, money, or position are lured by the complex set of emotional and symbolic ties that internally order their members. Buddle problematizes the gang community, and in outlining how community-based programs that help ex-gang members embark upon the long process of remaking their "selves" and embedding themselves in new forms of relationality, she provides insight into how new forms of community arise in cities.

In various ways, the chapters in this volume contribute to conceptions of community as situationally diasporic and geographically rooted, fluid and relational, arising from different material, legal, and ideational contexts to claim or reclaim the power to define and create structures of belonging. Processes of becoming, then, are extended from individual to collective domains. Theoretically these articles draw upon diverse sources. Indigenous knowledge that arises from various "ways" structure understandings of how to live "the right way" in cities (Ryan 1994). The symbolic healing embodied in such "ways" constitutes a major thrust in Aboriginal theorizing about decolonization of minds and cultural production, as Flynn illustrates.

Darnell shows how Aboriginal hunting and gathering theory and practice (nomadic legacies) become reformulated and re-tasked in cities; however, her approach differs drastically from James Spradley's (1970) earlier conceptualization of "urban nomads" and Paul Letkemann's (2004) reformulation. While Letkemann acknowledges that the analogy of the survival strategies of homeless Native people in cities to hunting and gathering societies is not inconsistent with what he observed, he also takes account of the interdependence of rural and urban experiences in his focus on homelessness. Darnell's work is perhaps better situated in relation to Wilson and Peters' (2005) borrowing of the theories of transnationalism, which acknowledges the significance of networks, relationships, and travels across borders and over time, rather than the idea that Native people engage in lineal movement from reserve to city to oblivion.

Other contributors utilize non-Aboriginal theories in order to understand Aboriginal city life and to contribute to decolonization processes. Proulx, for example, utilizes critical discourse analysis to reveal the depth of non-Aboriginal racism in basic linguistic structures, claimed to be value-free, used daily in media representations of Aboriginal peoples in cites and how this constructs social contexts of domination and oppression. How these media practices contribute to democratic racism and neo-colonial regimes of disappearance is foregrounded by Proulx. Patrick and colleagues, using Bourdieu's concept of the habitus, frame how individual and collective practices operate in relation to larger state and political economic practices to produce specific racialized, ethnicized, and/or politicized behaviours and subject positions. They illustrate how these generative practices can be "emergent," "hybrid," and "local" and can also articulate with larger discursive state-sponsored, institutionally produced and historically based constructions of "Inuitness." The chapter also builds on recent theoretical discussions of space, place, and fixed essences to discuss the affects of the Aboriginal diaspora on identity and authenticity among Ottawa Inuit.

Miller uses the post-structural and diasporic theories of Stuart Hall on identity to discuss how the Papaschase Band, dispersed through colonial identity policies and land surrenders, reclaim their identity in the twenty-first century. Buddle critiques older forms of gang theory that tie gang development to social disorganization and economic deprivation. She employs a form of social field analysis to focus on a specific neighborhood, gang node, and family, and connect these with constructs that have been refined over a long tradition of gang scholarship. Her intent is to bring to light a practical understanding of the circumstances bearing on street agency in one subcultural Aboriginal context.

Ignace uses recent theorizing about the role of hip-hop culture and music, how it has been appropriated by young people from multiple ethnic backgrounds on different continents, and how Aboriginal artists weave the functions and messages of hip-hop music as art of resistance into very localized messages shaped by their particular histories, meanings, languages, and experiences. In this project she uses a form of interpretive interactionism, to grasp, understand, and interpret the perspectives and experiences of others. The "others" in this case are not outsiders to her community but others from a different generation. Her dialogic approach to the voices of youth allows us to feel the experiences of generational others' lives, experiences, and standpoints.

The chapters in this volume are based on research with and by Aboriginal peoples in urban contexts across Canada, yet we recognize and regret a gap in eastern representations. This said, we are extremely thankful to our contributing authors, who have made here profoundly rich, valuable, and innovative additions to the scholarly literature. We hope this makes up for uneven geographical coverage and inspires further research and dissemination in these areas. For the most part, the authors have either conducted extensive ethnographic research and/or have engaged their own lived experiences in the crafting of their contributions. They bring together Aboriginal and non-Aboriginal epistemological traditions to provide original perspectives on cultural transformation and continuity. Overall, this volume highlights the different and specific social, political, and legal forces that have shaped Aboriginal peoples' experiences of urban life in Canada.

Notes

A number of the chapters in this volume began as papers presented in a symposium organized by Howard and Proulx at the annual meeting of the Canadian Anthropological Society held in Montreal in 2006. These were supplemented with submissions from contributors who could not attend the Montreal meetings or who responded to our invitation to be included in this volume. We wish to acknowledge the valuable ideas and discussions inspired by all presenters, the audience, and our discussant, Marc Pinkoski, that day. We are grateful as well for the anonymous reviewers' very careful and insightful comments. Proulx also thanks St. Thomas University for research support during the creation of this volume.

1   The contributors herein use a number of terms to refer to Aboriginal peoples. Overall, we will use the appellation "Aboriginal peoples" or "Native" in order to encompass First Nations, Inuit and Métis, status and non-status peoples in cities. Occasionally, we will use terms like "urban Aboriginal communities" or "contexts" as a short-hand with the understanding that these comprise the diversity of perspectives of the authors in this volume, including both objections to (Darnell) and accentuation of (Flynn) the term "Urban Indian."

Works Cited

Andersen, Chris, and Claude Denis. 2003. "Urban Natives and the Nation: Before and after the Royal Commission on Aboriginal Peoples." *The Canadian Review of Sociology and Anthropology* 40 (4): 373–90.

Amit, Vered. 2002. "Reconceptualizing Community." In *Realizing Community: Concepts, Social Relationships and Sentiments*, edited by Vered Amit, 1–20. London: Routledge.

Amit-Talai, Vered, and Henri Lustiger-Thaler, eds. 1994. *Connections: The Ethnographic Challenge*. Toronto: McClelland and Stewart.

Appadurai, Arjun. 1991. "Global Ethnoscapes: Note and Queries for a *Transnational Anthropology.*" In *Recapturing Anthropology: Working in the Present*, edited by Richard G. Fox, 191–210. Santa Fe, NM: School of American Research.

Buddle, Kathleen. 2005. "Aboriginal Cultural Capital Creation and Radio Production in Urban Ontario." *Canadian Journal of Communication* 30 (1): 7–40.

Clifford, James. 2001. "Indigenous Articulations." *The Contemporary Pacific* 13 (2): 468–90.

Culhane, Dara. 2003. "The Spirit Lives within Us: Aboriginal Women in Downtown Eastside Vancouver Emerging into Visibility." *American Indian Quarterly* 27 (3/4): 593–606.

Curry, Bill. 2006. "No-Race-Based Commercial Fishery, Minister Says." *The Globe and Mail*. Friday, 14 July: A8.

Deleuze, G., and F. Guattari. 1986. "What Is Minor Literature?" In *Kafka: Towards a Minor Literature*, translated by Dana Polan. Minneapolis: University of Minnesota Press.

Furniss, Elizabeth. 1992. *Victims of Benevolence: The Dark Legacy of the Williams Lake Residential School*. Vancouver: Arsenal Pulp Press.

Garroutte, Eva Marie. 2003. *Real Indians: Identity and the Survival of Native America*. Berkeley: University of California Press.

Gupta, Akhil, and James Ferguson. 1992. "Beyond 'Culture': Space, Identity and the Politics of Difference." *Cultural Anthropology* 7 (1): 6–23.

Hall, Stuart. 1996. "Introduction: Who Needs Identity?" In *Questions of Cultural Identity*, edited by Stuart Hall and Paul du Gay, 1–17. London: Sage Publications.

Halperin, Rhoda. 1998. *Practicing Community: Class Culture and Power in an Urban Neighborhood*. Austin: University of Texas Press.

Hanselmann, Calvin. 2001. *Urban Aboriginal People in Western Canada: Realities and Policies*. Calgary: Canada West Foundation.

Harding, Robert. 2006. "Historical Representations of Aboriginal People in Canadian News Media." *Discourse and Society* 17 (2): 205–35.

Henry, F., and C. Tator. 2000. "The Theory and Practice of Democratic Racism in Canada." In *Perspectives on Ethnicity in Canada: A Reader*, edited by Madeline A. Kalbach and Warren E. Kalbach, 285–302. Toronto: Harcourt Canada.

Howard, Heather A. 2004. "Dreamcatchers in the City: An Ethnohistory of Social Action, Gender and Class in Native Community Production." Unpublished Ph.D. thesis. University of Toronto, Department of Anthropology.

———. 2009. "Women's Class Strategies as Activism in Native Community Building in Toronto, 1950–1975." In *Keeping the Campfires Going: Native Women's Activism in Urban Areas*, edited by Susan Applegate Krouse and Heather A. Howard, 105–24. Lincoln: University of Nebraska Press.

Jackson, Deborah Davis. 2002. *Our Elders Lived It: American Indian Identity in the City*. DeKalb: Northern Illinois University Press.

Kaplan, Caren. 1987. "Deterritorializations: The Rewriting of Home and Exile in Western Feminist Discourse." *Cultural Critique* 6: 187–98.

Knauft, Bruce M., ed. 2002. *Critically Modern: Alternatives, Alterities, Anthropologies*. Bloomington and Indianapolis: Indiana University Press.

Krouse, Susan Applegate, and Heather A. Howard. 2009. *Keeping the Campfires Going: Native Women's Activism in Urban Areas*. Lincoln: University of Nebraska Press.

LaPrairie, Carol. 1994. *Seen but Not Heard: Native People in the Inner City*. Ottawa: Communications and Consultation Branch, Department of Justice of Canada.

Lawrence, Bonita. 2003. "Gender, Race, and the Regulation of Native Identity in Canada and the United States: An Overview." *Hypatia* 18 (2): 3–31.

———. 2004. *"Real" Indians and Others: Mixed-Blood Urban Native People and Indigenous Nationhood*. University of Nebraska Press and Vancouver: University of British Columbia Press.

Letkemann, Paul G. 2004. "First Nations Urban Migration and the Importance of "Urban Nomads" in Canadian Plains Cities: A Perspective from the Streets," *Canadian Journal of Urban Research* 13(2): 241–56.

Lobo, Susan. 2001. "Is Urban a Person or a Place?: Characteristics of Urban Indian Country." In *American Indians and the Urban Experience*, edited by Susan Lobo and Kurt Peters, 73–84. Lanham: AltaMira Press.

Lobo, Susan, and Kurt Peters, eds. 2001. *American Indians and the Urban Experience*. New York: Altamira Press.

Monture-Angus, Patricia. 1994. "Alternative Dispute Resolution: A Bridge to Aboriginal Experience?" In *Qualifications for Dispute Resolution: Perspectives and Debates*, edited by Catherine Morris and Andrew Pirie, 131–40. Victoria: UVic Institute for Dispute Resolution.

Nader, Laura. 1997. "Controlling Processes: Tracing the Dynamic Components of Power" *Current Anthropology* 38 (5): 711–23.

Norris, Mary Jane, and Stewart Clatworthy. 2003. "Aboriginal Mobility and Migration within Urban Canada: Outcomes, Factors and Implications." In *Not Strangers in These Parts: Urban Aboriginal Peoples*, edited by David Newhouse and Evelyn Peters, 51–78. Policy Research Institute. http://dsp-psd.pwgsc.gc.ca/Collection/CP22-71-2003E.pdf.

Peters, Evelyn, J. 1996. Urban and Aboriginal a Contradiction? The Social Construction of Aboriginal Peoples in Relation to the City. In *City Lives and City Forms: Critical Research and Canadian Urbanism*, edited by Jon Caulfield and Linda Peake, 47–62. Toronto: University Of Toronto Press.

———. 2002. "'Our City Indians': Negotiating the Meaning of First Nations Urbanization in Canada 1945–1975." *Historical Geography* 30: 75–92.

———. 2004. "Three Myths about Aboriginals in Cities." Canadian Federation for the Humanities and Social Sciences Breakfast on the Hill Seminar Series. Ottawa, ON, 25 March. http://www.fedcan.ca/english/pdf/fromold/breakfast-peters0304.pdf.

Peters, Evelyn J., and Oksana M. Starchenko. 2005. "Changes in Aboriginal Settlement Patterns in Two Canadian Cities." *Canadian Journal of Urban Research*. 14 (2): 315–37.

Proulx, Craig. 2003. *Reclaiming Aboriginal Justice, Community and Identity*. Saskatoon: Purich Publishing.

———. 2006. "Aboriginal Identification in North American Cities." *The Canadian Journal of Native Studies* 26 (2): 403–36.

Ramirez, Renya. 2007. *Native Hubs: Culture, Community, and Belonging in Silicon Valley and Beyond*. Durham, NC: Duke University Press.

Rice, David A. 2004. "Mediating Colonization: Urban Indians in the Native American Novel." Unpublished Ph.D. thesis. Storrs: University of Connecticut. http://digitalcommons.uconn.edu/dissertations/AAI3144605/ (27 September 2006)

Royal Commission on Aboriginal Peoples. 1993. *Aboriginal Peoples and the Justice System: Report of the National Round Table on Aboriginal Justice Issues*. Ottawa: Minister of Supply and Services Canada.

———. 1996. *Bridging the Cultural Divide: A Report on Aboriginal People and Criminal Justice in Canada*. Ottawa: Minister of Supply and Services Canada.

Ryan, Joan. 1994. *Doing Things the Right Way: Dene Traditional Justice in Lac La Martre, N.W.T.* Calgary: University of Calgary Press.

Sahlins, Marshall. 1999. "Two or Three Things I Know about Culture. *Journal of the Royal Anthropological Institute* 5 (3): 399–421.

Sanderson, Frances, and Heather Howard-Bobiwash. 1997. *The Meeting Place: Aboriginal Life in Toronto*. Toronto: Native Canadian Centre of Toronto.

Silver, Jim, Kathy Mallett, Janice Green, and Freeman Simard. 2002. *Aboriginal Education in Winnipeg Inner City High Schools*. Manitoba: Canadian Centre for Policy Alternatives.

Sinclair, Murray. 1994. "Aboriginal Peoples, Justice and the Law." In *Continuing Poundmaker and Riel's Quest: Presentations Made at a Conference on Aboriginal Peoples and Justice*, edited by Richard Gosse et al., 172–84. Saskatoon: Purich Publishing.

Spradley, James P. 1970. *You Owe Yourself a Drunk: An Ethnography of Urban Nomads*. Boston: Little, Brown.

Statistics Canada. 2005. "Study: Aboriginal People Living in Metropolitan Areas." *The Daily*, 23 June. http://www.statcan.ca/Daily/English/050623/d050623b .htm.

Tax, Sol. 1980. "Introductory Remarks: The Relocation Act and Its Effects." Proceedings of the Third Annual Conference on Problems and Issues Concerning American Indians Today: Urban Indians, 6–20. Chicago: Newberry Library.

Warry, Wayne. 1998. *Unfinished Dreams: Community Healing and the Reality of Aboriginal Self-Government*. Toronto: University of Toronto Press.

Weaver, Hillary. 2001. "Indigenous Identity." *American Indian Quarterly* 25 (2): 240–55.

Weibel-Orlando, Joan. 1999. *Indian Country, L.A.: Maintaining Ethnic Community in Complex Society*. Revised edition. Chicago: University of Illinois Press.

Williams, Raymond. 1981. *Marxism and Literature*. Oxford: Oxford University Press.

Wilson, Kathi, and Evelyn J. Peters. 2005. "'You can make a place for it': Remapping Urban First Nations Spaces of Identity." *Environment and Planning: Society and Space* 23: 396–413.

2
Urban Life
Reflections of a Middle-Class Indian

David R. Newhouse

I am an urbanite and proud of it. I have lived in cities all of my adult life. I left my Indian reserve community at the age of 19, three and a half decades ago, in 1972, to attend university. I have not returned either to live or work. In three cities, I encountered and became part of small and vibrant Aboriginal communities. Many, like me, came from Indian reserves to the city to study, to join family who had preceded them, to take care of family or friends, to take a job, to explore what the city had to offer. We came to the city for the most mundane of reasons—for the same reasons that people have come to cities for the last few thousand years. Many of these people lived comfortable middle-class lives and like middle-class people wanted to give back to their communities in concrete and beneficial ways. We volunteered in Friendship Centres, worked in Aboriginal political and service organizations; some ran their own businesses, some worked in those owned by others. All wanted to live good lives not just as individuals but as Aboriginal persons. Few I encountered over the years had renounced their Aboriginal identity. Most saw themselves as part of a larger Aboriginal community or nation, even if they were physically distant from it.

In each city, the small community was diverse. I met expatriates, ex-reservers, so to speak, longing to return to the reserve that would always be home—a place where they felt comfortable, could live among family, where they would be accepted, would not always feel different or out of place—the reserve as Cheers (where everybody knows your name). In the early years, we were students who wanted to return home to change our birthplaces, to make them better places to live and work—Indian Martha Stewarts or Indian reformers, so to speak. Thirty years later, some of us see the reserve as a place to return to upon retirement from work. My colleagues talk of "returning home" and some have done so quite successfully, becoming involved in local politics and community life.

Others I encountered expressed no desire to return to the reserve: they found the reserve too small, too cloistered, too far away from the action, too close, too backward, too limiting in opportunity, either in terms of jobs or schooling—all the things that city people have said about rural life over the last few hundred years. Some who came were trying to rebuild lives after illness, separation from partners or acts of intolerance; some wanted what the city had to offer: safety, services, better schooling, jobs, income, and better lives. Some had never lived on a reserve, having being raised in families that had left a generation ago for reasons of marriage or military service or careers. Many of those with reserve connections retained strong ties with family and friends back home, moving back and forth with regularity, visiting "home" often, renewed and re-energized by the visits or disillusioned by the slow pace of change or the lack thereof.

While many of the people I encountered and became friends with lived in the cities, they were not of the city; it would be unfair to call them urbanites. The city was a stopping place, a place to live and work but not to call home; home was and would always be the reserve or a rural community where they were born. They were just passing through to go to school or to look for a job. For me, though, the city became home; it was the place I wanted to be. I revelled in it and became immersed in its life; the rhythms of the city became a part of me. I felt comfortable and alive amid the noise, busyness, and distractions. At no time did I feel less "Indian" or "Aboriginal" as a result of my desire to live in the city nor did I feel that I had lost something by my move. In fact, I felt that I had gained something.

Over the years, we asked each other, "Where are you from?" The answer was always elsewhere. None of us came from Ottawa or London or Peterborough or Toronto. Even now, after three decades of city life, I hesitate when answering the question: do I say Six Nations of the Grand River or Peterborough? I come from Six Nations, will always feel an affinity for it, but I live and work in Peterborough. I am part of a Six Nations diaspora though with no desire to return there to live even in retirement. The city has become an essential part of me. I would be lost without it.

I enjoy the city and have no desire to live in the country. I like the rhythm of life of the city—its sights and sounds, its multicultural offerings.

As an urbanite, I rejoice in the city, feel energized by it, enjoy its pleasures, and work to minimize its sufferings.

I live a privileged life of a university professor in a small city in eastern Ontario with easy access to Toronto. My experience of the urban has been mostly positive although I have encountered racism and homophobia over the years and seen it in action, both visibly and invisibly throughout the country. My life is solidly middle class and not representative of the vast majority of Aboriginal people. I am able to move about the social scene of the city and university with ease and with a solid and firm identity as an Aboriginal person, to be more specific, as an Onondaga. I teach my mainstream business classes as an openly Aboriginal person, using ideas and teachings from my own cultural heritage as well as those from the vast management literature. I participate in all aspects of urban life as an Aboriginal individual. Others recognize and acknowledge me as an Aboriginal person.

The city for me was an escape, not from family—although like middle-class adolescents, as I imagined I was despite my low economic status at the time, I longed to escape the confines of family, if only temporarily—but from the oppression of peers, unwilling to accept the differences I exhibited from a young age. I continually expressed no desire to follow in the footsteps of my father into high steel, given my fear of extreme heights. The city was a place where I could be myself, where I could live in relative obscurity away from the peering eyes of neighbours. It was a respite from the panoptic gaze of tradition. In my experience, the rural reserve community was oppressive and restrictive: My school peers did not accept my interest in books and academics and taunted and bullied me constantly for it. In high school, my bus-mates denigrated my participation in high school life and my mostly white friends. Adults in my life did not attempt to stop any of these things. There were high expectations that I would live a life similar to my father and his father before, becoming a member of the longhouse and perhaps assuming a position within it over time. My move to the city was not difficult or problematic or imbued with a sense of loss. I thought of it in terms of opportunity and openness. I saw not only the negative aspects of the city, well described by my father, but its positive attributes as well.

The urban communities I encountered were welcoming. In London and Ottawa, there was an Indian friendship centre that served as the most visible Aboriginal institution in the city, playing a role as a community centre for the small community. In both cities, Ottawa in particular, there was a community of Aboriginal public servants (in all aspects of the public sector:

Canada, Ontario and Aboriginal), many who had lived there for decades. There were opportunities to build community and to meet people from around the world. I volunteered in friendship centres (again, a middle-class action that I now conceive of as consistent with Indigenous traditions of sharing and contributing) along with others, both Aboriginal and non-Aboriginal. I sat on city council subcommittees, became active in the HIV/AIDS education movement, and learned about different Indigenous cultures and traditions that I would otherwise not have encountered if I had remained to live and work at Six Nations. I choose to participate in urban life and to take advantage of what it had to offer. My participation was made easier by my university education, which rested on a solid foundation provided by the Six Nations school system. It taught, based upon the education philosophy of its long time superintendent, Dr. Joe Hill, that one needed to be grounded and educated in one's own history and culture as well as that of the rest of Canada. A solid identity as an Iroquoian person would enable one to live well anywhere in the world.

My experiences and views were not those that permeate the literature on urban Aboriginal peoples I have encountered over the last three decades of my life. They were also different from the reality that I encountered when I served as Chair of the Working Group on Aboriginal Peoples in Urban Settings in Ontario in the early 1980s. This study showed urban lives of poverty and marginalization, marked by racism and prejudice. Despite much effort, it is still part of the reality of the vast majority of Aboriginal people living in cities. What the literature did not show was a desire to live a good life as an Aboriginal person and the effort to advance this goal. The academic literature still does not show the resilience, determination, and community building that I have encountered over the last few decades. My reality is a middle-class one; even as a student, my life was a middle-class life of relative privilege. I am not advocating urban life for everyone; what I advocate for is the ability to choose. Urban life provided me with a panoply of choices and a modicum of skills and knowledge with which to choose. Racism, like extreme poverty, takes away the privilege to choose.

In the early 1990s, as an executive member of the National Association of Aboriginal Friendship Centres (NAFC), I encountered another part of urban Aboriginal reality. We invited the national chief of the Assembly of First Nations (AFN) to our AGM. Our desire was to create an alliance with the AFN, to work together in improving the lives of city people. We asked the national chief if this would be possible. He replied that he had no mandate to do so and that because we left our communities we have to live with the consequences. Somehow by moving to the cities, we turned our back on our homelands and our people. When, I asked, did ruralness become a defining and essential characteristic of Aboriginality? (In a sense, the AFN was following the policy of the state that defined Indianness and residence on reserves as linked. Those who moved away from reserves moved away from their Indianness and no longer deserved the support of the state as they were no longer Indians.) The national chief cited our relationship to the land in reply as a defining characteristic. It is hard to maintain that relationship in a city. Stalemate.

Unwilling to give up, I tried a different tack. As an urban resident of a First Nations community, I told the national chief, I can vote for the prime minister of Canada, the premier of a province, and the mayor of the town where I live, but I cannot vote for the national chief. I am disenfranchised from the Assembly of First Nations. Urban dwellers are pushed away, so to speak, living in exile, not welcome in the political process that selects a national Aboriginal leader. Why would we do this to ourselves? Why would we divide ourselves using the criteria of the state? We debated: Your connections to your home communities are lost and since you don't live there, you should not have a say in how they're governed. As a Canadian, if I move away, I can still vote and participate in the governing of Canada. Come home and help. Don't waste your talent in the city. What about the 50 percent of us who live in the cities? Who will look out for us? Who will speak for us? Can we not use our talents to build good communities in the cities? Can we not have good lives in the cities? Yes, but my mandate comes from the Chiefs and I cannot go back and ask them to revise it. End of debate.

In response to this exclusion from local, regional, and national Aboriginal politics, the Congress of Aboriginal Peoples (CAP), formerly the Native Council of Canada, emerged, somewhat controversially, as a representative body for urban Aboriginal peoples. CAP has a difficult time in gaining respect for its claims in this area. The National Association of Friendship Centres (NAFC), with 122 centres located in most cities and towns with significant Aboriginal populations, makes no claim to represent urban Aboriginal peoples and focuses on its service mission. They stake out a claim to provide services to all Aboriginal peoples regardless of government-defined status. It is a way to survive in a divisive political environment and a way to resist the state definitions of Aboriginality.

Many questions remain: who speaks for the diverse urban Aboriginal populations? Is it possible to have one group to represent such a geographical and diverse cultural group? More importantly, how are Aboriginal voices represented in local politics? Local politics most often affects the daily life of urban residents in more profound ways, but many of us do not participate in local city politics, either as individuals or collectively through our businesses or organizations. We are not usually landowners in the cities. We are disenfranchised not only from national Aboriginal politics but also from local politics. Is it possible to maintain a distinctive political presence that is effective and representative in contemporary urban politics? Is this a worthwhile political goal? How can we claim the city as our own?

The support of local elected councillors was important to the establishment of two friendship centres that I had the pleasure of working with. They were helpful in locating properties, interpreting bylaws, providing capital and operating grants, and helping to create good relationships with other community members. In many western Canadian cities, local Aboriginal councils, comprising mostly representatives of Aboriginal social service organizations, have emerged as effective voices to speak on behalf of communities and to speak to city councils and other service agencies. Aboriginal service organizations in an emergent network of, while not overtly political, are also able to influence local politics by creating alliances with mainstream agencies to get institutional attention for Aboriginal quality of life issues. The creation of Aboriginal institutions, serving urban Aboriginal needs and participating in the politics of the city, is a way we make the city ours as well. Evelyn Peters and I, in "Not Strangers in these Parts: Urban Aboriginal Peoples" (2003), point out that the sites of many Canadian cities are traditional gathering places for Aboriginal peoples. Our move to the cities, then, can be seen not as exile or escape but a return to a familiar place—a home of sorts.

Over the last three decades, I came to define myself as an Urban Indian. It is hard to say Urban Aboriginal Person. My cultural heritage is Iroquoian-Onondaga; I grew up on the Six Nations of the Grand River community near Brantford, Ontario. My family has been strong supporters of the Iroquoian Confederacy and members of the Longhouse since before our move to Canada around 1790. My great-grandfather, grandfather, and father worked with a successive group of anthropologists in documenting, in English, much of our intellectual and cultural heritage and knowledge. Growing up in southern Ontario, about forty-five minutes away from Toronto, one could say that I was always urban. After all, growing up at Six Nations means being surrounded by more than 3 million people within a half-day's travel. It is a rural area but by no means remote. Some may argue that the move from rural to urban was not a large leap at all.

My earliest encounters with the urban occurred in the city of Brantford primarily, if my memory serves correctly, through the farmers market that took place on Saturdays at the former Market Square. There I encountered a variety of people and goods that I found intriguing. The market was enticing. I enjoyed the excitement, the constant movement, the noise, the colours, and the fact that it was a small oasis of Six Nations land in the heart of the city. It was this early experience with the market that was to serve as the basis for my conversion into an urbanite.

Relatively few Six Nations residents lived in Brantford during this time. The few who did were seen as having left the reserve and their heritage behind. We spoke of them in disparaging terms, believing that they had somehow changed as a result of their choice of residence. They thought that they were better than the rest of us and had turned away from their own people. My own family however had roots and branches in urban areas surrounding the reserve: Caledonia, Hamilton, Fort Erie, Vineland, Buffalo, Niagara Falls, London, Toronto, and Oakville as well as Miami, Nashville, Windsor, Chicago, and Montreal.

Many of my mother's brothers lived in the small town of Caledonia. Her father had enfranchised the entire family in the 1930s, hoping that this act would lead to a better life for all of them. It did, in their eyes: all had long work careers, good homes and families; none expressed regret at the actions of their father, and none wanted to live on the reserve. Interestingly, none took up the provisions of Bill C-31 for reinstatement of their Indian status. Their children, my cousins, are all now solidly middle class, living throughout Canada. Of my mother's eleven siblings, only two (women) moved back to the Six Nations community, all upon marriage. My mother was born a status Indian, became a non-status Indian upon enfranchisement, and became a status Indian again upon marriage to my father, a status Indian. As a result of the arcane membership rules of the Indian Act, I am considered to have 50% Indian blood, 50% non-Indian Blood. My mother's family was mostly urban, and only one of her three sisters lived on reserve. For the most part, they have created good urban lives for them and their families.

My father's only sibling lived in the Six Nations community and expressed no desire to live anywhere else. My father's mother's family lived in various urban centres across the continent; none lived at the Six Nations community. My father, as an ironworker, travelled frequently and worked in many of the major urban centres in North America. He considered life away from the reserve community to be an economic necessity and found much to dislike about large cities. It was his urban experience that led him to counsel me to seek a career in ironworking; in this way, he could ensure that I would remain tied to the community and family. As a father, he saw my growing interest in life and events away from the reserve and knew that I would eventually leave. Despite living at Six Nations, the urban was a part of my family's life experiences even before I encountered it in significant ways as a high school student.

I attended high school at Brantford Collegiate Institute and Vocational School, located in the heart of old Brantford. My classmates were members of Brantford's elite. I found myself involved in many of the high school clubs, much to the disdain of my bus companions from the reserve. I was introduced to a world that I didn't know existed. In this group of upper-middle-class students everyone was expected to go to university, and I joined the crowd. The desire to go to university had been set in grade eight when a foresighted teacher asked us to write to universities to obtain calendars and then choose courses to take. My father argued that we were too poor to afford university for me and tried to convince me to consider a job as an ironworker. The white world, he also argued, was not a supportive place for Indians. I would encounter too many problems to succeed. Going to university required me to leave the reserve and move to a city, a place he considered a necessary evil, a place to visit and work but not a place to live or study. For my white high school friends, going to university was simply a move from one city to another, not a move from rural to urban areas or a move across cultures. While university was a culture shock, it was filled with people with whom I was already familiar with as a result of my high school experiences.

My Aboriginal university colleagues all expected to return to their home communities upon graduation. The city was not home, and in their view never could be; there was something strange about my desire to remain in the city. City life was not for Indians: it would rob us of our culture. Over the next thirty years, I encountered this and other notions over and over again—the city as place to visit, a place to acquire something to take home, and a place where one lost something important. Many of my Aboriginal university friends felt that they did not belong in the city, feeling a profound discomfort at the urban way of life. They felt disconnected from the land they grew up on, that they were not accepted by urban residents, and they believed that Indians were not meant to live in the cities. For those who practised what we have come to call Aboriginal spirituality, the landscape was unfamiliar and not conducive to spiritual practice. Many remarked on the feeling of always being watched.

I often challenged these ideas, much to their dismay, asking questions about the origins of the idea that we were not meant to live in cities (making analogies to our attendance at university, which was not part of our experience, yet here we were, in the heart of the beast, so to speak. Would it not change us as well?). As it turned out, what was behind their ideas was a fear of not being accepted by their communities upon their return home. They would be seen as different and changed and, as a result, would no longer fit in. I asked them why we could not practise our spirituality in the city. After all, I had seen Longhouse ceremonial leaders conduct ceremonies in city apartments, opening windows to let the tobacco smoke out, or using electric burners to burn tobacco, among other concessions to the city. Could not our healing spirits find their way to our homes? Why were they confined to the boundaries of the reserve? (I was tempted to ask on many occasions if they needed a pass to leave, and if so, why a pass was denied to them, but my good sense and desire to remain intact and violence-free prevented me from doing so.)

The questions are still good questions, and today I would frame them in terms of cultural change rather than loss. Every day we negotiate the boundaries of our culture and accept what we like, that makes life easier, or reject what doesn't fit or we don't understand or doesn't make sense. As urban Aboriginal residents, we are engaging in a practice that our ancestors have always done: we adapt to the world we find ourselves in.

I became involved in the friendship centre movement in 1978 and remained so for the next two decades. Federal funding for Indian friendship centres was provided through the Migrating Native Peoples Program. The main purpose of the funding was to provide assistance to those who were new to the cities and needed help in finding housing and jobs and who experienced discrimination. The idea of an urban Aboriginal community was not part of the intellectual foundations of the policy. In 1982, when the policy was renewed, we set out as the fundamental policy principle the idea of urban Aboriginal institutions as legitimate institutions in their own right that would not have to justify their existence on a yearly basis. We established the idea that there were urban Aboriginal communities with institutions developed by community members to serve our own needs. We argued for urban Aboriginal peoples and institutions to be seen as legitimate part of the urban landscape. It was a tough sell. Institutions meant that Aboriginal peoples were planning on living in cities permanently. How could we know this since we had only recently migrated to them? The linking of Aboriginal peoples and ruralness was and still is firmly entrenched in Canadian social consciousness: Indians live on reserves not in cities. I keep asking, who says so?

While advocating for the needs of a growing urban population, friendship centres evolved into one of the key urban Aboriginal organizations responsible for the development of a community of other institutions that grew up around them. I have served as president of two centres, one in London, Ontario, and another in Ottawa. The centres, funded as social service agencies, adopted as much as possible a community-development approach to their work and rapidly became important actors in municipal politics, representing and speaking on behalf of the local urban Aboriginal community. The centres prided themselves on not being "political organizations" and kept their efforts focused on meeting the social, economic, and cultural needs of all urban peoples. The apolitical stance was adapted to avoid the divisive debates about identity and status that continue to rage. The centres could then serve all identity communities: Status Indian, Métis, Inuit, and Non-Status Indians. The non-political stance also extended to partisan politics, allowing the centres to advocate freely without regard for the political stripe of the governing party. It was easier to be non-partisan than to be non-political, however. Aboriginal organizations other than the AFN kept claiming to represent different sectors of the Urban Aboriginal population, usually the part that was consistent with their own mandate. We kept the debate focused on the client, to use a social-service term, who had needs and desires, rather than the client's status. The focus on service also kept the friendship centres clearly out of Aboriginal Representative Organizations Program (AROP) funding and hence out of competition for funding from the major national Aboriginal organizations.

Throughout Canada, a small urban Aboriginal middle class began to emerge in the 1980s. The members of this group, comprising a growing cadre of workers in urban Aboriginal organizations, both service and political, served on the boards of centres. Their needs were expressed in the increasing emphasis on traditional and cultural teachings and a turn to elders as sources of knowledge about how to live in the world. There was much discussion about the development of distinct Aboriginal organizational cultures, informed by traditional teachers and inclusive of elders. The annual general meetings had workshops that dealt with these ideas and suggested ways that they might be put into practice. The social service aspects (employment, housing, health care, employment equity, access to welfare, etc.) of the centre's mission began to compete with these needs and desires for cultural development. Finding a balance between two disparate sets of activities became an important board activity, essential to maintaining the legitimacy of the centre in the eyes of its communities.

What I find interesting is that during this period, we did not discuss the notion of urban Aboriginal culture(s). We spoke constantly of urban Aboriginal communities, without much definition and with a sense that we knew what these were. These communities included both individual families and the set of institutions that had emerged by the end of the twentieth century. It was unclear in our discussions whether we were speaking of neighbourhoods, cultural communities, class communities, political communities, or other possible communities. The idea of community is a powerful one, consistent with the ideas of relatedness and connection taught in traditional teachings. Even as we moved to cities, we used ideas from our own cultures to structure the environment. We did not use the term "neighbourhood," a term extant in the sociological literature of the time. Or perhaps our speakers read a different literature.

The idea of an urban Aboriginal culture means that those who feared that we might not return or those who feared that we would be changed by the city were right: the city has changed us. But had the city made us unrecognizable to our rural counterparts? Was ruralness an essential part of the characteristic of being an Aboriginal person? The 1996 Report of the Royal Commission on Aboriginal Peoples notes that the markers of Aboriginality for urban peoples are different from those of rural residents: an Aboriginal spiritual ethos, speaking an Aboriginal language, maintaining a connection with an ancestral territory and land, the presence of elders, the use of traditional values in daily life, a family centered life, and an active ceremonial life to reinforce traditional values and spirituality. These seem to me to elements of a culture and a distinct way of life. Ruralness is not part of it.

My life in the city has not made me less of an Aboriginal person. It has made me a different Aboriginal person. My encounter with Buddhist spirituality has deepened my understanding of aspects of Aboriginal spirituality. My desire for Starbucks rather than Tim Hortons coffee can be fulfilled more easily. I am not far from nature. (One of my colleagues remarks that everywhere we are as close to nature as we're going to get and I agree.) I am keenly aware of the absence of Aboriginality in the landscape of cities. Yet I believe that we must be here in a visible substantive sense; these are our cities as well. More than 50 percent of us live in these places; many of us call them home. Our institutions are here: political representative organizations, social service agencies, businesses, schools, friendship centres, community organizations, art galleries, community development organizations. Our families and homes are here as along with a sense of community, albeit not neighbourhoods. The AFN has finally recognized our existence and asked, as part of its renewal exercise in 2005–2007, what its role with regard to us ought to be. The final report indicates that it ought to represent urban First Nations people, a step toward ending the disenfranchisement.

For the past decade and a half, I have taught a first-year course in Native studies. Despite the overwhelming evidence to the contrary, it is difficult for students to accept the fact that we have become an urban people. They enter the class with images of Aboriginal peoples as rural or northern, images that are supported by the popular and mass media. Even among my colleagues the idea that we ought to start the course with this urban reality is a difficult one to accept. We have a course on urban Aboriginal peoples that until recently was called "urbanization." I want to start with a lecture on urban Aboriginal hip hop and rap, presenting it as evidence of a continued ethic of adaptation and innovation that allowed us to survive across the centuries and to show that the focus of Aboriginal life has shifted. The accepted way to discuss Aboriginal peoples is as if they were rural and to talk of issues surrounding urban Aboriginal peoples as "urbanization," using the perspectives and tools from sociology. I have also suggested, to little avail, that we ought to talk of urbanism, as urbanization appears to be almost complete. What we ought to explore, I suggest, is the way Aboriginal cultures and communities are changing as a result of their encounter with and accommodation of the urban experience.

My personal experience, my academic experience with colleagues in the university, and my encounter with the academic literature in this area suggest to me a strong resistance to the notions of urban Aboriginal cultures and communities—the idea that one can live a good life in the city and still retain core elements of Aboriginality and the idea that the urban environment does not always result in loss of identity. Like the members of the Supreme Court who measure Aboriginality in terms of practies extant at the time of initial contact, the urban features little in contemporary non-Aboriginal versions of Aboriginal life. It is hard to practise agriculture or fishing or hunting in the city, unless one counts gardening, aquaria, or supermarket shopping as extensions of these activities. I began to understand that the urban was not seen or experienced by many Aboriginal people as a neutral environment. The urban, in all of its manifestations, was not part of the historical experience of Aboriginal peoples, nor was it meant to be. Somehow it was capable of transforming people into something else, a person who lacked Aboriginality. If the city caused us to lose our Aboriginality, then it was to be avoided; yet many have come to cities. Many live good lives—fewer than those who live on the margins, yet we come again and again. Those who believed it was transformative were correct, but not in the sense that they feared. It did not result in a loss of Aboriginality but an addition to it. Urban experiences have been added; they have not replaced rural or reserve experiences.

The historical literature on urban Aboriginal peoples is what I call a "study in lack." Lack indicating an absence of a desired characteristic is a dominant theme of these texts. It isn't until the work of Aboriginal scholars emerges at the end of the century that the urban environment is characterized in positive terms. These new scholars turn to central ideas in Indigenous thought—community, relationships, interconnectedness—which are used to describe urban experience in a different light.

The urban environment, in the findings of the RCAP, is now a site of established, long-standing urban Aboriginal communities, essential to the maintenance of Aboriginal identities. The words used to describe these communities are telling, however: "Following three decades of urbanization, development of a strong community remains largely incomplete" (RCAP 1996, 530–31) and "with little collective visibility or power" (ibid). Lack again.

Rejecting the idea of the absence of the urban in Aboriginal North America, Forbes, in Lobo and Peters (2001), discusses the "urban tradition" in Native America, focusing on the Indigenous civilizations of Mexico and South America. He argues that there were large urban centres in North America prior to the arrival of Europeans and our notions of urban, based to a large extent upon European/North American notions of "city" ought to be rethought to include Indigenous notions of the urban. The urban in Aboriginal history has been systematically erased because it would allow for the idea of "Aboriginal civilization," a notion that would have been inconsistent with European thought of the day. He seeks to bring the idea of historic urban Aboriginal communities into our understanding of Aboriginal peoples. The idea of the urban is not lacking in Aboriginal thought or history, only in European ideas about Aboriginal peoples.

Lobo (2001), Weibel-Orlando (1991), and Proulx (2003) conceive of the urban as a positive force in Aboriginal peoples' lives. Although there are problems, the urban should not be inconsistent with our notions of Aboriginality, they argue. There are problems in European cities as well but that does not prevent Europeans from being European. Creative adaptation has always been a part of Aboriginal life. The contemporary urban environment is another aspect of the continuous transformations that

Aboriginal peoples live within. There is no doubt that it can be accommodated and adapted to.

What has been accomplished, over the last decade in particular, I think, is a refutation of the notion that the urban is inconsistent with the idea of being Aboriginal. The urban environment is seen as a place where Aboriginal people can live good lives as Aboriginal peoples provided there is a strong community that supports the core elements of urban Aboriginal identity: spirituality, language, land base, values and tradition, family, and ceremonial life" (RCAP 1996, 533). Various scholars document histories of urban Aboriginal communities (Proulx 2003; Lobo and Peters 2001; Fixico 2000; Howard-Bobiwash 2003; Sanderson and Howard-Bobiwash 1997; Weibel-Orlando 1991). Shorten (1991) documents the life stories of a dozen urban Aboriginal individuals living in Edmonton. Any doubt of the existence of urban Aboriginal communities is made problematic by the forty-year history of the development and work of Aboriginal friendship centres. The RCAP final report grapples with the complexity of the urban Aboriginal community and how it ought to be governed. It also conceives of urban Aboriginal governments as "community of interests" governments. The urban site then is seen as a site of Aboriginal governance, clearly refuting the idea that Aboriginality and urban are inconsistent. Urban had become, by 1996, "the framework though which an individual approaches all issues" (RCAP 1996, 2) and, more importantly, a distinct framework or perspective through which one sees and experiences the world.

Barron and Garcia (1999) examine a relatively new phenomenon: urban Indian reserves. The urban is seen as a site of opportunity for reserve-based governments. They are sites of economic development that permit the harvesting of urban wealth for reserve purposes. In an interesting twist, reserves that were seen as holding sites for Indians (until they died or were assimilated) are now seen as ways of breathing life into small towns by attracting industry and commerce through the establishment of urban Aboriginal sites. It is now the cities that are demonstrating lack.

The movement of Indians to cities was first brought to public attention through the Survey of the Contemporary Indians of Canada, commonly known as the Hawthorn Report (1966), and the early investigations of anthropologists and sociologists. The encounter with the urban was seen as difficult and incompatible to Aboriginal peoples and in some sense inconsistent with commonly held notions of Aboriginal. Forty years later, despite some holdouts, the idea of urban is no longer inconsistent with the idea of being Aboriginal. The RCAP final report argues that

Aboriginal peoples and their communities are important to the health and vibrancy of Canadian cities (1996, 521). Hawthorne states: "The Indian does not come empty handed to the modern situation" (1966, 10).

The recent literature begins to accord with my early experience of the urban environment. Newhouse and Peters (2003, 5) remark that "city life is now an integral component of Aboriginal peoples' lives in Canada." At the same time, though we live with the legacy of lack and struggle to overcome it.

Politically, the AFN renewal process of 2004–2005 asks whether or not urban Aboriginal peoples should be represented by the AFN. The Congress of Aboriginal Peoples still claims to represent urban Aboriginal peoples. The Federation of Saskatchewan Indian Nations claims to represent all Saskatchewan First Nations people, regardless of residence. They argue that Aboriginal friendship centres ought to be brought under their purview. The urban Aboriginal site is become a site of contestation for representation. While I still cannot vote in AFN elections, or in congress elections without purchasing a membership, I can now vote in Six Nations band council elections, a recognition by the courts that I am still an Indian, regardless of residence.

We are now, I think, becoming more comfortable with the idea of urban Aboriginal peoples than we were three decades ago. We are also becoming more comfortable with the idea of middle-class Aboriginal peoples. When we meet other Aboriginal people these days and ask, "where are you from?" we don't mean what reserve community but what part of the city.

Works Cited

Barron, F. Laurie, and Joseph Garcea, eds. 1999. *Urban Indian Reserves Forging New Relationships in Saskatchewan*. Saskatoon, SK: Purich Press.

Fixico, Donald L. 2000. *The Urban Indian Experience in America*. Albuquerque: University of New Mexico Press.

Forbes, Jack. 2001. "The Urban Tradition among Native Americans." In *American Indians and the Urban Experience*, edited by Susan Lobo and Kurt Peters, 5–26. New York: Altamira Press.

Howard-Bobiwash, Heather. 2003. "Keeping the Campfires Going: Urban American Indian Women's Community Work and Activism." *American Indian Quarterly* 27 (3/4): 566–82.

Lobo, Susan, and Kurt Peters. 2001. *American Indians and the Urban Experience*. Walnut Creek, California: Altamira Press.

Newhouse, David, and Evelyn Peters. 2003. *Not Strangers in These Parts: Urban Aboriginal Peoples*. Ottawa: Policy Research Initiative.

Proulx, Craig. 2003. *Reclaiming Aboriginal Justice, Community and Identity*. Saskatoon, SK: Purich Publishing.

Royal Commission on Aboriginal Peoples. 1996. *Bridging the Cultural Divide: A Report on Aboriginal People and Criminal Justice in Canada*. Ottawa: Minister of Supply and Services Canada.

Sanderson, Frances, and Heather Howard-Bobiwash, eds. 1997. *The Meeting Place: Aboriginal Life in Toronto*. Toronto: Native Canadian Centre of Toronto.

Shorten, Lynda. 1991. *Without Reserve: Stories from Urban Natives*. Edmonton, AB: NeWest Press.

Weibel-Orlando, Joan. 1991. *Indian Country, L.A.: Maintaining Ethnic Community in Complex Society*. Chicago: University of Illinois Press.

3
Nomadic Legacies and Contemporary Decision-Making Strategies between Reserve and City

Regna Darnell

This chapter argues that contemporary First Nations decision-making strategies are continuous with the nomadic hunting and gathering traditions of the Anishinaabeg and that the Haudenosaunee (Iroquois) agricultural traditions sustain relationships to land that transcend permanent settlement. Today, the exploited resources are more likely to include education, employment, and access to medical or social services than moose, fish, or geese; nonetheless, the world continues to be conceived as an abundant source of resources to be exploited on a temporary but recurrent basis. This model of human-to-nature interaction constitutes a "nomadic legacy" that has stood the test of time and remains available for application to new domains.

Conceptual Framework

There is, of course, more than one way to be urban and Aboriginal in contemporary Canada. My understandings of the dynamic relationship of Native people with residential movement from a reserve-based identity to one of mobility and urbanity arise from particular experiences and ethnographic encounters. My own residential locations in northern Alberta and, more recently, London, Ontario, intersect with these theoretical, methodological, and ethnographic concerns. What I call nomadic legacies apply to the Aboriginal patterns of traditional subsistence and forms of urban residence with simultaneous ties to home place. I have found this thematic and hermeneutic recurrence in the stories people have told me over almost four decades now (Darnell 2004; Darnell and Manzano-Munguia 2005).

Despite caveats about generalizing, I am convinced that, for many contemporary Native people whose ancestors were hunters and gatherers, decisions are made today within a value system that is deeply embedded in tradition and continuously embodied and adapted to new, including urban, circumstances. The "urban Indian" has become, for me, an incoherent category, part of the problem rather than the solution, because its reification by academics masks the agency of people who attempt to maximize their resources and choose their futures within alternating forms of reserve and urban community. Urban residence does not entail assimilation.

My argument emerges from the particular quality of First Nations research at the University of Western Ontario and the policy implications deriving from it. A number of initially discrete projects have proved in their implementation to be interrelated and exhibit an underlying coherence of both theory and method. Some of this coherence probably arises from my standpoint as observer. Situated knowledge is not, however, random. From my standpoint and its ethnographic specificity I can engage the argument with other contexts, times, and places, such as those in other chapters of this volume.

Southwestern Ontario is a fascinating place to be engaged with First Nations peoples and their home communities. I came to the University of Western Ontario in 1990 after teaching for twenty-one years at the University of Alberta in Edmonton. In northern Alberta and Saskatchewan, where the pressures of white settlement occurred later and were less intense, the Plains Cree have, on the surface, at least, preserved their language and culture more effectively than the Anishinaabeg and Haudensaunee people in agricultural southwestern Ontario, which quickly became a crossroads for trade and industry. Certainly, there were individuals who had lost their ties to home community and traditional language and culture, but accessible places remained where elders still held traditional knowledge and welcomed those who wanted to return. The communities I worked in during those years were secure, for the most part, in their identity and heritage despite forced settlement, residential schools, and the absence of opportunity on small isolated reserves (Darnell 2006).

Having begun as a linguistic anthropologist, I expected things to be very different in southwestern Ontario as a result of the more intensive exposure to assimilative pressures. And indeed few children came to school speaking Anishinaabemowin or a Haudensaunee language. Just beneath the surface, however, I found that what I first perceived as the invisibility and unintelligibility of First Nations languages and cultural traditions obscured continuities similar in London, Ontario, and environs to those I had observed in Edmonton. Native people lived in both cities, but in neither case did the static category of "urban Indian" capture the hybridity, complexity, and mobility of their experience.

My research program over the last twenty years has focused on cross-cultural miscommunication between First Nations peoples and the Canadian mainstream among whom they currently subsist. There is a pernicious belief within the Canadian mainstream that First Nations peoples exist/ed primarily in the past but that they are now very much like anyone else. It is true, indeed, that many of the approximately ten thousand Aboriginal people living in London are likely to eat pizza and speak English in addition to living away from their home reserves. Almost all, regardless of generation, have lost their traditional languages (Ojibwe, Potawatomi, Delaware, Odawa, Mohawk, Oneida, Cayuga, Onondaga, Seneca) as a result of residential school coercion that is now widely defined at the personal level as abuse and at an Aboriginal community level as genocide (Darnell 2006). In southwestern Ontario, this is true whether the survivors live in the city or on their home reserve.

Most non-Native Canadians have difficulty understanding why Aboriginal rights established by treaties should persist and draw a facile parallel between First Nations peoples and immigrant ethnic groups coexisting within the multicultural framework of Canadian confederation. This is an instance of fundamental miscommunication. At the very least, "the Honour of the Crown" is at stake; treaties are contracts, and their terms have been ignored, circumvented, and arbitrarily modified in the experience of virtually every First Nations community. First Nations peoples are not like immigrants crucially because they do not have a homeland elsewhere to which they could return if conditions in Canada did not suit them. Their prior stewardship over the land, which most believe to have been stolen from them through the colonial process regardless of the particular circumstances of transfer, is not, according to the near-universal tenets of Indigenous knowledge, subject to extinguishment. That many First Nations individuals do not consider themselves Canadians comes as a shock to the mainstream majority. Assimilation policies have failed because Native people do not want to become second-class copies of their oppressors.

I belabour this context because I believe that all research, even so-called objective statistics, is necessarily political. The goal of my research program, in both the short and long term, is to demonstrate that urbanness does not eradicate Aboriginality or Aboriginal rights. Indian (in the meaning of the Indian Act), Inuit, and Metis people who identify themselves as

Native hold inherent Aboriginal rights, according to the Canadian constitution, regardless of their life circumstances. Native people choose to remain distinct from the mainstream and to transmit this distinction to their children for the seven generations into the future, for which each individual holds personal responsibility inherited from seven generations past.

Language and Land

Language and land are most often identified as the pillars of contemporary Native identity. Crucially, neither can be maintained by an individual in isolation. Maintenance and revitalization of language and culture inevitably depend upon family, community, and, for many, the reserve as home place, regardless of present residence.

Accordingly, between 1990 and 2001, my colleague Lisa Philips [Valentine] and I (later also Allan McDougall) spent a decade studying Native Englishes in southwestern Ontario (Darnell 2004). We argued that everything, from sound systems and vocabulary to the principles of discourse organization and what I have called "interactional etiquette" (Darnell 1988), has been transposed into English in a communicative economy that is adapted creatively to Aboriginal purposes in everyday interaction and in public contexts. Thus, Dolleen Manning (2005) argues that she is a native speaker of Anishinaabemowin because of her mother's traditional teachings in English over her lifetime. The philosophy transmitted by the late Rosalie Elijah Manning was harder to express in English, of course, and has increasingly led her youngest daughter back to the language and the cultural practices from which it was originally derived.

What appears to make sense to mainstream ears because words and sentences are familiar too easily glosses over the fundamental incommensurability (at least in the absence of translation) of an English spoken from a ground of profound cultural difference. There is no single "Indian English," because the languages, cultures, and traditions of the First Nations differ among themselves. The condition of "reinventing the enemy's language" (Harjo and Bird 1997) has had a local and "tribal" flavour everywhere. To note a few examples from southwestern Ontario, terms such as "well-being," "healing," and "spirituality" carry resonances for Aboriginal speakers of English that are missed by non-Aboriginal interlocutors. The familiar invocation of "all my relations" goes beyond human kinsfolk to the land and the living beings on it. When Native people speak of their responsibilities to seven generations in both directions from themselves, this is literal as well as metaphorical. The scale of human responsibility is vastly greater than that of the usual mainstream scientific definition of ecological responsibility.

The question of expressing Aboriginality in English led me to study social cohesion in relation to rapid cultural and technological change. As in the case of language, continuity just below the surface was masked by the appearance of homogeneity with the mainstream. Technology seemed to be part of the shared experience of Native and non-Native people in Canada, because the technology itself was the same. But differences in the use and value of technology and ways of responding to change draw upon culturally specific assumptions about how the individual is framed within relationships of family, community, and subsistence strategies. Since such differences are not obvious to outsiders, the invisibility of social cohesion has been exacerbated by increasing surface similarity to the mainstream.

Aboriginal claims to land too often have been understood by the mainstream as nostalgic but unrealistic efforts to revitalize outmoded subsistence economies. Many Native persons and communities in regions across Canada, however, still do rely on traditional subsistence for substantial portions of their diet; moreover, the resources of "country food" are distributed throughout the community in accordance with traditional patterns of kinship and responsibility for neighbours (see, for example, Asch 1988). Some individuals continue to hunt as their primary livelihood.

Most of the people who move between city and reserve are not subsistence hunters. For them, change is grounded in a different kind of continuity with Native traditional practices. The relations of European-derived settler-colonists to land clearly have changed over the centuries since contact, so it seems reasonable to acknowledge that the same must be true of Native relationships to land. Thus, I focus on contemporary decision-making strategies in which traditional land-based practices are modified and adapted across the urban–rural divide.

Nomadic legacies evoke habitual culturally inherited forms of thought that privilege movement of people among resources in a seasonal cycle with local variations depending on changes in the available resources, for example, in response to fluctuating game populations or natural disasters, with or without human intervention. Today, of course, few Native people in southwestern Ontario make their living directly and fully off the land, although "country food" remains highly valued by many and often is shared with family and community when available. This dramatic change in everyday diet, especially in urban contexts, does not mean, however, that former nomads have abandoned forms of decision-making that evolved over millennia within their traditional lifeways. Rather, their form has changed to reflect new resources and new directions of mobility and citizenship.

A shifting relationship of particular land or location to the needs of individuals, families, and communities was both normal and normative for semi-nomadic hunters and gatherers. The size of the community under traditional subsistence conditions varied dramatically around the seasonal cycle. Extended family hunting units away for much of the winter commonly came together for sociality and political interaction in the summer (although there are many local and regional variations in the details of seasonal cycles as well as changes over time within the same resource area).

Today in many places, the spring and fall goose hunt or summer fishing continue to take many members of the community away from the reserves that appear to be their places of permanent residence, in ways that draw literally on traditional forms of subsistence resource exploitation. I have modelled this historically attested form of social organization as an accordion (Darnell 1998), with an ebb and flow of group size in relation to resources (some "traditional" and others not) and territory. Significantly, however, the movement is recurrent rather than random. People come back to the same resources in due course. Some individuals go out seeking resources and return to a home camp or home place, a pattern of return intensified under reserve conditions. As long as someone maintains the community's claim to a home place by their presence there, others with (usually kinship-based) rights to group membership and local resource exploitation are authorized to return. This pattern of ebb and flow continues to be reflected in contemporary decision-making strategies—despite the invisibility of such strategies to the mainstream.

Thus, the reserve system in its present form has been adapted (perhaps even subverted) to familiar previously nomadic assumptions, its meaning reinterpreted to serve contemporary needs. The reserve functions as a home place to which people return periodically over their lives. Band members "belong" to that place regardless of where they are living at a given time (which has a far more accidental quality than allegiance to the home place). What appears at first glance to be a rigidly bounded territory controlled by the band becomes in practice a permeable and dynamic set of relationships among people, land, and resources on the land that changes over time. The artificial marking off of a space as belonging to a particular community by the imposed reserve system adapts itself to nomadic patterns by ensuring that some community members are always in residence, whereas others come and go. One need only be present at the swelling of community membership accompanying a wedding or a funeral to see ties being activated that have never ceased to exist as potential. Rarely is anyone surprised, except possibly the visiting anthropologist.

Within their own interactional etiquettes, Native people track the multiple places people belong. For example, the question "where are you from?" does not mean "where did you last live?" or "where do you live now?" Rather, it asks where you grew up, where you have a right to return, where you belong. It enables people to place one another in relation to known persons, places, and resources. Residence is not serial, as it usually is in the increasingly mobile mainstream population, but cyclical in relation to resources. One may go out for various reasons, seeking other known persons or other places known to harbour desired resources. One may return home (or continue to stay away) for various other reasons, for example, for retirement or because of ill health. This right is inherited, although challenged, and often is confirmed by the choice to activate it. This normative question is complicated in practice since 1985 by the implicit genocide built into the C-31 revisions of the Indian Act and its concomitant limitation of additional local resources to support the returnees. Although C-31 allowed women who had married out to reclaim Indian status for themselves and their children, the next generation loses Indian status with marriage to a non-Native person and cannot pass it on to their children.

The Urban Indian

Reflections on social cohesion and cultural continuity led me to the question of the "urban Indian." Whereas my colleagues in sociology accurately document a stable distribution pattern of population numbers and sociological characteristics of age, gender, occupation, education, and so on, my own more qualitative bent leans me toward mapping the ongoing process of turnover in who is here in London, how long they will stay, where they come from and where they will return (or not).

Aboriginal place of residence is what sociolinguist William Labov (1972) called an "ultra-rich topic." People of all ages, both on the reserves and in the city, frequently are eager to talk about why they are living where they are, how they expect this to change in the future, and how their decisions intersect with those of other persons around them. Life histories (of individuals, families, and by inference communities) provide overwhelming evidence of movement back and forth between city and reserve for most of the individuals living in London or on nearby reserves. In London, several reserves are close enough to commute to jobs or school, or to leave children at home, most often with grandparents, and return on weekends or holidays. Such choices rarely involve being fully urban or fully reserve over the course of a lifetime. Most people do not move far from home. These residential decisions make sense to me as nomadic legacies.

The same individuals, therefore, are sometimes "urban Indians" and sometimes not. Moreover, they are practising some aspects of their traditional culture regardless of the point at which we observe their residential choices. Too many efforts to study "the urban Indian" have reified the residence of individuals and families whose actual affiliations to both space/place and kindred are multiple and alternating. The importance of family and community is underscored because the ties acquired through birth and socialization are maintained, indeed nurtured, over considerable distances. Community does not necessarily involve geographical contiguity or immediate co-presence.

The implications for self-government are considerable. If anyone who retains ties to a home place holds rights there, both personally and on behalf of their descendants, then it follows that living off-reserve is not necessarily an obstacle to full First Nations citizenship. Indeed, many bands today are expanding the rights of voting, office-holding, and so on, to non-resident members (supported by the 1999 Corbiere decision of the Supreme Court of Canada). In Indigenous terms, the process is an inclusive one, validated by the actions of particular individuals and families as they enact their community ties, often to multiple places simultaneously.

The Royal Commission on Aboriginal Peoples (RCAP) argued a decade ago that only First Nations peoples with large contiguous populations could expect something like municipal government within the foreseeable future. Little progress has been made over the decade for most communities; indeed, it appears that more and more people are seeking enhanced opportunities off-reserve. This does not necessarily mean that they want to leave home (though in some cases it might) but that resources are not available at home. My colleague and collaborator Dan Smoke, Seneca journalist, put it this way:

> The mobility patterns and the alliances that First Nations people build in the modern society [mean that they] have to leave the reserve due to there not being an economy on the reserve. In the same way, in the old days, the old people would travel and mobilize where the hunting and gathering and the agriculture were resourceful [i.e., full of resources]. This would determine the resources of a location and would determine lengths of stays in territories. So the ... claim that First Nations people are leaving the reserve to find a better life, is untrue. They go in search of a better economy until

one is created in their own home, where they can work and develop their own economy. So, this pattern of leaving the reserve is not holding true, when you see so many people returning home to resources ... The old patterns of our ancestors are very similar to the resource tracing patterns of our present day populations. And ... people are returning home to help develop businesses and resources in their own communities. (personal communication, September 2003)

Not all Native people who move between city and reserve are as self-conscious as Dan about the process, but the traditional character of the pattern of movement is pervasive.

The "urban Indian" cannot be understood exclusively within the city. Native people living in the city do not form a closed population that can be sampled in any meaningful way. To take their urbanity as always already existing is to obscure its emergent and shifting constitution through individual, family, and community decision-making processes. The explanations for observed demographic profiles/correlations are complex and, I would argue, largely inaccessible in the aggregate. These hypotheses call for a methodology that combines the quantitative and the qualitative, the latter with particular emphasis on what people say about themselves and their lives.

A Nomadic Academy?

At the University of Western Ontario, we have been developing ways of combining disciplines and methodologies through our recently established interdisciplinary First Nations Studies program. It has been my privilege to have served as founding director, then co-director, with my colleague Anishinaabe historian Karl Hele, from 2003 to 2006. A four-year honours degree in First Nations Studies was introduced gradually over several years and fully in place for 2006–07, with the first graduates in 2006.

Disciplinary collaborations at the curricular level already include anthropology, history, English, kinesiology, visual arts, media studies, women's studies, political science, and law, with relevant research in sociology, health sciences, medicine, and education, among others.

I suggest, somewhat whimsically, that the university has become a nomadic resource that can be differentially exploited by First Nations students combining the study of their own traditions, histories, and contemporary circumstances in ad hoc but ultimately cohesive ways. The majority of our Native students are Haudensaunee or Anishinaabe (i.e., fairly local), and many make their residential decisions in line with the processes I have been delineating. The collaboration of the First Nations Studies program with Native organizations and individuals working in London as well as with students' home reserves opens up potential further elaborations of the nomadic legacies model.

I continue to emphasize, however, that this model is not intended to explain the decisions or affiliations of any—or every—Native person, even in London and environs. My claims are normative and characterize the behaviours and decision-making strategies of many individuals and sometimes their idealized (and thus consciously formulated) understandings of how things ought to be done. I believe that the decision-making strategies of many individuals now defined as Metis will also make sense under this model, although those of mixed descent may not always be able to identify their personal roots. Native people who come from further away have more difficulty accessing and retaining ties to their home communities. Large cities, particularly Toronto, Winnipeg and Vancouver, have much more heterogeneous Aboriginal populations that, in the aggregate, do not relate in such systematic ways to the home places of people who live there. Yet they reconstitute community in ways that recapitulate traditional practices in new forms and contexts.

The inclusion of the Inuit and Metis in the legal definition of "Aboriginal" under the Canadian Constitution Act of 1982 challenges us to further deconstruct the "urban Indian," to seek out people whose experiences follow other patterns. As in the methodology used in this research, listening to the stories of urban Native people in Toronto, for example, would be expected to produce repeated themes and a limited number of patterns of relationship to home place and traditional culture (Howard 2004). One of these would be a pattern of nomadic legacy.

An important ongoing concern in many reserve communities is that of band membership and participation. The RCAP (1996) proposed a move from blood quantum or lineal descent as defined by the post-1985 Indian Act to custom adoption as a locally relevant and locally controlled principle of membership. Although these issues are evolving constantly, with considerable variation in local protocols, the increasing urban residence of Native community members requires serious consideration of the implications for performing Nativeness in both reserve and city.

Finally, I turn to the latest wrinkle in this evolving research program. The intersection of several projects in our ongoing collaboration with Walpole Island First Nation (WIFN) near Wallaceburg, Ontario, clarifies the permeability of these boundaries and distinctions. WIFN is located on the St. Clair River downstream from Sarnia and is subject to massive and frequent chemical spills. The community has been a pioneer in maintaining its wetlands ecology and in monitoring pollution levels of water and air quality. A team from Western, based in the Ecosystem Health program of the Schulich School of Medicine and Dentistry, Department of Pathology, where I hold a cross-appointment, has actively worked with WIFN to link environmental degradation to health outcomes. On the qualitative side, Christianne Stephens and I examined community risk perception, especially in relation to water quality (Stephens and Darnell 2005, forthcoming; Stephens 2009). We assisted in a study of fish consumption, levels of contamination, and risk perception within the community. We also worked with the island's fluent speakers of Anishinaabemowin to catalogue seventy-six endangered species of plants and animals using the Indigenous knowledge encoded in the language (WIFN 2006). We have also been working on uniting the research and service access objectives of the WIFN health centre with the ecological focus of the Heritage Centre. Sufficient longitudinal data from health records and pollution monitoring suggests the possibility of identifying particular contaminants and the temporal trajectory of their impact on community health.

Although ecosystem health on one reserve may seem distant on the surface from the nomadic legacies that play into the residential decisions creating fluid interchange between city and reserve, we are finding regularities of health care access and health outcomes that show how biomedicine differs in these two contexts, and how individuals maximize the resources available to them by moving from one place to another. Again, the "urban Indian" fails to stand as a monolithic category. People may come to the city to access better medical services. If their health declines, they may move back home in expectation of better care and more local services geared toward chronic conditions and prevention. The same individuals turn up in health records at their home places and in the city. Follow-up care, of course, is impeded because this kind of movement makes tracking patients and their care difficult. Coordination of services and organizations seems critical, and indeed would not be impossible if we remain open to resource-directed mobility as a positive exercise of agency rather than a refusal to stand still and be counted.

Conclusion

This chapter has developed a model of nomadic legacies that mediate between traditional First Nations subsistence patterns and the contemporary urban residence of many Aboriginal people. Language and land emerged as the key issues of identity formation, with resource exploitation encompassing both city and reserve. The relationship of community collaboration to nomadic residence and concomitant decision-making strategies was illustrated by ongoing ecosystem health research that draws on Indigenous knowledge where the boundaries of academic disciplines have become barriers. This model foregrounds First Nations engagements with ongoing dynamic processes of change and adaptation.

Note

I gratefully acknowledge the Social Science Research Council of Canada for its continuous and ongoing support since 1991. Our research teams have included graduate students from Anthropology, Political Science, and the Centre for the Study of Theory and Criticism and community collaborators in London and from several nearby reserves. Our present work on ecosystem health arises from collaboration with the Schulich School of Medicine and Dentistry at the University of Western Ontario. A Killam Research Fellowship made it possible to integrate this long-term work in a more systematic manner.

Works Cited

Asch, Michael. 1988. *Kinship and the Drum Dance in a Northern Dene Community*. Edmonton: Boreal Institute for Northern Studies.

Canada. 1996. *Report of the Royal Commission on Aboriginal Peoples*. Ottawa: RCAP.

Corbiere v. Canada (Minister of Indian and Northern Affairs). 1999, 2S.C.R. 203.

Darnell, Regna. 1982. "The Interactional Consequences of Power." In *Native North American Interaction Patterns*, edited by R. Darnell and M.K. Foster, eds., 69–77. Ottawa: Canadian Museum of Civilization.

———. 1998. "Rethinking the Concepts of Band and Tribe, Community and Nation: An Accordion Model of Algonquian Social Organization." *Papers of the 29th Algonquian Conference*, 90–105. Winnipeg: University of Manitoba.

———. 2004. "Revitalization and Retention of First Nations Languages in Southwestern Ontario." In *Language Rights and Language Survival*, edited by Jane Freedland and Donna Patrick, 87–102. Manchester, UK: St. Jerome.

———. 2006. "Residential School Discourses and the Discourses of Self-Government: Changing Political Resonances of Language and Land in Algonquian Narrative." *Papers of the 37th Algonquian Conference*. Winnipeg: University of Manitoba.

Darnell, Regna, and Maria Manzano-Munguia. 2005. "Nomadic Legacies and Urban Algonquian Residence." *Papers of the 36th Algonquian Conference*. Winnipeg: University of Manitoba, pp. 173–86.

Harjo, Joy, and Gloria Bird, eds. 1997. *Reinventing the Enemy's Language: Contemporary Native Women's Writing of North America*. New York: W.W. Norton.

Howard, Heather A. 2004. "Dreamcatchers in the City: An Ethnohistory of Social Action, Gender and Class in Native Community Production in Toronto." Unpublished Ph.D. dissertation, University of Toronto.

Labov, William. 1972. *Sociolinguistic Patterns*. Philadelphia: University of Pennsylvania Press.

Manning, Dolleen. 2005. "The Give: Hunting for Moose in the Mouth of Nothingness—An Anishinaabe Philosophy of Slips, Slides, and Simultaneity." Unpublished M.A. thesis, University of Western Ontario.

Stephens, Christianne. 2009. "Toxic Talk at Walpole Island First Nation: Narratives of Pollution, Loss and Resistance." Unpublished Ph.D. dissertation, McMaster University.

Stephens, Christianne, and Regna Darnell. 2005. "Water Quality Issues and the WIFN Community." In *Feasibility of Conducting Epidemiological Studies to Assess the Health Risk of the Walpole Island First Nation Community from Exposure to Environmental Contaminants*, Jack Bend et al. Report to the Environmental Contaminants Health Program, First Nations and Inuit Health Branch, Canada.

Stephens, Christianne, and Regna Darnell. Forthcoming. "Assessing Environmental Health Risks through Oral Histories: The Water Quality Issue at Walpole Island First Nation." In *The Nature of Empires and the Empires of Nature*, edited by Karl Hele. Waterloo, ON: Wilfrid Laurier University Press.

Walpole Island First Nation. 2002. *Species at Risk on the Walpole Island First Nation*. Wallaceburg and London, ON: Bkejwanong Natural Heritage Program and the Centre for Research and Teaching of Canadian Native Languages, University of Western Ontario.

4
The Papaschase Band
Building Awareness and Community in the City of Edmonton

Jaimy L. Miller

How does a band, dispersed through colonial identity policies and land surrenders, reclaim their identity in the twenty-first century? This chapter investigates how the Papaschase Band asserts their existence and identity as a Cree First Nation in Edmonton despite not having a land base. In addition, it explores how this Cree Band has re-emerged and is now actively community building after being misidentified as Métis during the North West Half-Breed Scrip Commissions (1885–1886). This misidentification led to the erasure of their status as an Indian band and the loss of their reserve. Currently the Papaschase Band is pursuing a land claim that would restore that status if successful. As Stuart Hall has eloquently put it, "cultural identities are a matter of 'becoming' as well as 'being'"; they have a history, and like everything historical they undergo transformation (Hall 1990, 225). Some of these histories are told everyday; others have been silenced. This is especially true for Indigenous peoples, like the Papaschase Band, living in the aftermath of the colonial endeavour. The "New World," Hall argues, is the beginning of "diaspora, of diversity, of hybridity and difference" (235); and although he is speaking primarily of the experiences of African and Afro-Caribbean peoples, I suggest that hybridity and diaspora are also part of the experience of an Indigenous people such as the Papaschase Cree. This particular band has been subjected to over a century of policies, and therefore lived experiences, based on the Canadian government's notions of identity.

As a person of both European and Indigenous ancestry, experiences of diaspora, hybridity, and difference are a part of my own experience of history and identity. Furthermore, as I explore in this chapter, I can see that they have played a role in the experience of the Papaschase Cree, who, having been separated along the lines of identity during the colonial period and nation-building process, have now come full circle to reclaim their history, culture, and identity. Because of their history, their identities have not been, and could not be, static. Indigenous identities are in a constant process of negotiation; negotiations within selves, with settler societies, and with nation-states that can grant rights and take them away. Indigenous identity is a highly contentious subject between Indigenous and non-Indigenous peoples alike, largely because of the rights that flow from such an identity and the status that accompanies it. The Papaschase Band, through their very presence in Edmonton and particularly through their involvement in political issues such as the Rossdale/Fort Edmonton Reburial, denies the attempts at silencing their history.

When I began this research, the Papaschase Band was in its sixth year as a re-formed First Nation, and as of August 2006 there were 895 registered voters in the band.[1] As a descendent of the band myself, I felt that I was in an interesting post-colonial situation of identity. I had grown up on what was my ancestors' traditional territory, and yet I knew very little about it—hardly anything about the history of what happened during the reserve era in Edmonton, and almost nothing about Cree culture (other than a few words in Cree that my Father had taught me). Growing up I thought my Grandmother was Métis or generically Native, and I could not say where she and her family had come from or what band or community they had belonged to. It was only through genealogical efforts, spurred by the re-formation of the Papaschase Band in 1999, that the connections between my family and Papaschase came out. Since my own experience of silence and absence of knowledge was my starting point, it was a logical step to move beyond myself and ask, In the face of these silences in our collective history, how is the Papaschase Band reclaiming its identity in Edmonton today?

The Papaschase Band, as a dispersed Indigenous people, is in an interesting moment in its collective history. They are "calling people home," reclaiming identity as a band, and fighting for their rights in the legal system. The very existence of the Band today questions the legitimacy of the Indian Act and the Scrip Commissions (explained below), and demands that we rethink our ideas of what an Indigenous community is and can be, and how people go about reclaiming an identity. Being interested in the band's project of re-formation and self-determination, I set out to learn about people's experiences of reclaiming Papaschase identity, and about how government policy and the legal system have affected Indigenous identities now and in the past. During my research I found that an important venue in which Papaschase identity was being asserted was the Rossdale/Fort Edmonton Reburial Project, and in this chapter I consider this political action and the occupation of public space in Edmonton as a vital aspect of their reclamation of identity.

A Brief History of the Papaschase Band[2]

Chief Papaschase and the Headman Tahkoots (the chief's brother, also spelled Takootch) signed an adhesion to Treaty Six on behalf of the Papaschase Band on 21 August 1877 at Fort Edmonton. The chief, Tahkoots, and several other headmen were the children of John Quinn (known as Kwenis) and Lizette Gladu, two mixed-blood Crees from the vicinity of Lesser Slave Lake, and at the time of the adhesion the band consisted of 202 members. The band had migrated toward Fort Edmonton in the 1850s to work, reside, and hunt near the fort, and the area continued to be a site of usual use and occupancy for the band since that time, although it is also possible that the band's association with Beaver Hills, as the area around Edmonton was know to Cree people, goes back even further. During this time they associated and lived with other Crees and "Mixed-Bloods" that came to Edmonton House from areas around Saddle Lake and Lac la Biche in the two decades before the signing of Treaty Six (Tyler 1979).

The reserve had been established across the river from Fort Edmonton because the Papaschase Band had occupied and used this territory since at least the 1850s. During the 1870s and 1880s the hunt failed almost completely; the buffalo disappeared from the prairies in what is now Alberta, and local game became greatly depleted. People began to starve, and the bureaucratic machinery of Indian Affairs slowly began to respond by providing rations for the Indian bands around Edmonton. It was during this time that the Papaschase Band decided it would be most advantageous to have their reserve immediately across the North Saskatchewan River from Fort Edmonton, since the bands closest to the agency often received the most rations and their concerns with respect to their transition to agriculture were more likely to be addressed (Tyler 1979). After signing the treaty, Chief Papaschase selected a site a few miles to the south of the river. In 1878, when M.G. Dickieson (clerk and assistant to the lieutenant governor of the North West Territories) came to pay treaty annuities to the Papaschase Band, he found that some of the band had tried to farm with their treaty implements, but had done very poorly, and he reported that hunting still seemed the surest means of support. It was also recorded that the great majority of the Papaschase Band were practising traditional Cree beliefs, and the Papaschase reserve was the centre of "Indian religious dances and festivals" (Tyler 1979; also see Dempsey 1984).

The official survey of the Papaschase reserve commenced on 2 August 1880 and was calculated by surveyors to be forty-eight square miles; however, they missed eight individuals on the band annuity pay sheets, and the reserve was should have been 49.8 square miles. On the same day, the new Indian Agent, T.P. Wadsworth, came to pay treaty annuities to the band. He found that Chief Papaschase would not accept any treaty money until the problem of the reserve size (among others) was addressed, and so Wadsworth left the chief, crossed the river, and exacted his revenge. He created a new band called the "Edmonton Stragglers" that included eighty-four members of the Papaschase Band and other Crees around Edmonton. Wadsworth could then tell Chief Papaschase that the population of his band was now lower, and that no more than forty square miles would be allocated for his reserve. In addition, he stated that the Stragglers were merely Indians who "loitered" around Edmonton, and could not expect any land to be set aside for their benefit (Tyler 1979).

The next blow to the band would be the Scrip Commissions that first came to Edmonton in 1885. Beginning in 1880, Treaty Indians who could claim or "prove" that they were the children of "half-breeds," or of mixed European and Indigenous parentage, were allowed to withdraw from treaty status and take scrip. The "scrip" they received was a one-time payment of money or land "without any recognition on the part of Canada of their collective Indigeneity" (Lawrence 2004, 84). Speculators closely followed the Scrip Commissions, ready to buy scrip certificates from people on the spot, often at half the amount they were worth (Tyler 1979; also see Hatt 1986). By 1886, Cree bands around Edmonton such as Chief Bobtail's, Samson's, and Ermineskin's bands had many members that requested scrip, and Chief Papaschase and his band, as well as Enoch's band, had even moved to camp at the Scrip Commission (Tyler 1979).

More than half of the Papaschase Band was discharged from treaty in 1886 (102 members, leaving 82 members in the band), and in just two years they would lose their reserve as well. When Chief Papaschase and his headmen took scrip, they were classified as "Métis" and were no longer permitted to live on the reserve by law, and the band found itself without solid leadership. The diasporic nature of the band today can be traced to this event. Indian Affairs agents even had the authority to use the North-West Mounted Police to evict scrip takers from the reserve, and when faced with the agent's power, the chief and headmen left. Other Papaschase Band members then moved to other reserves such as Enoch's, Samson's, Louis Bull, Saddle Lake, Onion Lake, Kehewin, Beaver Lake, and many others. Other band members dispersed to the northeast in the region near Lac la Biche, and their descendents now reside on Métis Settlements such as Elizabeth Settlement, Kikino Settlement, East Prairie Settlement, and others. Provisions were soon made to hasten the removal of people from the Papaschase reserve to Enoch, and by the end of 1887 all members had left. On 19 November 1888 the reserve was officially surrendered to the Crown—the reserve and band erased to make way for settlement. Until the 1970s and the formation of the Papaschase Historical Society, band members found themselves living in a variety of situations on reserves, Métis settlements, and other communities. The oppressive poverty and regulations many Indigenous peoples faced in first half of the twentieth century, along with the geographic dispersal of the band, prevented any attempts at re-formation and often helped internalize imposed identities (Tyler 1979).

The legality of the surrender of the Papaschase reserve is questioned in the Papaschase Band's current land claim; however, their land claim was initially dismissed in 2004, largely because of notions of identity and the diasporic nature of the band. Many Papaschase Band members simultaneously identify as members of other bands and communities, a form of hybridity that does not fit Western and legal notions of identity. Rather than being considered Cree people from the Edmonton area, historian Clint Evans and Justice Frans F. Slatter declared them "Métis from Lesser Slave Lake" without a "cohesive" community (due to the dispersal) and therefore with no legitimate claim to land in Edmonton (Evans 2003). The court decision is now being appealed. Although descendents of the Papaschase Band have been publicly active since the 1970s in reclaiming their history and identity in Edmonton, in 1999 an election was held for chief and council of the Papaschase Band. The band had "officially" re-formed, received recognition from the Treaty Six Confederacy, and launched a land claim. Prior to 1999, some descendents of the band had created a Papaschase Descendents Council, and today members are still sometimes referred to as "descendents." According to the band's website, the mandate of the Chief and Council is to "govern the Papaschase Descendents affairs, to defend and advance their treaty rights and legitimate interests of the Papaschase Descendents, and to take all necessary steps to obtain a just settlement of the unlawful surrender of Papaschase I.R. 136 in 1888" (Papaschase Band, Welcome).

Creating Awareness in the City of Edmonton

The band's process of reclaiming identity has resulted in political activism, a presence in the media, and the occupation of public space within the city. Although the band is not recognized by the federal government, they have received recognition as a band from the Treaty Six Confederacy, members of the Blackfoot Confederacy, and the City of Edmonton through their involvement in the Rossdale/Fort Edmonton Reburial project. In addition, the band was recognized as the host band of the Day of Commemoration held by the Aboriginal Healing Foundation in Edmonton on 8 July 2004, and Chief Rose Lameman of the Papaschase Band gave a welcoming address to the participants that included prominent Aboriginal political figures such as Phil Fontaine, National Chief of the Assembly of First Nations, and George Erasmus, President of the Aboriginal Healing Foundation and Co-Chair of the Royal Commission on Aboriginal Peoples.[3] Aboriginal peoples and elders from around the country participated in the event, and the message was clear that the foundation and the Aboriginal community in Canada accept and respect the Papaschase Band.

The band has also asserted its presence in Edmonton through participation in Aboriginal Day events in Edmonton, rallies and public protests outside the courthouses in response to legal decisions regarding their claim, the creation of a website, organizing Papaschase Band reunions, and involvement in the Fort Edmonton/Rossdale Reburial project. EPCOR, the major energy company in Edmonton, announced plans in the late 1990s to expand the power generating station on the Rossdale Flats near the North Saskatchewan River and downtown Edmonton. This was immediately met with resistance from the Rossdale Community League, members of the Aboriginal community, and the Alberta Historical Board, as the Rossdale Flats was the site of Fort Edmonton as well as its cemetery. When the Papaschase Band officially re-formed in 1999, they became involved in the fight to stop the expansion. This proved to be an issue very close to the band, as several of its members had been buried there and the Papaschase reserve was just across the North Saskatchewan River from the site. It was an important opportunity for the band to assert its presence and identity as a First Nation in Edmonton.

Rossdale Burial Grounds and Oral History Project

The Rossdale Oral History Project and Reburial Ceremony was the result of agitation from local First Nations, Métis, and French activists and stakeholders in Edmonton, and was sponsored by the Edmonton Aboriginal Urban Affairs Committee. The purpose of the project was to "properly honour the memory of the people resting in the Rossdale Flats and to provide necessary information that links the past to the present and create a valuable resource for future generations. Originating at the request of members of Edmonton's Aboriginal communities, the Rossdale Flats Aboriginal Oral Histories Project (RFAOHP) research team began collecting and transcribing oral histories related to the traditional burial site/Fort Edmonton Cemetery in the Rossdale Flats area" (Pelletier et al. 2004a, 2).

The report is extensive, and by the project end date the oral history project team had "travelled to different parts of the province for presentations, attended city and stakeholder meetings, and hosted two gatherings. By this time, the team had also interviewed twenty-seven participants: Aboriginal elders, community members, descendants of people interred at the Fort Edmonton Cemetery, Rossdale residents, and historians." The report also discusses the significance of the site for Aboriginal peoples, a significance that predates the fur trade and the arrival of Europeans. The report, prepared by Jacqueline Pelletier and a team of researchers for the Edmonton Urban Aboriginal Affairs Committee, states that "long before the Rossdale Flats contained the Fort Edmonton Cemetery, this area in Edmonton's river valley was a pehonan, a 'gathering place,' for Aboriginal peoples ... the Flats were the location for sacred ceremonies that included the Goose Dance, Sun Dance, and Pow-Wows" (2004a, 2–3). The Rossdale Flats also had an excellent crossing site on the North Saskatchewan River, and was important not only for Aboriginal peoples but also for the fur traders who came to the area.

Significantly, the Papaschase Band was recognized and approached by Aboriginal activists (including Duane Good Striker and members of the Blackfoot Confederacy and Phillip Coutu of the Métis Nation of Alberta), and was treated with respect, because this area was seen as the Papaschase Band's traditional territory. Papaschase councillor Calvin Bruneau was interviewed as part of the Rossdale Oral History project on 7 October 2003, and reported that:

> I believe it was February 2000. We were approached by Duane Good Striker. I was newly elected the year before in '99 in August to the Papaschase Council. We were having some structural problems, and just

basically trying to get the leadership issue settled. During that time while we were in the process of doing this, Duane found out that ... the closest Band, you know where there's a burial ground that the closest Band is to look after that issue. He heard about us; he could have gone to Enoch [reserve], but he came to us instead because we were based out of Edmonton and he thought of us because we had a reserve on the south side. So we were newly elected and all that, so he came to us. He showed us pictures of human remains and skeletons that were unearthed and the burial grounds being desecrated. He told us that EPCOR wanted to do some work there, and because there was to be a significant amount of further desecration, he wanted our help. (Pelletier et al. 2004b)

The Papaschase Council was asked to send a letter of objection to Edmonton City Council and the Energy Utility Board (EUB), and asked to become interveners and attend stakeholder hearings with the Energy Utility Board and the Edmonton City Council.

An Energy Utility Board pre-hearing (2000) and hearings (2000/01) were requested when a number of stakeholders came forward to protest EPCOR's proposed expansion. At first, the Energy Utility Board (EUB) approved EPCOR's expansion plans, but after the Alberta Historical Board made recommendations to Alberta Community Development, Community Development Minister Gene Zwodesky stopped the expansion. The expansion was primarily halted to protect the historic buildings on the flats that were built for power generation, but it did result in a victory to protect the burial grounds as well. The Alberta Historical Board was moved to this action by presentations from the Papaschase Band and other stakeholders and activists concerned about the burial ground. Since their initial pleas had not been heeded by the EUB or city council, they strategically found another avenue through which to protect the area, designating the buildings historic properties and thereby halting desecration of the burials. It also helped the band's cause that human remains were found on EPCOR's property in May and October 2000, which resulted in EPCOR being held accountable and unable to dig in the area without an archaeological permit (Papaschase Band, Rossdale). After the hearings, the First Nations, Métis and French activists approached then-mayor Bill Smith at a meeting at city hall to protect the burial ground. At first, EPCOR's arguments against it swayed Mayor Smith and council, but they changed their minds after seeing pictures of archaeologists digging human remains on EPCOR's property (Papaschase Band, Rossdale). As a result, meetings were commissioned between representatives of the city of Edmonton and the community stakeholders to discuss how best to deal with the burial.

The hearings with the Energy Utility Board were intense and confrontational, and Councillor Bruneau reported to the Rossdale Oral History Team on 7 October 2003 that:

> There were a lot of different groups; there was a coalition of environment, historical, and descendent groups. There was the Rossdale Community, different community league groups, homeowners, people like that. Basically we were all against what was going on so it was confrontational ...We had made our best presentations but it seemed time to ... it just wasn't good because there were people being attacked personally ... The Hearings were pretty intense and there were a lot of Elders there backing and supporting us and we made some good presentations and we threw what we could at them. We were disappointed by the decision the EUB made. At the same time, too, we did make a presentation to the Alberta Historical Board, in August of that year, later that year. There were a few of us that made passionate presentations, and they went to the Alberta Community Development and made their recommendations to them and what they did was they overturned it by designating some buildings there at EPCOR's site historical properties. So that effectively shut it down. (Pelletier et al. 2004b, 49–50)

As a result of this agitation by the Papaschase Band and other stakeholders, a portion of Rossdale road was shut down, and traffic is no longer allowed to drive over this sacred area. The remains that had been uncovered were held at the University of Alberta and at the Medical Examiner's Office, and on 28 August 2005 they were finally returned to rest in the burial ground. Other activist techniques were employed as well. During the spring of 2001 Aboriginal activists (including some members of the Papaschase Band) put up white crosses along Rossdale road in time for morning commuters to see that they were driving to work over a cemetery (Edmonton Urban Aboriginal Affairs Committee, Backgrounder). An elder connected with the Papaschase Band was interviewed as part of the Rossdale Oral History Project on 9 September 2003 and remarked that:

> I'm thinking that part of the burial grounds was associated with the reserve that was across the river there of the Papaschase. I haven't been down there recently. I went down when Duane Good Striker was bringing a cross, and I brought a wreath. I haven't been there for a long time now.
>
> There were a bunch of crosses planted there at one time, little crosses ... I'm trying to think of when Calvin (Bruneau/Desjarlais) and them went down there and I think Gerald Delorme went down there too. They had some crosses there ... those were put there to commemorate the dead that were there and somebody—well those were there for a little while. Then somebody went there and knocked those crosses down which aggravated me. And then I don't know if it was in the papers or—yes it was in the

papers I guess. I heard this remark, "Why don't those Indians quit raising heck down there?" I thought to myself, "If your relations were down there, you'd make some noise." So this is why we're making noise and we're going to keep making noise!

Of course when I come over that bridge I always take a look down there. I look there to see what's happening because I will not go over Rossdale Road. (Pelletier et al. 2004b, 43–44)

The crosses erected by Papaschase Band members and other Aboriginal activists were damaged and knocked down by unknown people, but not before their physical and symbolic impact was felt. Professor Heather Zwicker from the University of Alberta, referring to this makeshift memorial, states that "first of all, it's there, a physical reminder that our colonial accounts are not settled. Second, its construction—it just appeared one day—suggests a bold reclamation of public land by the people. Third, its very makeshift nature is productively shocking, especially since it is located directly alongside a major traffic thoroughfare" (Zwicker 2004). The memorial served to remind anyone aware of the Rossdale issue that Edmonton's history was full of silences and that Aboriginal peoples would no longer allow their lives and histories to be erased from public memory. It was a demand to correct the injustices of the past, and brought curiosity and consciousness to those who had never heard of the burial site or the Papaschase Band before. This type of agitation, along with the efforts of the Aboriginal stakeholders at the EUB meetings and with the Alberta Historical Board, led to the Rossdale/Fort Edmonton Reburial Ceremony during which the remains that had been disturbed on EPCOR's property would be re-interred on a protected site. It was a victory for the Aboriginal community involved in the issue and for the Papaschase Band.

The Reburial Ceremony

The reburial ceremony was held on 28 August 2005 on the Rossdale Flats in Edmonton. It was an incredibly hot day: temperatures were well above thirty degrees Celsius and no clouds were in the sky. The event began at 2:30 p.m. with a procession in which a few hundred people walked along the Rossdale Road following Red River carts that carried the eight caskets to be buried. Six of the pine caskets contained the partial remains of individuals, while two caskets contained bone fragments from an unknown number of individuals. The remains had been in the care of the University of Alberta and the medical examiner's office for many years, and they were wrapped in simple cotton blankets and placed on a bed of buffalo hair because unidentified hair had been found with the remains. Grave goods that were found alongside the bodies were also placed in the caskets, and the caskets were permanently sealed with wooden pegs. No metal was used; such luxuries as metal hinges were not used on caskets in Fort Edmonton during the 1800s. Pendleton blankets were draped over the caskets at the request of descendents, and the Edmonton city council provided flowers to sit on each of the caskets. The caskets' small size was probably the first thing that people noticed. The pallbearers were people known to be descendents of people who were historically recorded as buried at the site during the 1800s, and this included several members of the Papaschase Band.

When I arrived at the starting point of the procession, Chief Rose Lameman, the councillors, and other members of the Papaschase Band were getting ready to begin. The chief was having her hair braided, and others were changing clothes and preparing for their journey ahead as pallbearers. The media was present; I saw many cameras, tape recorders, and people being interviewed and photographed. Horses, trucks, lawn chairs, and a couple of tipis were set up on the grounds. A large tent was also set up, where the mayor and other dignitaries and descendents would make some remarks after the burial. The carts were slowly lined up, the pallbearers took their places, and the sound of bagpipes signalled the beginning of our walk through this historic site and to the place where our ancestors would be laid to rest again. Earlier in the day Cree and Blackfoot elders performed a traditional pipe ceremony over the burial site, and our procession would take us to the burial location for a multi-faith ceremony.

As we walked in the procession, I tried to concentrate on why I was there, I thought about my Métis and Papaschase ancestors and what their lives might have been like. I thought about my research with the Papaschase Band, and how I refuse to let my family be forgotten for who they were. I thought about the silences in our collective history, and I thought about how I would not let the project of assimilation be completed. Most of all, I hoped that my ancestors understood why I was doing this, that they could see my good intentions and my choice to stand up and represent them. I looked around, and it was amazing to see so many communities come together and remember a time when they were linked through Fort Edmonton. While I walked I was also conscious of the tremendous heat and the numerous people watching and recording us from the sidelines. The entire event was photographed and filmed, except for the actual burial of the caskets themselves. When we reached the site of the multifaith service, we were able to sit down and listen to speakers from all the communities involved. The caskets were placed in front of us, and on the stage prayers were offered in Cree, Blackfoot, English, and French. Songs were sung in these languages as well, and there were Aboriginal singers and drummers, a French-Canadian fiddler, and Scottish bagpipes.

Archaeologists and employees of Alberta Community Development who knew the parameters of the site selected the location of the graves. The graves and caskets were kept as small as possible so that opening the graves would not disturb the other remains at the site. After the multifaith ceremony we followed the pallbearers to the gravesite, and the caskets were laid in the ground on beds of buffalo sage. Cree Elder Louie Rain drummed and sang as the caskets were laid to rest, and we were invited to walk past the graves, pay our respects, and throw dirt, tobacco, and sweetgrass into the burials. Afterward, people slowly made their way over to the large tent where Mayor Stephen Mandel, Alberta Aboriginal Affairs Minister Pearle Calahasen, Duane Good Striker of the Blackfoot Confederacy, and Papaschase Councillor Calvin Bruneau made some concluding remarks about the steps taken to get to this day, and what lay ahead.

At the reburial ceremony, Chief Rose Lameman and Councillor Calvin Bruneau confirmed that the Papaschase Band had at least thirty-one members who were buried at the Fort Edmonton burial ground during the nineteenth century (Papaschase Band, Rossdale). The band's involvement in the Rossdale/Fort Edmonton reburial also created an arena in the media and urban community to assert Papaschase identity; for example, I was able to listen as Chief Rose Lameman as she sent out this message to the media and descendents of the Papaschase Band:

Chief Rose Lameman: What I need to say to the descendents, and everybody here, is that it is not only an honour [to be here], but it is also of personal, historical, and cultural significance. Not only for the three pallbearers behind me and myself, but also for people in the community of Edmonton. And it is important, because I am the chief of the Papaschase Band, and the people behind me are councillors for the Papaschase Band, and this is our cultural and traditional ground. We camped here; we lived here, lived and died here. This is significant and why we are here today ... I myself am a great-great-granddaughter to the chief, and so are the councillors behind me.

Interviewer: So Rose, what are you going to be thinking about during the procession, as you work your way around this burial ground? What will be going through your mind?

Chief Rose Lameman: I'll be thinking about the people that lived and died here, who settled here, who gathered here, from the time before settlement right through until now. I will think about all the people who are buried here, and the people that are here to represent their ancestors. About how we are going to honour them and give them dignity and the respect that they deserve, because to us—our people, once they were buried it was sacred ground and was never to be touched—we left and never looked behind. And in this situation we are doing something of historical and cultural significance, because we have never had to rebury our people, so this is a very historical event for us. There is nothing in Cree tradition that indicates we reburied people. So this is very important to us, and we are doing the best that we can, in terms of doing what is right for our people, the Cree people.

It's a step toward a new beginning, a new day, a new dawn, and a new tomorrow. And I will be singing to the ancestors, to my family, to the chief's family, and everyone that is buried here. To ensure that they have a good journey and can go forward. And that we can go forward, that it will give us life to go forward.

Later, at the Papaschase Band meeting on 1 October 2005, a different band member reflected on the experience of the reburial as well:

I have met a lot of family here, I've learned how to connect, this is where I belong, the people here—I'm proud to represent you, and also, the good things—the reburial, the four of us … carrying the coffin, and you were thinking very hard during the procession to the graveyard, hanging on to this person, and you were thinking, "if only this person could talk," all the answers we need to find out. But I believe people are here, our elders, they're here, they are out there, and we need to get the stories and histories so that we can prove we were a band. But the difficulty [is] that we are running on a limited budget … (personal communication)

On the day of the Rossdale/Fort Edmonton Reburial Ceremony, many people in the Papaschase Band wore traditional dress as well as shirts that said "Papaschase First Nation" and had the symbol of the woodpecker. In the Cree language Papaschase means woodpecker, Papastes meaning small woodpecker and Papastew meaning large woodpecker (Papastew is phonetically "Papastayo"). The spelling "Papaschase" is actually a European attempt at the name, and as one can see in fur trade records, Europeans spelled Indigenous words and names in a plethora of ways. The symbolism of the Papaschase crest represents a way to create a bond and an understanding between members of the Papaschase Band. It is a visual account of the values important to the band and its history, and it drew attention and united the Papaschase Band at the ceremony.

Conclusion

Occupying public space has been a key element in reclaiming Papaschase identity, and at no time was this more apparent than during the Rossdale/ Fort Edmonton reburial issue. The band's involvement was not only about protecting and honouring the lives of our ancestors but also about asserting the existence of the Papaschase Band and its members as the living descendents of the people that lived and died at this site. The Rossdale Flats was always a significant place to Aboriginal peoples, and though Justice Slatter argued that the Papaschase Band were "Métis from Lesser Slave Lake" new to Edmonton in the mid-nineteenth century, as Aboriginal people the Métis understood its cultural significance and even held sun dances and gatherings on the site. As Cree people they too made this special place their home and honoured its scared ground. Their people were buried on the flats, and the Papaschase reserve was just across the river from the site. This was their home. The members of the contemporary Aboriginal community, including the Treaty Six Confederacy, the Métis Nation of Alberta, and the Blackfoot Confederacy, understood this and respected the Papaschase Band, respected that this area was the Papaschase Band's traditional territory. The City of Edmonton municipal government, through its involvement in the Rossdale/Fort Edmonton reburial issue, also recognized the legitimacy of the Papaschase Band in claiming this site as part of their traditional territory.

The band has actively worked on building a community through its involvement in Aboriginal Day festivities, the Day of Commemoration held by the Aboriginal Healing Foundation, its website, band reunions, and the creation of the Papaschase Band's symbols. Although this community may be diasporic in nature and members are often members of other bands and communities, the Papaschase Band sees itself as a Cree First Nation that is, in the words of Chief Lameman, "going to go forward." People in the band have donated an immense amount of time and effort to foster this community—travelling at their own expense, fighting for the respect of those buried at Fort Edmonton, governing the affairs of the band, and contacting descendents who have been dispersed and misidentified by the policies and actions of a colonial government. The historic actions of the government have resulted in the diasporic nature of the band, as well as members' need to "become who they really are." This can be seen as a part of the "being and becoming" nature of identity that Stuart Hall has discussed (1990). Their hard work on the Rossdale/Fort Edmonton Reburial Project has resulted in more descendents coming forward and recognition from many different groups; the only aspect lacking is legal recognition of their identity, although this in itself is problematic, with legal Indigenous identity often constrained.[4] Finally, the diasporic quality of the Papaschase Band has made public assertion of identity through the Rossdale/Fort Edmonton Reburial project a vital aspect of community building, and just as importantly it has been a place to "be" Papaschase.

Notes

1 Papaschase Band Councillor Calvin Bruneau, personal communication, 21 August 2006.

2 The history of the Papaschase Band is complex. Kenneth Tyler's master's thesis in history provides a thorough account of the origins and dispersal of the Band, and in research separate from this particular paper I explore the history of the Band in greater detail.

3 See the website for the Aboriginal Healing Foundation for video of Chief Rose Lameman of the Papaschase Band giving a welcoming address to the Day of Commemoration delegates. Participants at the event included George Erasmus, Phil Fontaine, and the federal minister responsible for residential school survivors. http://www.ahf.ca/e_commemoration.aspx.

4 For more exploration into the legal demands on Indigenous identities, see publications such as Asch 1997; Clifford 1986; Culhane 1998; Feit 2001; Macklem 2001; and Mackey 2001; 2005. Also useful is the article "The Politicization of 'Culture' in Anthropology Today," by Susan Wright (1998), which discusses "old" and "new" concepts of "culture" and how they are used.

Works Cited

Asch, Michael. *Aboriginal and Treaty Rights in Canada: Essays on Law, Equality, and Respect for Difference.* Vancouver: University of British Columbia Press, 1997.

Clifford, James. *The Predicament of Culture: 20th-Century Ethnography, Literature, and Art.* Cambridge: Harvard University Press, 1988.

Culhane, Dara. *The Pleasure of the Crown: Anthropology, Law, and First Nations.* Burnaby: Talon Books, 1998.

Edmonton Urban Aboriginal Affairs Committee, BackGrounder. http://www.aboriginal-edmonton.com/PDF/BackgrounderRossdale.pdf.

Evans, Clint. "Report on the Origin and Dissolution of the Papaschase Band." Unpublished report prepared for Department of Justice Canada, Edmonton Regional Office, 27 January 2003.

Feit, Harvey. "Contested Identities of 'Indians' and 'Whitemen' at James Bay, or the Power of Reason, Hybridity, and Agency." *Senri Ethnological Studies* 66: 109–26, 2004.

Hall, Stuart. "Cultural Identity and Diaspora." In *Identity: Community, Culture, and Difference,* edited by J. Rutherford, 222–37. London: Lawrence & Wishart, 1990.

Hatt, Ken. "The North-West Rebellion Scrip Commissions, 1885–1889. In 1885 and Beyond: Native Society in Transition edited by F. Laurie Barron and James Waldram,189–204. Regina: University of Regina Canadian Plains Research Center.

Lawrence, Bonita. "Real" Indians and Others: Mixed Blood Urban Peoples and Indigenous Nationhood. Lincoln: University of Nebraska Press, 2004.

Macklem, Patrick. *Indigenous Difference and the Constitution of Canada.* Toronto: University of Toronto Press, 2001.

Mackey, Eva. "Universal Rights in Conflict: 'Backlash' and 'Benevolent Resistance' to Indigenous Land Rights." *Anthropology Today* 21 (2): 14–20, 2005.

———. *The House of Difference: Cultural Politics and National Identity in Canada.* Toronto: University of Toronto Press, 2001.

Papaschase Band, *Rossdale.* http://www.papaschase.ca/rossdale.html.

Papaschase Band, *Welcome.* http://www.papaschase.ca/index.html.

Pelletier, Jacqueline, et al. 2004a. *Rossdale Flats Aboriginal Oral Histories Project, Part 1.* Edmonton: Edmonton Urban Aboriginal Affairs Committee. http://www .aboriginal-edmonton.com/PDF/Aboriginalhistoryproject.pdf.

———. 2004b. *Rossdale Flats Aboriginal Oral Histories Project, Part 2.* Edmonton: Edmonton Urban Aboriginal Affairs Committee. http://www .aboriginal-edmonton.com/PDF/Aboriginalhistoryproject.pdf.

Slatter, Frans F. *Reasons for Judgement of the Honourable Mr. Justice Frans F. Slatter, Citation: Papaschase Indian Band (Descendents of) v. Canada (Attorney General), 2004 ABQB 655.* http://www.papaschase.ca/text/summary.pdf

Tyler, Kenneth James. 1979. "A Tax-Eating Proposition: The History of the Passpasschase Indian Reserve." M.A. thesis, Department of History, University of Alberta.

Wright, Susan. "The Politicization of 'Culture.'" *Anthropology Today* 14 (1): 7–15.

Zwicker, Heather. 2004. *Dead Indians, Power Conglomerates and the Upper Middle Class: Commemorating Colonial Conflict in Edmonton's Rossdale.* http://culturalstudies.ca/proceedings04/pdfs/zwicker.pdf.

5

"Regaining the childhood I should have had"

The Transformation of Inuit Identities, Institutions, and Community in Ottawa

Donna Patrick, Julie-Ann Tomiak, Lynda Brown, Heidi Langille, and Mihaela Vieru

This chapter explores the production of urban Inuit identities and the construction of an urban Inuit community in Ottawa. These processes are seen as mutually reinforcing relationships that dynamically link identity formation, ethnicity, and institutional discourses and practices. "Identity" and "community" formations are conceptualized as reciprocal processes that are constituted by discourses, historical developments, institutional practices, and everyday life. Our discussion is based on preliminary research conducted on the shifting and complex nature of urban Inuit identity and community and, more specifically, identity formation in youth in Ottawa. In this urban context, state processes overlap with local cultural and social practices to shape social institutions, networks, and communities in new dynamic ways. Thus, "community" cannot be assumed to be an unproblematic or fixed entity but seems to be conceptualized more abstractly by members who are part of the social networks, cultural practices, and the institutional landscapes that form this non-geographically bounded community (Lobo 2001; Howard-Bobiwash 2003; Proulx 2003; Weibel-Orlando 1999). Complex and multiple processes taking place in urban settings are not only redefining but also enriching and expanding notions of Inuitness, as will be elaborated on in the next section. Overall, this chapter emphasizes the diversity and complexity of transnational, diasporic, and local processes that constitute and reconstitute Inuit identities and communities in this specific urban environment.

In what follows, we situate urban Inuit realities within larger societal and political economic contexts. We first discuss how Inuitness is contingently constructed, and then briefly describe the urban Inuit community in Ottawa. The experiences of two of the authors, Lynda Brown and Heidi Langille, who are urban Inuit bring the key issues raised in this chapter into perspective.

Inuitness, Identity, and Community-Building

Our analysis takes social and cultural identity to be a contingent, strategic, and positional process (Hall 1996). Contrary to essentialist views, identities are not always "there," waiting to be "discovered"; they emerge in the context of specific discourses, social interaction, and political economic constellations. Thus, subject positions establish points of temporary attachments to particular identities, which are produced within specific discursive formations. Identity can therefore be conceptualized as a collective social project that requires investment by actors in specific temporal and spatial operating frames (Bourdieu 1991; Calhoun 1995). Articulations of identity are also social struggles in, through, and about place and spatial struggles in which ideas of race, class, ethnicity, gender, and community are formed (Jacobs 1996; Keith and Pile 1993).

A number of related concepts are useful for understanding the complex nature of the shifting, positional Inuit identities in southern, urban contexts. One is the concept of community building and, more specifically, the construction of the Inuit community as an imagined community to which individuals belong (Anderson 1983). A second is that of habitus, which can be seen as a set of dispositions and a socialized capacity for generating "thoughts, perceptions, expressions and actions" (Bourdieu 1990, 55). Although the embodied dispositions of the habitus do not determine behaviour, "they do predispose us to respond in particular ways to both new and familiar situations" (Freeland and Patrick 2004, 12). A "product of history," these "individual and collective practices" (Bourdieu 1990, 54) operate and are defined in relation to larger state and political economic practices producing specific behaviours and subject positions. In the context of emerging urban Inuit identities, as discussed later in this chapter, these generative practices can be "emergent," "hybrid," and "local" and can also articulate with larger state-sponsored, institutionally produced and historically based constructions of Inuitness—a general term that we use to capture the panoply of practices, beliefs, and attributes of being Inuit.[1]

The concept of Inuitness allows us to account for the multiple ways in which Inuit identity is constructed. In addition, since it involves both a sense of "being" and "doing," it can account for the ways of "being Inuit" (i.e., defining oneself as Inuit) and for the enactment of cultural and discursive practices that construct ethnicity and the social category of "Inuit" in particular social contexts. Thus, it captures the socio-cultural relations and practices of individuals operating in social groups and the larger discursive processes involved in community building.

The imagined community of Inuit in Canada is both a strategic and political construction, as Inuit have mobilized across time and space for recognition within the Canadian state and, more specifically, for title to and jurisdiction over their lands. Inuitness in this political-geographical sense is characterized not only by localized cultural practices that have persisted over centuries in northern Canada but also through relationships and interactions with traders, missionaries, government officials, and the state. The state in particular became more involved after a 1939 Supreme Court of Canada ruling that extended the federal government's jurisdiction to include Inuit under section 91(24) of the BNA Act—to make laws for "Indians, and Lands reserved for the Indians."[2]

Despite being subsumed under this federal responsibility, however, Inuit have always remained a separate category in Canadian political-legal discourse, distinct from First Nations and Métis. Historically, geographically, politically, and legally, Inuit have been imagined and positioned as distinct peoples inhabiting the Canadian Arctic. Through the land claims and political processes, Inuitness is now often defined in relation to the traditional land bases and according to territorial and provincial boundaries— Nunatsiavut (Labrador), Nunavik (Quebec), Inuvialuit (NWT), and Nunavut (NT). In these geographical imaginings, urban Inuit in southern Canada often get sidelined, not only with respect to national bodies dealing with Inuit but in the public imaginary as well.

The assumed associations between peoples and place are the unstable products of historical and social processes rather than the outcome of pre-given, fixed essences (Jacobs 1996; Gupta and Ferguson 1997). While the increased movement of people and information has complicated dominant concepts of place, the ways in which space and identity are imagined have become real concerns for dispersed groups—particularly for those for whom notions of authenticity and questions such as "who counts as a 'real' group member?" become central to diasporic life.

For Inuit, who counts as a "real Inuk" is embedded in language ideologies whereby speaking particular forms of Inuktitut might classify one as more or less "real Inuk." In the Arctic, a real Inuk or Inummarik possesses the cultural and linguistic knowledge to pursue a traditional way of life based on traditional harvesting practices—an identity that was not an option for many Inuit who were educated in southern urban centres (Ipellie 1993, vii). In southern contexts, we refer to Inuit identities as forms of Inuitness, a notion that is shaped by cultural practices that define oneself as Inuk and are recognized by others as such. In these acts of identity, the representations of Inuit, as they have been constructed through centuries of textual and discursive production by Europeans and Euro-Canadians, including countless stereotypes and images that have shifted across time and space in an "imaginary North," can also come into play and can be resisted, reproduced, and/ or subverted in daily life (Graburn 1969; Brody 1975, 1987; Patrick 2003).

The ways in which urban Inuit construct Inuitness, particularly for those who have been brought up in the South (either as the children of parents who came south or as children who were adopted into southern families), are particularly relevant to our understanding of community and the process of community building. While there might be a noticeable tension between the Northern- and Southern-born Inuit, based on their geographic, historical, and cultural positioning, there are nevertheless community-based processes that unify Inuit as a recognizable, important force in the Aboriginal urban landscape. Tensions between forms of desired symbolic capital that Northern-raised Inuit possess (linguistic and cultural knowledge that could define "authentic Inuitness") versus that of Southern-raised Inuit (the language, literacy, and social capital necessary for urban life) might create a boundary between community members, but the boundary is fluid and becomes more salient at certain times than others. In the following section, we look more closely at these and other forms of heterogeneity of the Ottawa Inuit community. Despite the diversity and complexity of the community, urban Inuit have unified and mobilized for particular social and community services, consistent with their historical positioning and relationship to the state.

Inuit in Ottawa

Well over a thousand Inuit are estimated to live in the Ottawa area (Tungasuvvingat Inuit 2005); however because of high rates of mobility in the urban environment, the exact number of Inuit is difficult to pinpoint. Similar to First Nations and Métis urban communities, there is great diversity, with Inuit taking up residence in different parts of the city. Some stay for short periods, while others have been in Ottawa for most of their lives or have always lived in the South. Many Inuit come to the city temporarily (for medical reasons or post-secondary education), or more permanently for employment. Some also come for family reasons.

An understanding of the highly mobile and dispersed Inuit population, both demographically and socio-economically, becomes important given the need to develop adequate programs and allocate sufficient funding to existing programs. The fluid nature of the urban Inuit community in Ottawa, however, has made it difficult to map in a more definitive sense.

Rather than suggest the existence of a single, cohesive urban Inuit community in Ottawa, we stress the heterogeneity of Inuit realities in the city. Inuit who move to Ottawa for jobs or higher education navigate the city differently from those who have been marginalized in the North, fled from abusive homes, or spent time in Ottawa for medical reasons. Social stratification and different reasons for migrating determine the positionalities of individuals and families in the urban context, which translates into a myriad of experiences, perceptions, and ways of dealing with the realities of urban life. Ottawa, as the federal capital, provides a particular dynamic—Aboriginal professionals participate in the public service, as well as national Aboriginal organizations, to promote First Nations, Inuit, and Métis interests. For Inuit, then, Ottawa might offer a more socio-economically polarized picture of an urban Inuit community than, say, Montreal or Edmonton. The national organizations and the people working in them can, to some extent, shape the politics of Inuitness through their access to resources and dominant discourses via these institutional infrastructures. Differences based on class, gender, place, or other factors, however, may not preclude solidarity or successful mobilization around notions of Inuitness; for example, class mobility has been instrumental in creating Indigenous spaces in the city and in delivering services to urban Aboriginal populations considered at risk (see Howard-Bobiwash 2003).

Although we situate urban Inuit experiences within the broader social category of "urban Aboriginality," we also argue that the experiences of Inuit are worth examining on their own terms. We recognize Inuitness as a separate set of experiences based on the specificity of Inuit historical, cultural, and geographical circumstances and because the umbrella "Aboriginal" category tends to homogenize and essentialize the myriad of experiences and difference among Indigenous peoples living in urban environments. Although it is recognized that First Nations, Inuit, and Métis experiences and identities in Canada are shaped by particular colonial (racialized and gendered) processes of social categorization (see Lawrence 2003, 2004; Miller 2004), and that urban identities are faced with even more complexity in this regard (Jackson 2002; Proulx 2003), we argue here that Inuit urban experiences—although similar to First Nations and Métis experiences—are also set apart in some respects.[3]

The dynamics of trans-regional migration are different for Inuit in comparison with many First Nations and Métis residents in the city. One of the key differences lies in the ability of members in the latter groups to return to their home communities on a more regular basis. The prohibitive costs of Arctic travel make these connections less viable for a large number of Inuit in Ottawa, especially for those without high-paying jobs and for those from small Arctic communities. Despite these geographical and economic constraints, relationships to home communities are often maintained through various communication technologies. These communal ties continue to be important elements of imagined geographies and shape urban Inuit realities (c.f. Jackson 2002 on the role of home communities for urban American Indians). Thus, major organizing principles of social networks in cities are not only economic and cultural but geographical as well. For instance, people with relatives from particular regions tend to be identified with particular locales. In the mapping of urban Inuit networks, people coalesce at certain times around these geographical identities.

In many ways, social identities for Inuit have much in common with those of transnational migrants.[4] Access to services is rendered particularly problematic for Inuit at times as a result of geographical dislocation, socio-cultural and linguistic barriers, and other factors that shape one's ability to get by in a new environment. Although Tungasuvvingat Inuit (TI) offers initial support, not all Inuit have access to the information and resources needed to end up at the right place for services.[5]

Accessibility to services can be affected by language barriers because many Inuit arrive in the city without the fluency and vocabulary in English necessary for dealing with urban life. Economic realities also affect mobility, since money is needed for transportation and, unlike in Northern communities, it is often impossible to "get a lift" or walk the extraordinary distances to access services. This adds to the psychological difficulties that arise in the transition from "knowing everyone" to feeling "isolated" and losing one's sense of groundedness and mobility in the urban environment. Although these sorts of social challenges are probably echoed in other diasporic communities (Aboriginal or non-Aboriginal), we argue here that overlapping geographical, historical, linguistic, and cultural factors heighten Inuit experiences of struggle (both personal and political) when dealing with urban realities.

In the urban environment, there is also an increased reliance on social (often kin-based) networks, and a kind of informal economy can develop in order to access "country food," childcare, and income through crafts production and so forth. In short, symbolic resources, including friendship, support, and solidarity networks become vital in linking familiar social strategies (from the North) to the new ones in the city.

In the process of urban community building and the mobilization around Inuit-specific symbolic and material resources, Inuit struggles over institutional representation not only foster belonging and a collective consciousness but can also exacerbate tensions and divisions within the community, since this involves normalizing the urban Inuit community as a homogeneous entity.

Reclaiming Inuitness

The increased visibility of Inuit in southern Canada seems to be linked to larger transformations in the relationships between the Canadian state, Canadian society, and Aboriginal populations. These transformations coincide with the increased political mobilization among First Nations, Inuit, and Métis groups in the late 1960s and 70s—mobilization that was largely based on protecting Aboriginal and treaty rights, which were enshrined in the 1982 Constitution Act of Canada. The relatively slow and arduous struggle for legal and civil recognition of these rights and the lack of progress on the resolution of land disputes also culminated in violent clashes between Indigenous protestors and police. The most significant of these, with respect to media awareness, was during the summer of 1990 and has come to be known as the Oka crisis. It involved the deployment of the Canadian Armed Forces against Indigenous protestors and the exchange of gunfire that resulted in the death of a police officer.

Soon after these events, the Royal Commission on Aboriginal Peoples (RCAP) was established (1991–1996), with a comprehensive mandate to investigate the relationships between First Nations, Inuit, and Métis peoples and the Canadian state. These developments in the political and social climate in Canada, in combination with the efforts of Indigenous leaders, we argue, increased the public awareness of Aboriginal issues in Canada and, more specifically, favoured the institutional promotion of Inuit culture and language in northern schools, media, and administrative domains. These efforts also enhanced the presence of Inuit in urban social, political, and administrative realms.

These broader socio-political transformations had a significant impact on the shift in the perceptions of and attitudes toward Inuit. Over the last three decades of the twentieth century, Inuit language and culture gained legitimacy through such valorizing practices as federal funding and programming in media, schools, and other institutions. Negative stereotyping of traditional Inuit customs and beliefs was gradually supplanted by the valuing of Inuit cultural forms as part of an emerging Canadian national identity, based on more inclusive forms of national heritage (Mackey 2002). This practice of valuing Inuit heritage and cultural forms is not unambiguous, however. One of the clearest illustrations of this is the inclusion of the Inukshuk as the official symbol of the 2010 Olympic Games. While it promotes Inuit inclusion in Canadian cultural projects, it also represents an appropriation of an Inuit symbol by the dominant culture.

Urban Inuit Narratives

This section is based on the narratives of co-authors, Lynda Brown and Heidi Langille, who, in the telling of their life histories, strongly identify as Inuit. This telling can be seen as part of a "process of identification," that is "something that happens over time, that is never absolutely stable, that is subject to the play of history and the play of difference" (Hall 1991, 15). As we shall see, these life stories show how identification has shifted over time and support our argument that the reclaiming of Inuit identity is shaped by wider historical, political, and economic developments in relations between the Canadian state and Aboriginal peoples.

This broader historical, social context, formed through developments at the global, national, and local levels, shaped Canadian institutional practices such as those in the visual (sculpture and painting) and performing arts, the media, the administration of health and social services, community centres, legal aid centres, and education. These transformative institutional practices have played a partial but important role in the shaping of subjectivities, including those of students and teachers in classrooms, as demonstrated in the narrative accounts below. Before examining these in more detail, however, we consider two other points. The first is that, although they represent individual cases, the experiences are echoed in other narrative accounts (see Jackson 2001). The second lies in the fact that it became acceptable to publicly express a heightened interest and pride in Inuit heritage only when the Canadian political and social climate became less hostile to Aboriginal self-identification.

This latter point is reflected in the 2001 Canadian census, which saw a 22 percent increase from the 1996 census in the reporting of Aboriginal identity (Siggner 2003). While the overall Aboriginal-identified population has grown considerably, this growth has occurred predominantly in urban areas (Guimond 2003; Siggner 2003). Research shows that the growth in this urban population cannot be attributed to factors such as natural increase and migration alone but is also due to "ethnic mobility"—the "phenomenon by which individuals and families experience changes in their ethnic affiliations" (Guimond 2003, 35). Changes in reporting behaviour, that is, choosing Aboriginal ancestry and/or Aboriginal identity categories on censuses and surveys, have been part of a discernable trend over the last several censuses (Siggner 2003; Guimond 2003). As Guimond (2003, 43) notes, ethnic mobility could account for up to 60 percent of the urban Aboriginal population growth in Canada. Similar developments can also be identified for Aboriginal populations in the United States and Australia. The link to the larger socio-political context is crucial for an understanding of this phenomenon, as we discussed in the previous section.

All these factors contribute to the socio-cultural and political climate in which self-identification with new forms of non-essentialized, non-static forms of ethnicity has taken place. They also inform the subjectivities and identification processes elaborated on in the following accounts.

Lynda Brown was born in 1974 in Iqaluit, Nunavut, to a Scottish father and an Inuk mother. Her family moved south in 1981 for a better education for Lynda and because she "was getting beaten up a lot up North apparently by both Inuit and non-Inuit kids." The reason given for this was that she did not fit in either category because of her mixed heritage. After graduating from Trent University with an honours degree in psychology and a minor in Native Studies (1993–1998), Lynda started her career at Tungasuvvingat Inuit, an Ottawa-based community centre. She then worked with Pauktuutit Inuit Women of Canada, managing the health and community files and most recently has become a community worker at the Ottawa Inuit Children's Centre (OICC).

Lynda has seen a resurgence of Inuit performance arts and is proud that she can continue to sing and dance and that her two young children can participate as well. She has trained as a performer through cultural performance lessons in Ottawa and elder teachings. She educates and entertains audiences in the art of throat singing, drum dancing, and traditional games. Some of the most valuable teachings come from her close ties with the Inuit community around the Inuit Head Start, a culturally appropriate early education program that has been in existence since 1998. She is the proud mother of two sons, one a graduate from the Head Start program and the other currently attending. According to Lynda, "Head Start is the best program out there for kids—it gives them a sense of who they are and pride, something that I didn't have when growing up. Inuit Head Start is especially important for children who haven't been up North, to give them the sense of what it means to be part of a community."

Heidi Langille was born in 1979 in Ottawa, to a Dutch mother and an Inuk father (Labrador) whose community was shut down by the federal government in 1956. Her parents moved to Ottawa in 1978 for employment reasons. After graduating from high school in 1997, Heidi moved to Nova Scotia where she attended college. She returned to Ottawa with her two older children in 2003. It was in Ottawa that she found the environment for developing her professional career within the urban Inuit community and for asserting her link to this ancestry. She has worked for various Inuit organizations, such as Tungasuvvingat Inuit Family Resource Centre, Inuit Head Start, Pauktuutit Inuit Women of Canada, as well as Odawa Native Friendship Centre and Indian and Northern Affairs Canada. She currently does community outreach work for the Ottawa Inuit Children's Centre.

As both Lynda and Heidi point out, their sense of Inuitness developed later in life, during their school years and was not something that was fostered by an urban Inuit community or recognized by Canadian society at large when they were growing up. During their childhood they felt that negative perceptions of who they were had an impact on their sense of self as Inuit. As children of mixed heritage who were born and/or raised in the South and in a city, they experienced conflicting identities at a time when the general discourse downplayed the value of their Inuit background. The negative stereotypes about Inuit were internalized throughout their childhood. For Heidi it was that Inuit were perceived as "alcoholics" and "always at risk of suicide." For Lynda it was the idea that Inuit were "raw-meat eaters who still lived in igloos with penguins and drove a team of dogs to the ice flow to drop off Grandma." Heidi states "I was just as disgusted as my friends and ashamed of my ancestors," and Lynda notes, "I had become embarrassed by my own culture." It made the two girls perceive themselves as profoundly different at an age when, as Lynda put it, "you notice that you are different, but you don't want to be different."

The perceptions in the immediate (school) community—undoubtedly linked to and fed by the public discourse in the media and at the political level—made Lynda and Heidi deny their Inuit heritage and develop roles that would be valorized by their peers. Heidi was able to identify herself as First Nations, since "that was promoted everywhere," and she would accordingly teach her colleagues "the first ever traditional sacred Inuit 'rain dance,' about dream catchers and pow-wows, bow and arrows, and lacrosse," while Lynda found that taking on a Chinese persona would secure her a respected place among other kids: "'Pull harder!' I demanded from my mother, as she braided my hair. If done properly, just the right amount of tension would give the added appearance of slant to my already almond-shaped brown eyes. I found that most in my classes revered the

Chinese. For most it was the food, then the fireworks, and the Wall. That was about all anyone knew about China when I was ten—which was three times more than anyone knew about Inuit."

As children, both Lynda and Heidi learned to negotiate the urban environment much faster than their parents, who had lived in the North for most of their lives. As is often the case with urban Inuit youth, they acted as guides for their parents to enable them to navigate the labyrinth-like geographic and social landscape in the city. Lynda remembers how she "helped her mother learn English and assimilate into the suburbs of Edmonton," where they lived for a while. Heidi also recollects how "my dad was complaining that he couldn't see the stars, so he didn't know what was where. He would get lost five minutes away from our home, where we had been living for sixteen years, so I would always help him manage."

While the social horizon in the urban environment remains mainly closed and restricted for parents raised up north, the children manage to penetrate it by learning the rules of socialization quickly; that is, they have acquired the valued cultural capital required to negotiate the urban geography and taken on identities that are valued by the mainstream and their peers in their quest to "fit in." Despite these processes, children and youth from minority backgrounds are always at risk of internalizing negative stereotypes or negating their family cultural background and practices, which may influence their development and sense of self, sometimes permanently. This is exemplified in the following extract from Heidi's narrative: "I didn't know much about the Inuit culture. My childhood home was filled with artefacts that I took for granted and did not inquire about. I didn't know the first thing about igloos or sled dogs, hunting or sealing, carving or throat singing. So, when people did find out about my Inuit heritage and asked questions, I just made things up."

Heidi's experiences as a child reflect the formative influence of dominant discourses within the school system on shaping (mis)representations of Inuit culture. For example, Heidi did not see Inuitness as significant in defining who she was. This excerpt reinforces our point that awareness of the Inuit cultural background has to be taught and highlighted not only as valuable but also as distinct in relation to other Aboriginal or non-Aboriginal cultures. In this process, the resources for early childhood education are crucial for identity formation in Inuit youth. Lynda recollects how positive reinforcement from her teacher provided the possibility for her later assertion of her Inuk identity:

It was not until my last year of high school, in a small classroom in rural Ontario, that I found the pride and excitement for my culture, which had been missing all my life. My homeroom class was doing a project on Inuit and native art. My father had secured himself an impressive collection during his years with HBC. I brought in what I could to shock and awe them all, especially my wide-eyed teacher. It was his excitement and reverence for my culture that was immediately transferable to me. His knowledge and inquiries were serious and academic, most of which I could not answer. This experience made me want to learn more about what it meant to be Inuk.

The positive reinforcement of cultural backgrounds in schools (in this case Inuit heritage) is historically and politically situated, prompted by political and social development in the 1990s that fostered valorization of cultures through institutional mechanisms. For instance, Inuit Head Start was set up in 1997 to address the development of Inuit preschool children and to foster positive parenting through support and education. According to the Ottawa Inuit Children's Centre website, the mission of the Inuit Head Start is to provide each child and parent with a "supportive learning environment that promotes Inuit culture and language." The establishment of such institutional support coincided not only with more people asserting their Aboriginal identity but also with the increased awareness and visibility of Inuit culture overall.

Heidi says that in some contexts, she asserts her Inuit identity more than her Dutch background, since "that is what people see." She adds that "people seem more interested in Inuit culture" since this is an identity that is also more prevalent in Canadian political discourse. Despite the fact that Inuitness seems to be dominant, however, Heidi still teaches her kids Dutch traditions. As Lynda notes as well, "this does not mean dismissing the other heritage, but Inuit appears to be at the forefront."

For Inuit who have grown up in urban settings, "northern" practices and knowledge are desired forms of cultural capital that validate identity claims. For instance, throat-singing and other performances of Inuitness become central activities that demonstrate cultural pride and belonging both to other Inuit and to audiences across Canada and internationally. As the following statement illustrates, acquiring cultural knowledge and participating in community activities is seen as vital to creating a sense of collective Inuit identity for Heidi and her family: "As an adult, I am striving to learn the more tangible cultural traditions. A good friend of mine is teaching me to throat sing and as my children hear and absorb everything around them, they are learning, too."

The more tangible traditions provide the means to develop a sense of community through shared cultural practices. As urban Inuit—particularly those born and raised in the city—learn about the Inuit customs and beliefs, they learn how to reconcile their sense of Inuit identity with dominant understandings of it. At the same time, they are also expanding and enriching what it means to be Inuk.

Because of political mobilization in the Inuit homelands, a territorialized identity politics has developed, which has deprived the urban Inuit from enjoying social recognition as such. By making Inuit cultural practices part of everyday life, urban Inuit are asserting their belonging to a collective identity that transcends narrow conceptual boundaries and geographical distance.

The Importance of Identity-Based Organizations

The centrality of identity-based institutions in constructing community for urban Inuit cannot be overstated. Similar to pan-Aboriginal, First Nations, and Métis organizations in cities, Inuit organizations and service providers offer contexts in which identities are validated and, in effect, become the "community context" (Weibel-Orlando 1999; see also Jackson 2002). Culturally relevant social services, therefore, have become important sources of community and empowerment, offering services and employment opportunities (Lobo 2001). Stressing the importance of organizations, Susan Lobo (2001, 75) defines urban Indigenous community not as a specific geographical location but as "a widely scattered and frequently shifting network of relationships with locational nodes found on organizations and activity sites of special significance." The social and cultural spaces provided by urban Aboriginal institutions are crucial sites where Aboriginal identities are shaped and valorized (Belanger et al. 2003). Heidi's story illustrates how working for Inuit-focused organizations has had a positive impact on her identification as an Inuk and on her family's participation in community activities: "At sixteen I worked for the Department of Indian Affairs and Northern Development and at eighteen I worked with the summer youth program at the local Inuit Centre. I have since been a part of the Inuit Community in Ottawa, volunteering, working, living, playing, and raising my children."

Similar to Heidi's experiences, Lynda's story also involves working for Inuit organizations and active participation in community building: "Upon graduation I moved to the nation's capital. I started working as an employment counsellor, helping Inuit find jobs. Soon I moved on to an Inuit preschool [Head Start], where I stayed for several years. It was like regaining the childhood I should have had. We taught the children their language, their culture, everything to instil in them that they should be extremely proud to be Inuk."

National organizations, such as Inuit Tapiriit Kanatami (ITK) and Pauktuutit, and local organizations, such as TI and the Ottawa Inuit Children's Centre that houses the Head Start program, foster a growing sense of Inuit collectivity in Ottawa. These are also sites in which cultural capital is transformed into social and economic capital in the sense that Inuitness is becoming valorized by institutions that legitimize forms of Inuit linguistic and cultural practice and are, in turn, legitimized by Inuit participation. Both "northern" and "southern" practices and knowledge are essential in this process, but southern-based skills (higher education, English, computer literacy, etc.) are crucial for being able to benefit from these opportunities. This is not to suggest, however, that North and South, or rural and urban, exist as rigid dichotomies; rather, they are flexibly and contingently combined in the everyday lives of Inuit in Ottawa.

There is a highly reciprocal and mutually beneficial relationship between Inuit identity, community, and institutions that offer programs and services. In the process of representing Inuit interests, national and local institutions offer spaces in urban environments where a range of Inuit identities are validated. Even though the interests of all sections of the Inuit population may not be equally represented, Aboriginal and Inuit organizations are vital in creating shared spaces and collective visibility in the urban landscape.

Conclusions

This chapter has examined some of the social, geographical, and cultural complexities of the urban Inuit community in Ottawa. Using examples from two urban Inuit life histories, we have seen how emergent processes of Inuit identification are situated in the larger historical, political, and economic Canadian context. In particular, institutional structures have shaped the construction of new forms of Inuit identity and community. With this emergence of "new ethnicities" (Hall 1992)—identities constructed through cultural hybridity and fluidity within and across social groups, and performed in localized, interactional practices—we can map out individual trajectories over time, which parallel changes in the political and social climate and the resurgence of Aboriginal nations in Canada. More specifically, Aboriginal institutions—especially those that are Inuit-specific—have played a pivotal role in valorizing Inuitness outside of the Arctic North by enhancing urban Inuit identities through Inuit language and cultural practices.

Many questions remain to be addressed in further research, particularly with respect to Inuit understandings of urban community. It appears that in Ottawa such a community is in flux, and social interaction and positioning yield different understandings of the urban Inuit community. It cannot be assumed to be a straightforward or fixed entity; rather, it seems to be conceptualized more abstractly by Inuit who are positioned differently within social networks and institutional formations.

Despite the fact that this Inuit community is non-geographically bounded (Lobo and Peters 2001), tensions still arise based on geographic trajectories. These include the tensions between Inuit coming from the North and those born and raised in the South and the related tensions between English-language fluency, Inuktitut fluency, and English-Inuktitut bilingualism and between traditional cultural capital (traditional knowledge, abilities, and social networks) and urban social and cultural capital (including urban networks and the ability and knowledge to access urban resources). Despite these tensions, however, forms of collective identity and cohesion develop, in part, through the unifying forces of the national and local institutions, which play a key role in urban Inuit experiences. The complex and multiple processes that are taking place in urban settings are thus not only reproducing but are also redefining notions of Inuitness.

Notes

1   See Bucholtz (2002, 538), where the terms "local" and "hybrid" are used to characterize new ethnicities.

2   This ruling, in fact, favoured the province of Quebec, which took the federal government to court, insisting that Inuit were like other Indigenous Peoples in Canada and the responsibility of the federal government. The case was motivated by the extreme hardship and material needs of the few thousand Inuit in Northern Quebec (Backhouse 2001).

3   In particular, see Miller (2004) chapter 1, "Designer Labels: Shaping Aboriginal identity," 1–51.

4   Podlasly (2002) makes a similar point concerning urban movements of Aboriginal peoples in general, likening urban Aboriginal communities to transnational "expatriate communities." While his point emphasizes the linkages between "expatriate and homeland communities" or between "urban Aboriginal to reserve communities," we would emphasize the social and cultural displacement and the subsequent social barriers and conflicts that sometimes arise among urban Inuit. The experiences that we emphasize would be more akin to those of transnational migrants or refugees, who are economically vulnerable and keenly focused on negotiating their way in new and unfamiliar terrain.

5   Tungasuvvingat Inuit was established in 1987 and operates as an Inuit "friendship centre." Its mandate is to enhance the lives of Inuit residing in Ontario. TI operates as a community-based resource centre. Its services and programs include counselling, employment services, Urban Inuit Diabetes Awareness and Prevention, the Inuit family resource centre for pre- and post-natal care, Inuit Head Start, a youth program, the Mamirsavik healing centre, and Pigiarvik House for drug and alcohol treatment, drop-ins, and a monthly lunch.

Works Cited

Backhouse, Constance. 2001. "'Race' Definition Run Amuck: 'Slaying the Dragon of Eskimo Status' Before the Supreme Court of Canada, 1939." In *Law, History, Colonialism: The Reach of Empire*, edited by Diane Kirkby and Catherine Coleborne, 65–77. Manchester and New York: Manchester University Press.

Belanger, Yale, Liz Barron, Charlene McKay-Turnbull, and Melanie Mills. 2003. *Urban Aboriginal Youth in Winnipeg: Culture and Identity Formation in Cities*. Ottawa: Canadian Heritage.

Bourdieu, Pierre. 1990 [1980]. *The Logic of Practice*. Translated by Richard Nice. Cambridge: Polity Press.

———. 1991. *Language and Symbolic Power*. Translated by Gino Raymond and Matthew Adamson. Edited and introduced by John B. Thompson. Cambridge: Harvard University Press.

Brody, Hugh. 1975. *The People's Land: Eskimos and Whites in the Eastern Arctic*. Harmondsworth: Penguin.

———. 1987. *Living Arctic: Hunters of the Canadian North*. Vancouver: Douglas and McIntyre.

Bucholtz, Mary. 2002. Youth and Cultural Practice. *Annual Review of Anthropology* 31: 525–52.

Calhoun, Craig. 1995. *Critical Social Theory. Culture, History, and the Challenge of Difference*. Malden: Blackwell Publishing.

Freeland, Jane, and Donna Patrick. 2004. "Language Rights and Language Survival: Sociolinguistic and Sociocultural Perspectives." In *Language Rights and Language Survival*, 1–33. Manchester: St. Jerome Press.

Graburn, Nelson. 1969. *Eskimos without Igloos: Social and Economic Development in Sugluk*. Boston: Little, Brown and Company.

Guimond, Eric. 2003. "Fuzzy Definitions and Population Explosion: Changing Identities of Aboriginal Groups in Canada." In *Not Strangers in These Parts: Urban Aboriginal Peoples*, edited by David Newhouse and Evelyn Peters, 35–49. Ottawa: Policy Research Initiative.

Gupta, Akhil, and James Ferguson, eds. 1997. *Culture, Power, Place. Explorations in Critical Anthropology*. Durham/ London: Duke University Press.

Hall, Stuart, 1991. "Ethnicity: Identity and Difference." *Radical America* 13 (4): 9–20.

———. 1992. "New Ethnicities." In *"Race," Culture, and Difference*, edited by James Donald and Ali Rattansi, 252–59. London: Sage.

———. 1996. "Introduction: Who Needs 'Identity'?" In *Questions of Cultural Identity*, edited by Stuart Hall and Paul Du Gay, 1–17. London/Thousand Oaks/New Delhi: Sage Publications.

Howard-Bobiwash, Heather. 2003. "Women's Class Strategies as Activism in Native Community Building in Toronto 1950–1975." *American Indian Quarterly* 27 (3/4): 566–82.

Ipellie, Alootook. 1993. *Arctic Dreams and Nightmares*. Penticton, BC: Theytus Books.

Jacobs, Jane M. 1996. *Edge of Empire: Postcolonialism and the City*. London and New York: Routledge.

Jackson, Deborah Davis. 2001. "This Hole in Our Heart: The Urban-Raised Generation and the Legacy of Silence." In *American Indians and the Urban*

Experience, edited by Susan Lobo and Kurt Peters, 189–206. New York: Altamira Press.

———. 2002. *Our Elders Lived It: American Indian Identity in the City*. DeKalb: Northern Illinois University Press.

Keith, Michael, and Steve Pile, eds. 1993. *Place and the Politics of Identity*. London and New York: Routledge.

Lawrence, Bonita. 2003. "Gender, Race, and the Regulation of Native Identity in Canada and the United States: An Overview." *Hypatia* 18 (2): 3–31.

———. 2004. *Real Indians and Others: Mixed-Blood Urban Native Peoples and Indigenous Nationhood*. Lincoln: University of Nebraska Press.

Lobo, Susan. 2001. "Is Urban a Person or a Place?: Characteristics of Urban Indian Country." In *American Indians and the Urban Experience*, edited by Susan Lobo and Kurt Peters, 73–85. New York: Altamira Press.

Lobo, Susan, and Kurt Peters, eds. 2001. *American Indians and the Urban Experience*. New York: Altamira Press.

Mackey, Eva. 2002. *The House of Difference: Cultural Politics and National Identity in Canada*. Toronto: University of Toronto Press.

Miller, J.R. 2004. *Lethal Legacy: Current Native Controversies in Canada*. Toronto: McClelland and Stewart.

Ottawa Inuit Children's Centre. Website, http://www.ottawainuitchildrens.com.

Patrick, Donna. 2003. *Language, Politics, and Social Interaction in an Inuit Community*. Berlin/New York: Mouton de Gruyter.

Podlasly, Mark. 2002. "Canada's Domestic Expatriates: The Urban Aboriginal Population." Paper presented at Searching for the New Liberalism, Munk Centre, University of Toronto, 27–29 September.

Proulx, Craig. 2003. *Reclaiming Aboriginal Justice, Community and Identity*. Saskatoon: Purich Publishing.

Siggner, Andrew. 2003. "Urban Aboriginal Populations: An Update Using the 2001 Census Results." In *Not Strangers in These Parts: Urban Aboriginal Peoples*, edited by David Newhouse and Evelyn Peters, 15–21. Ottawa: Policy Research Initiative.

Tungasuvvingat Inuit. 2005. National Urban Inuit One Voice Workshop, Ottawa, 26–27 October. Ottawa: Tungasuvvingat Inuit.

Weibel-Orlando, Joan A. 1991. *Indian Country, L.A.: Maintaining Ethnic Community in Complex Society*. Revised edition. Chicago: University of Illinois Press.

6
The Friendship Centre
Native People and the Organization of Community in Cities

Heather A. Howard

In 2002, a report on programs and services available to Native people in Toronto, produced by management-level workers at the Native Canadian Centre of Toronto, indicated how its authors perceived their roles not just as providers of adequate services to random, needy Native clients but as political leaders in the "continued growth and sustainability of the community" (Native Canadian Centre of Toronto 2002, v). Based on twenty-five interviews with "key informants," the report concluded that "the community" identified the following "internal gaps":

- a lack of Aboriginal unity-dispute resolution,
- a need to break the bonds of colonialism by Government acknowledging, respecting and supporting Aboriginal people and their self-governing aspirations in urban areas,
- no mechanism in place for community members to have their voices heard,
- weak community involvement and accountability with a need for Native agencies to be transparent and accountable to community members, and
- leaders' or organizations' (board of directors) lack of understanding around their roles (Native Canadian Centre of Toronto 2002, vi–vii).

The leaders who produced the report concluded with their "common belief that ... we can create, foster, sustain and build on a strong Aboriginal community within the Greater Toronto."

This chapter examines the socio-political history and culture of the Native friendship centre, the organization that most often serves as the focal point of urban Native communities in Canada. An ethnographic perspective on the history and formation of one of the first friendship centres, the Native Canadian Centre of Toronto, provides a case study through which a number of aspects are explored. The transformation of Native socio-political and cultural organizing at the centre is discussed in terms of identity politics, class mobility, the production of community, and the diversification of gender roles. These aspects of urban Native community organizing are described in relation to the dialogical character of local and national Aboriginal issues as they impact Native people who live in cities, and in relation to the dynamics of the production of community by and for Native people in urban contexts.

The Native Canadian Centre of Toronto as a Place and Space of Community Production

I introduce the Native Canadian Centre of Toronto by situating it in relation to broader questions about the conceptualization of community among Native people in the urban context. Gupta and Ferguson (1999, 1992) politicize space and its socially constructed meanings through an analysis that examines meaning-making as practice, rather than one that situates, positions, and thus tends to fix and polarize the locations, identities and therefore the interpretations of anthropologists and their subjects. Likewise, Kathleen Kirby prompts researchers to ask, "In what ways are subjects the effects of spaces?" (1996, 5) and "How is subjectivity lived as a space by people, and lived differently by different kinds of subjects?" (1996, 124). These seem particularly salient questions through which to explore "the Native community" in Toronto, where there are few visible community markers and no significant population densities or Native enclaves. If there is one key characteristic that could be used to describe the Native community in Toronto it would be diversity. Dozens of Indigenous cultures from across Canada as well as the United States and other parts of the Americas are represented in the Toronto Native community. The community is also socio-economically diverse and includes both a substantial homeless population and a considerable middle class. Native people in Toronto have created a vast social service network, a strong arts community, and a small yet influential political and cultural presence. The dimensions and dynamics of community are multiple, continually changing, and subjectively experienced and acted upon. I prefer therefore to speak of community in terms of its production, emphasizing its political and creative processes. The Native Canadian Centre of Toronto is the oldest Native organization in the city of Toronto and provides for a longitudinal perspective on the production of community.

Nonetheless, other groups and individuals challenged and negotiated the production of Native community as led by the centre, particularly in the 1960s and early 1970s. A complete review of these dimensions is beyond the scope of this chapter, however, and I have discussed them elsewhere (Howard 2004, 94–147).

Officially incorporated in 1962, the centre grew from a social club of the YMCA, the North American Indian Club, started in 1950. The "club" had itself existed informally for at least two decades in the form of casual gatherings at key households around the city (see Lobo 2009), such as the Jamieson residence on Bleeker Street and Millie Redmond's home in the 1940s (see Howard 2004, 148–86). Since its founding, the centre has moved locations three times and has been at 16 Spadina Road, the former Ontario Bible College, since 1976. It is only a few hundred yards from the north corner of Bloor Street in a downtown area and the popular and diverse neighbourhood called the Annex. Although the area surrounding the centre is highly gentrified and very few Native people have homes in the area, it also constitutes one of the few visible indications of the Toronto Native community. At the busy corner, one can often find familiar artists selling crafts, jewellery, and art prints. Just north from the corner on Spadina, a branch of the Toronto Public Library houses the city's largest collection of Native materials, and the name "Where the Books Live" is inscribed above the door in Ojibway. Nestled between the library and the Native centre is Wigwamen Terrace, a 120-unit housing complex for Native seniors. Along the stretch of a few hundred yards there are always a lot of Native people that visibly represent the multi-layered character of the Toronto Native community. There are young people and seniors, homeless, poor, middle-class, and elite members of the community, usually exchanging smiles and conversations, sometimes mixed in with uncomfortable aloofness and even the occasional fist fight.

In the driveway that circulates past the front door of Wigwamen Terrace and around the centre building, one can often find in the summer ongoing yard/craft sales put on by the seniors and fundraising barbecues organized by volunteers and staff of the centre's various programs. In the small park and walkway between the library and Wigwamen, seniors often mingle with staff from the centre and the library, people on their way to visit the centre, and some of the homeless people who live in the area. Until 2004, the focal point of this space was the veritable informal gateway into the community—the park bench that was Jim Mason's "office"—where Jim would jovially meet Native people who "might be too shy to walk up the intimidating steps of the centre ... He's there to listen and to share his experience [which included some very entertaining stories] with all those keen to learn" (Gajic 1997, 97). Jim was born in Toronto in 1920, the son of Mohawk and Ojibway parents. He led a rich and productive life, having raised a family, worked in high steel construction, as a trucker, and eventually as caretaker at the Native centre. He was eighty-four when he passed away, leaving a noticeable void in the community space around the centre.

The centre is seen by many as the centerpiece or metaphorical town square of the community and occupies a sacred place among Native people in Toronto. It is important symbolically as the "heart" or "mother" of organizations that form the infrastructure of what is considered "the Toronto Native community," which has no precise geographical location but is visible as a network of mostly social service delivery agencies and the programs and events they provide. The centre is referred to as a "home" for many people, and working at the Native centre is highly desirable.

When a position opens at the Native Canadian Centre of Toronto, there is usually an abundance of applicants, and many of those who are not hired feel dejected and often try again and again to be employed there. As an institution largely dependent on public funding, programs change relatively frequently, and this has taken its toll on staff turnover as well as on the internal dynamics of the centre as a workplace. Native people want to work at the centre for reasons beyond the desire to secure employment or for a vocation in social service. Unlike most of the other fifty Native organizations in the city there is a strong sense of community ownership of the centre. As such, staff and management must answer to the community both within and outside of the physical building. Centre employees are subject to a high degree of scrutiny in their private lives; for example, there are strict prohibitions against alcohol consumption on the centre premises, explained in terms of respect for the sacredness of the centre, as well as for the elders and the medicines and sacred items present there. On occasion, centre employees seen drinking alcohol in local bars have been reported to the executive director, suggesting that some community members feel that employment at the Native centre entails a special commitment to sobriety. Centre staff are responsible for their conduct and for care for the centre even when they are not at work.

The symbolic power of the centre can be understood in relation to the move in anthropological theory away from the concepts of "culture" and "place" as fixed or whole entities in which we observe people toward describing the unstable, fluctuating processes and relations people construct and deconstruct. This perspective is also problematic, however, in relation to the historical and socio-political relations between Indigenous people and nation-states, in which "deterritorialized" people work precisely to reclaim "culture" and their "place" on the landscape. As Hastrup and Olwig (1997) note, scholars are:

> preoccupied with de-essentializing the concept of culture, and deconstructing the notion of bounded, localized cultural wholes [just as] many of the very people we study are deeply involved in constructing cultural contexts which bear many resemblances to such cultural entities. Homelands and fishing villages [and I argue, community centres like the Native Canadian Centre, deserve that we examine the] historical and social significance of these "cultural sites" as focal points of identification for people who, in their daily lives, are involved in a complex of relations of global as well as local dimensions." (Hastrup and Olwig 1997, 11)

As the centre was described in one of its own publications twenty years ago, it is "to the people, much more than a name or a building. It has been a positive force in maintaining and developing a strong Native cultural identity within Metropolitan Toronto" (Obonsawin 1987, 25). The evolution of the centre over half a century underscores its agency in the production of urban Native community as both fluctuating process and re-territorialized cultural site.

Emergence of the Toronto Centre and Negotiations of Race, Class, Identity, and Citizenship

Beginning in the 1920s, many Native people came to Toronto from reserves, mainly in Ontario, to attend school and find work. They felt the city would provide them with a chance to make better lives than could be had on the increasingly economically and culturally depressed reserves. They formed a social network, which quickly came to include a wide diversity of cultures such as Anishinaabe, Haudensaune, Cree, Mi'kmaq, and others. They worked as nannies, housekeepers, and waitresses, in construction, truck driving, fruit and tobacco picking, and in factories, offices, or for the telephone company. Both Native men and women joined the military and war efforts in large numbers. Many pursued higher education (which meant beyond the limit of grade eight available on reserves) through their military training, and in technical schools, where they became nurses, teachers and secretaries. In turn, they contributed to the generation of a professional middle class (Howard-Bobiwash 2003). They actively sought to integrate into the cosmopolitan and consumer lifestyle of mainstream society in the city while valuing and promoting their Native heritage. They also tended to hold relatively conservative political views that would later come under fire by other Native people who formed the Red Power movement in the 1960s and 1970s (Obonsawin & Howard-Bobiwash 1997).

In its formative years, the centre's development and that of the community paralleled circumstances in other urban centres across the country. Although the members of the Indian Club were responding to immediate and local needs, developments on a national scale would eventually affect them and draw them into broad national participation. The 1950s were years of change for Aboriginal people across Canada. In 1958, Walter Curie, who was later a president of the centre's board of directors, made a presentation to the Special Federal Parliamentary Committee Examining the Status of Indian People in Canada. Aboriginal people began organizing more systematically for changes to the racist and unfair policies that dictated their lives, and to the deplorable conditions in which many lived on reserves. Many more people began migrating to the cities in search of employment and better opportunities. Following those in Vancouver (1955) and Winnipeg (1958), the centre, then named the Canadian Indian Centre of Toronto, became the third friendship centre in Canada.

Elsewhere, I have described the involvement of Native women in the early establishment of the centre, and their strategic collaboration with wealthy white women around differing concepts of citizenship (Howard 2004, 148–86; forthcoming). In the 1960s, many upper-class white women felt a duty to act benevolently and charitably toward the less fortunate in society and to contribute to the larger projects of Canadian nation building and patriotism. Programs were created that placed great emphasis on the concept of citizenship as a goal toward which Canadians should work as individuals and interest groups. A number of the women who had helped organize the North American Indian Club formed a "Ladies Auxiliary" at the centre, which positioned them as a gendered fundraising corps, both within the centre and in relation to the moneyed non-Aboriginal community. Working with organizations such as the Imperial Order of the Daughters of the Empire, the centre's Ladies Auxiliary promoted the idea that a sense of pride in Native heritage was a positive contributor to Canadian citizenship as it simultaneously affirmed citizenship in their own First Nations. "Playing Indian" stereotypes were an important part of these class and gender politics.

The North American Indian Club was frequented mostly by the members of this elite group of young working Native people who had moved to the city for work and higher education. Its primary function was to provide a space for Native people in the city to get together and socialize.

By the 1960s, the club organizers felt they should also take responsibility for facilitating the successful integration and settlement into urban life of the vastly increasing numbers of Native people migrating to the city. Through strategic alliances with non-Native people in Toronto, negotiated largely through the efforts of the Ladies Auxiliary, funding was secured to establish a community centre. At the newly established Canadian Indian Centre of Toronto, a social environment aimed at defeating isolation and loneliness continued to be offered; however, the centre also began to provide information and referral to other resources in the city, such as help with finding accommodations, employment, or training. The centre continues to offer these services today.

The philosophy of the centre in the early days promoted the value of the cultural distinctiveness of Native people but emphasized that this was not incompatible with their ability to integrate successfully into urban Canadian life. "Native culture" within the agency was largely abstract and intangible. It became visible mostly in the form of performance or display for outside audiences, such as at the Canadian National Exhibition. Internally, there were competing ideas around what constituted "authentic" culture. This was evidenced in some discussions that emerged around material culture such as crafts or regalia.

Much of what appeared publicly was designed to both educate and capture the stereotypical imaginations of non-Natives. Although "Miss Indian Toronto" contests were organized, largely reproducing stereotypical representations of Native women, there were other activities that attempted to debunk and eliminate stereotypes. In a 1966 *Toronto Star* article titled "Indian Centre Is Erasing 'Beads and Buckskin' Image," it was noted that "staff and volunteers work to bridge the gap between the widely different worlds of the Indian and the rest of society" (*Toronto Star* 1966). In this same article, an active youth member of the centre, described as "the son of a chief," said, "It makes me mad to see Indians bogged down in ideas and ways that have no relation to modern living. If the Indian is always referring to the past, he just won't make it today" (*Toronto Star* 1966). His critique referred to the centre's decision at that time not to erect a totem pole outside the centre. This was not because the board felt it was an inaccurate reflection of the local Native population but because the totem pole symbolized a stereotypical token of the past.

At the same time, however, in another newspaper report on the opening of the centre's second location in 1966, Governor General Roland Michener was pictured literally and symbolically "elevating" a seven-year-old Ojibway boy, Sheldon Driver, sporting a huge Lakota-style headdress and complete buckskin outfit straight out of a Hollywood movie. The caption quotes Michener's views that "Canadian Indians are capable of extending their contribution to the building of Canada by their own efforts and in accordance with their own viewpoint ... [O]ther Canadians should match 'this new pride and resolve of the Indians by greater consideration for Canada's native people'" (*Toronto Telegram* 1966).

These apparent contradictions in performances of identity within particular contexts, which characterized the public persona of the centre in the 1960s, were significant to the production of community for Native people then, but can also be compared with other contexts, such as those described by Ronald Niezen (2003) and Jonathan Friedman (1999). In the context of describing international Indigenous rights movements, Niezen writes, "There is still a seemingly unalterable core of popular romanticism that makes it advantageous for indigenous leaders to embody in every aspect of their demeanor the picturesque qualities of indigenous life" (Niezen 2003, 159). Similarly, Jonathan Friedman argues that when the state becomes

> the focal point of certain distributions of favours, funds and positions to an increasingly fragmented nation-state ... Regional, immigrant and indigenous minorities all become subject to this changing field of forces. The field tends to create new elites that move within the global sphere, ranked lower than the real big-shots, since they are clients to the real sources of power and money ... The articulation of verticalising and fragmenting process produces the paradox of class division at all levels, including movements that begin in urban ghettos. It is important to take these contradictions into account when trying to understand the trajectory of indigeneity in today's world. (Friedman 1999, 10–11)

The "paradox of class division" described by Friedman was manifest in the Toronto Native community of the 1960s through Native public dissension about the extent of non-Native involvement in the affairs of the Canadian Indian Centre of Toronto. As early as 1963, Native critics of the centre were concerned that the non-Native members of the board had an "unconsciously superior attitude," and that the centre was not reaching many Native people who really needed its services (*Toronto Star* 1963). The centre responded in vehement defense of its non-Native leadership by not only acknowledging their support but by also allying themselves politically against so-called "Native militancy." The non-Native director of the time stated, for example, that attempts by a neighbourhood Communist group to infiltrate the centre had been squashed and that he and "other officials at the centre agree that reports of 'Red power,' the label for Indian militancy, has no support among those Indians who frequent the centre. 'We believe in change ... but within the usual framework of things'" (*Toronto Star* ca. 1963).

Countering the "usual framework of things" was at the root of another critique of the centre's conservative approach by the Institute for Indian Studies, also known as the Nishnawbe Institute. This institute was founded in 1967 in connection with the establishment of the (in)famous Rochdale College, which emerged from the long-standing Campus Co-operative Residences of the University of Toronto. Wilfrid Pelletier, who had at one time served as president of the North American Indian Club, led the formulation and proposal for the establishment of the Nishnawbe Institute in connection with the Indian Ecumenical Conference (Treat 2003). The overlap of Native traditionalist and activist networks with those that were seen as "white-influenced"—the middle-class leadership of the Native centre and Christian-based groups involved in the establishment of some other Toronto Native organizations—illustrates the fluidity and flexibility of Native community production in the 1960s (Howard 2004). While some "traditionalist" voices were raised in criticism of the growing "white-like" middle-class Native community organizers (Harper 1974; Redbird & Dunn 1971), the Nishnawbe Institute provided a space in which this dichotomy was transcended through intellectual pursuits. As Treat writes:

> thus began Pelletier's activist period. He became a "professional Indian helper," and "Indian do-gooder," ... [and] he developed into a popular speaker and before long was a captain of the benevolent industry he would later refer to as "the Indian business—the business of making Indians acceptable to whites." The liberal reformers who had helped establish the Canadian Indian Centre of Toronto took control of the Centre's board and administration shortly after it opened, using the organization to "fill their own needs—the need of a cause to promote which would make them feel good." They also encouraged Pelletier in his attempts at community organizing, so long as he conformed to their assimilationist vision of social reform." (Treat 2003, 102–03; see also Pelletier and Poole 1974)

Pelletier felt that the "bureaucratic, hierarchical organizations did not serve the real needs of his intertribal community. Community organizing in the urban context could have little value to native people so long as it was guided by non-native values" (Treat 2003, 103). Likewise, Duke Redbird, another prominent figure in Toronto Native community organizing in the 1960s (now an arts reporter for Citytv), was also involved for a short time in the Rochdale community. He founded his own

"Thunderbird Club" as a counterbalance to the North American Indian Club. The Thunderbird Club was "an Indian social club, cum coffee-house, cum discotheque, and unlike most Indian social centres, which provided welfare services and only the most conventional social rituals, like ping-pong and dances, the Thunderbird Club encouraged its members to be what they were, in any context they pleased" (Redbird and Dunn 1971, 51).

As part of his "cultural self-esteem program," Redbird formed the Thunderbird Dance Troupe to which many young Native people gravitated to make their own outfits and work out traditional dances for performances both within and outside the club. The Thunderbird Club did not have a stable location, and "reaction to it wasn't all favourable. The fact that the Club stayed open all night and got a reputation for wild parties upset the more conventional members of the Indian community, but the young Indians loved it" (Redbird and Dunn 1971, 55). Redbird, Pelletier, and many others in the Toronto Native community, like the Indian Education for Indians movement led by Harold Cardinal (1969), saw self-determination, particularly over Native education and cultural development, as providing solutions and the basis for Native organizing.

Dosman (1972), Nagler (1970), and Ryan (1978) all note the inefficiency of friendship centres in these earlier years, either because they were poorly managed, or because they were seen as social clubs run by an elite club rather than as a way to attend to the social service needs of Native people in cities. The Toronto centre picked up this mandate very early in its history, however, and began delivering directly a wide range of social services such as hospital visitation, courtwork services, alcohol abuse counselling, housing assistance, and welcoming newcomers. The class divisions and parallel divides in cultural authority that emerged from the post–World War II migration and urbanization of Native people were instrumental in the negotiations of Toronto Native community production. They were the foundations for these programs and remain an important yet under-studied aspect of the Aboriginal urban experience.

The Toronto Centre and Native Urban Issues in the National Context

The centre was a founding agency in the national organization of urban Native social service delivery agencies known as the Friendship Centre Movement. On the national front during the 1960s urban Native community centres were established in numerous Canadian cities from Ontario westward. The National Association of Friendship Centres

(NAFC) was formed in 1971; Victor Peltier, program director of the Toronto centre, was named to its steering committee, and Roger Obonsawin, the Toronto centre's executive director (1974–1981), was elected as the first president of the NAFC. The Toronto centre was especially active in national lobbying for increased funding for friendship centres, including in the establishment of the Migrating Native Peoples Program through the Department of the Secretary of State in 1972.

By the early 1970s, discourse changed significantly with the rise of Native social movements. As Nagel has noted:

> The Red Power period of American Indian activism was an important force in the renewal of American Indian ethnicity, inspiring a resurgence in American Indian self-identification, kindling a renaissance of native culture, and speeding reform of federal Indian policy. By spotlighting Indian grievances, empowering Indian groups and individuals, and challenging prevailing definitions and evaluations of Indian rights and efficacy, Red Power redefined and revitalized Indianness ... the movement created both unity and tensions within and among Indian communities and multiplied the voices articulating diverse Indian realities. (Nagel 1996, 234)

The Red Power movement in Canada, which was heavily dominated by men, both coalesced and diverged around an urban–rural divide. As urban organizations and leadership distinguished themselves from their rural counterparts, they also had to find new ways to legitimize their authority as Native leaders and as Native communities. This had to take place both internally, to secure the support and solidarity of urban Native people, and externally in terms of gaining recognition as genuinely, distinct constituencies (see Newhouse, chapter 2 in this volume).

The controversy over white leadership at the centre, which had characterized the 1960s, was relatively short lived. In the early 1970s, it was apparent to many that there had been value in strategic alliances with elements of the white powerful elite of the city in early efforts to establish the centre, but by the mid-1970s that strategy was completely discarded. Leadership became almost exclusively made up of Native-only board members and managers and has continued this way since. The centre maintained its character as the epitome of a liberal reformer perspective and "respectable" middle-class Indian, but it was also more flexible and less afraid of controversial political campaigns.

In the 1970s, many at the centre worked hard to encourage pride in Native identity, and to provide information and rally support for causes such as the occupations at Wounded Knee, South Dakota, and the James Bay Cree's battles with Hydro-Québec. The centre's newspaper, the

Toronto Native Times (*TNT*), took on the national media, the justice system, and any others who promoted negative stereotypes and racism toward Aboriginal people. *TNT* also regularly published traditional stories and profiles of leaders in the community and in the history of Native North America.

Toronto Native voices of resistance to national government policy, and in harmony with Red Power activism elsewhere, were also raised during this era. In response to the Canadian government's White Paper on Indian Policy, which called for an end to Indian "special status" in order to bring Native people to an "equal" level with the rest of Canadians, Aboriginal people reacted with massive protest, including the "Red Paper" presented to Prime Minister Pierre Trudeau by the Indian Chiefs of Alberta and the B.C. Indian Position Paper coined the "Brown Paper." These documents outlined the damaging effects the proposed policy changes would have on Aboriginal rights, culture, economic development, and education. The White Paper was exposed as a deceptive tool with which the federal government could attempt to rescind its legal and fiscal responsibilities and obligations to Aboriginal people entrenched in the treaties signed with First Nations. In 1971, Jean Chrétien, then minister of Indian Affairs, retracted the White Paper. On these events, "Urban Elder" Vern Harper (born in Toronto in 1936) recalled in a 1983 interview: "Just the fact that people questioned the White Paper and looked at the Red Paper, the whole thing changed. Many people in the Church and the Government realized they had made a mistake; that you can't make a Mistawasis a Jones, and that it's criminal to do it. And there were government people who because of the Red Paper realized they were dealing with sovereign nations and should be treated that way" (Native Canadian Oral History Project 1983).

Verna Patronella Johnston, whose contributions to building the community I have discussed elsewhere (Howard-Bobiwash 2003, 1999), ran boarding houses for Native girls working and attending school in Toronto during the 1960s. She recalled the sense of "Indian awakening" during these times. In her biography (Vanderburgh 1977) she articulated how the experience of coming to the city, and the need to establish a sense of Native identity and community, contributed to the stimulation of both individual and collective consciousness:

> "I grew as a person in those ten years, and I don't mean just running the house for Indian students. I came into contact with Indians from other parts of Ontario, and other provinces. I found out that there were a lot of Indians working to help their own people. All the doors opened now because I was Indian." ... Verna says today that what she got caught up in was the upswing

of Indian consciousness. Indians were getting it all together, putting themselves forward to get public attention for their rights and their needs, and
to work out ways to get what they wanted ... She was on the board of the
Indian Friendship Centre [Native Canadian Centre] for a long time and that
place did good work, helping Indians find places to live, putting on special
recreation programs for them, getting them help from lawyers when they
were in trouble with the law. That is Indians helping Indians—it's not the
same as white do-gooders! Indians who have lived in the city know what
it's all about, they are the best ones to help people. That place always has
been great for Indian people. City Indians had really good ideas about how
to help their people adjust to city life. (Vanderburgh 1977, 122, 141)

As noted earlier, the centre's leaders played significant roles in the
organization of a national movement of urban Native centres. By the mid-
seventies over seventy urban Native community centres were members of
the NAFC. In 1988, the Migrating Native Peoples Program had become
the Aboriginal Friendship Centres Program, securing permanent funding
through the Department of the Secretary of State. In 1996 the role of ad-
ministering these funds was devolved from the federal government to the
NAFC. The NAFC represents over one hundred friendship centres and
seven provincial territorial associations (PTAs) across Canada (NAFC 1997).

Tensions soon surfaced at the national level over the degree to which
the friendship centre movement should be radicalized in its approaches
to dealing with the Canadian government, which was now the movement's primary funder. The majority of centres represented in the national
association took a conservative approach, tending to define the friendship
centres' roles in terms of social service delivery. On the other hand, the
Toronto centre's philosophy moved to one that connected the capacity to
respond to the local needs of Native people with initiating and influencing
national and even international struggles. In fact, in contrast to earlier
integrationist approaches, challenging the legitimacy of the nation-state
itself became central to the discourse of Native politics at this time. The
Toronto centre and a small contingent of other centres saw their roles in
terms of much broader community development, self-determination, and
cultural programming. In 1978, the Toronto centre and several others
withdrew from the provincial association and maintained independent
positions in the national association.

This divergence is evident in the different points of view taken in the
respective mission statements of the national association and the local
Toronto centre. The goals of the NAFC are "to improve the quality of life
for Aboriginal peoples in an urban environment by supporting self-determined activities which encourage equal access to, and participation in,

Canadian society; and which respect and strengthen the increasing emphasis on Aboriginal cultural distinctiveness." The Toronto centre, on the
other hand, has both "philosophy" and "vision" statements. The philosophy statement, which describes the purpose of the centre, reads: "The
Native Canadian Centre of Toronto is a community-based, non-profit
organization which provides a gathering place to deliver programs and
services for Native people while striving to reflect the traditional Native
cultural perspective." The Centre's vision statement elaborates on the
underlying principles guiding action:

> Our Native way has always given us life. On the foundation of this belief
> we can and will build a strong and healthy Native community. For the peo-
> ple who come from the four directions of our Nation we well make a good
> "centre." And from this place we will create the means to reach out to the
> people, to mend the hurt, lift the broken, to free the imprisoned—body,
> mind, and spirit, to challenge the young, to strengthen the families, to
> respect the Elders, past, present and future. We will do this by honouring
> the Native life way through commitment to self-determination, through
> striving for a life of quality, and by moving toward the empowerment of
> community.

Where the national association emphasizes the goal of improving "the
quality of life for Aboriginal peoples in an urban environment by supporting self-determined activities which encourage equal access to and participation in Canadian society," the Toronto centre's vision statement makes
no mention of the Canadian state and instead focuses on Native culture
as the nexus around which all its social action should revolve.

Rather than stress the potential of Native people becoming fully productive Canadian citizens, a view that dominated the discourse of Native
leadership in Toronto in the 1960s, the distinctive value of Native identity
and culture had become entrenched in the centre's approach by the end
of the 1970s. This 1977 *Toronto Star* article reflects media reports of the
day about the centre: "At the Native Centre a counsellor can explain ...
the strange ways of the white man and his obsession with time, money
and work ... In classes on ancestral customs they learn not only the chants
and drum rhythms, but a sense of pride in the achievements, of their fore-
fathers" (*Toronto Star* 1977).

The 1980s and 1990s: Local Affirmations and International Public Relations

For the Native centre, the 1980s marked the renewal and affirmation of traditional and spiritual teachings and practices. Speaking about Toronto specifically, anthropologist Rosamund Vanderburgh wrote in 1980:

> "Cultural maintenance" and "culture as a male activity" are important issues in the urbanization of Canadian Native people. In the Toronto Native community these issues are linked to class distinctions and gender conflicts.... Catering to the needs of the Toronto Native community provides many job opportunities for Native men and women at all levels of skill. The allocation of these jobs, where this lies within the Native community, is the major class determinant and source of power for urban Indians. [T]he focus of the struggle for leadership ... Prestige, is derived from spiritual power ... [and] those wielding spiritual power in Toronto, and in Ontario generally, are almost without exception men and these men are anxious to gain control of the funding/job allocation sources of power. (Vanderburgh 1980, 82–83)

An important role played by the centre over the years has been providing the non-Native community with speakers to discuss traditional and contemporary issues of concern to Native people. This movement toward a focus on culture is central to understanding the centre's adaptation to the changing socio-political context of the community, and the social services industry in Toronto, from the 1980s to the present. In 1986, the centre established the Elders and Traditional Teachers Advisory Council, which quickly became active and logged hundreds of hours of appointments with individuals as well as presiding over feasts and other cultural events.

Perhaps a most salient marker of the reversal of the centre's perspective on "culture" was that a totem pole was erected on the front lawn of the centre in the 1980s. This icon of Native cultural material had transformed from a stereotypical image disengaged from the Native community to one defined by the community to denote the strength and pride of Native culture in Toronto. As a product of community process, the pole now represents empowerment. The pole was "authentically" carved by a Haida artist, but the totems represented are those of the clans of the Great Lakes Native groups and so characterize more accurately the local First Nations. As tourists, journalists, and community members regularly flock to it for photo opportunities, today it serves as one of the key identifying symbols of the centre and of Native presence in the urban landscape. More than a stereotype, it is a symbol of the strength, pride, and power, and of nearly half a century of Native urban community production.

In the 1980s, as the Native population of Canada tried to grapple with issues of representation within a constitutional framework, it turned increasingly toward self-government. Aboriginal rights were recognized in the Canadian Constitution Act, and since that time Native people have turned to the courts to help define those rights. For the most part, urban Aboriginal people were left out of this process by national and provincial Native political organizations despite the fact that more than half of all Aboriginal people in Canada lived off-reserve (see Newhouse, chapter 2 this volume). No formal governing structure has successfully been formed to represent the Native people of Toronto. The Aboriginal Peoples' Council of Toronto (APCT), originally established in 1996, held its first elections in 2002, with eight seats to be filled by one male and one female for each cardinal direction; however, as of 2004, the APCT had not yet been able to fill four of its eight positions, and three of the remaining seats had been filled by acclamation rather than election. The quest to establish the infrastructure of urban self-government in Toronto has been long and difficult and the APCT represented only an unsteady step forward.

Bill C-31 was passed into law in June 1985 and had a tremendous effect for both reserve and urban Aboriginal populations. The bill was aimed at ending discrimination against Native women and their children who had lost their Indian status through marriage to non-Indians or through enfranchisement. The law also amended the Indian Act to strengthen band control of membership (see Weaver 1993). The government widely underestimated the numbers of people who would fall into the category of eligibility for status reinstatement, and this heavily increased pressures on bands that did not have the financial means to meet the demand of the many women and their families who sought to return to the reserve or apply for support such as for housing and education. This exacerbated divisions between reserve and off-reserve people, between Native men and women, and between their national organizations. In addition to the anger directed at each other, Native people were angry at the government for not supplying the support necessary to accommodate the changes brought on by the Act.

The Native Women's Association of Canada had mixed reactions to Bill C-31 and warned that while the government had upheld three important principles—the elimination of sexual discrimination, reinstatement of those who lost their rights, and band control of membership—many other provisions caused concern for Aboriginal women. Children of reinstated women would only regain status and not band membership, and leaving membership decisions entirely up to the band councils would exclude the very people for whom the decisions were relevant. These two aspects, they argued, perpetuated further inequalities.

Throughout the 1970s and early 1980s the issue of status and band membership was central to urban Aboriginal communities across the country. Jeanette Corbiere-Lavell, who was a youth counsellor at the Toronto centre in the late 1960s and helped the centre's youth group found the *Toronto Native Times*, gained national notoriety when she protested against being removed from her band membership list at Wikwemikong in 1970 after marrying a non-Native. She maintained that the removal of status from Native women contravened the Canadian Bill of Rights. Lavell won her case at the Federal Court of Appeal but the decision was challenged and struck down at the Supreme Court of Canada in 1973.

It was in Toronto that Mary Two-Axe Early, originally from Kahnawake, was presented with written confirmation of the reinstatement of her Indian Status, on 15 July 1985. She had battled for reinstatement since the early 1950s, and she was the first woman to regain her Indian status under the new law. A flood of applications followed, and the Native Canadian Centre of Toronto provided assistance in completing the necessary forms for reinstatement. The centre's newsletter reported congratulations on reinstatements well into 1988.

The slogan "proud of our past, committed to the future" was used on public relations material produced by the centre in the early 1990s, featured on information pamphlets aimed at a wide-ranging audience, both Native and non-Native, and both locally and nationally. The centre had recently celebrated its twenty-fifth anniversary, and a significant sea change was taking place in connection with its diverse and often contentious roles as a Native friendship centre. These roles include, but are not limited to, being responsible for the delivery of social services to Native people living in the city, manoeuvering the politics of the internally directed activity of serving as a "mother" of cultural renewal for urban Native people, and, playing the tricky and externally directed part of goodwill ambassador to non-Native society. In this latter role, Native identity continues to serve as cultural capital (Bourdieu 1986) in negotiations to secure financial and political support from non-Native sources to grow and maintain the Native community.

Concluding Thoughts

The Native population in Toronto is economically and culturally diverse. The ways in which the local friendship centre attempts to play an active role in the generation of a sense of unity, while also serving as an ambassador to non-Natives who are curious and interested in "Native culture," creates a politically charged space of complex competing discourses that reify, reinvent, and adapt concepts of Native "traditions" in the urban context. Urban Native people confront and often resist the ways in which their identity is relegated to a homogenized, romanticized, and static past by non-Natives. Yet "the past" is precisely the cultural capital drawn upon to build community for current and future generations. Asserting urban Native culture counters stereotypes and shapes power relations between Native and non-Native people, while also attempting to empower a distinct sense of community. The Native centre asserts its roles in these processes, striving to "honour the Native life way," as its mission statement says, while also packaging and showcasing Native culture for non-Native audiences. As Richard Lee has written on the politics of identity in post-Apartheid South Africa, "Where sheer survival is not an issue, encapsulated and marginalized peoples are turning to the reestablishment of their historical roots" (2003, 104). In Toronto, this process is underscored by the ways in which "indigeneity" is simultaneously fortified and contested. Here, I use Forte's definition of indigeneity as "feeling, believing and perceiving oneself as indigenous, the act of making such claims and of acting on those claims" (1998, 425). By comparing and contrasting moments from my historical research with my current observations, I am attempting to highlight some of the layers of both the tensions and the synthesis that characterize processes of producing community and culture for Native people in Toronto.

As Vanderburgh so astutely pointed out over twenty-five years ago, how individuals gain and wield political power through the formal organization of social service agencies is significant. Members of boards of directors, along with many of the managerial staff of these agencies, form a political elite. For the Native Canadian Centre of Toronto, winning and maintaining legitimate authority is a complex process of balancing its roles and responsibilities against the diverse, and often opposing, expectations of people inside, outside, and on the ever-shifting borders of the "community." Native culture, and how it is asserted, defined, reconfigured, and negotiated remains a key source of leverage in this political economy.

Geographer Evelyn Peters (1996) questions the assumption that being urban and Aboriginal necessarily constitutes an impossible and contradictory schism of identity. She counters the idea that the conditions of urban living subvert the possibilities of generating and sustaining "authentic" Native cultural communities in cities. My research agrees with Peters in that the history of the Native Canadian Centre of Toronto illustrates how Native people in the city strive to create and build places of Native community that are culturally rich, diverse, and strong. Generating "authentic" Native perspectives and values is a fundamental part of this community-building process. Against the socio-political backdrop of oppression from which urban Native people emerge, it is not surprising to see certain values essentialized in terms of Native culture. The capacity for conflict resolution and an emphasis on "sticking together" as a people in the face of adversity is one such value that permeates the history of the centre and contributes to understanding its particular position as a valued place in the community. It is not that the history of the centre is conflict-free; rather its history is precisely a living illustration of how conflict has been a catalyst for renewal through a range of dynamic struggles mediated by race, gender, and class relations with both non-Natives and within the Native community locally and nationally.

Note

I am extremely grateful for the collaborative support and assistance of the Native Canadian Centre of Toronto, and of the many volunteers and youth staff with the Toronto Native Community History Project who made research for this chapter possible. Financial support was provided through a Social Science and Humanities Research Council of Canada doctoral fellowship, a Formation des Chercheurs et Aide à la Recherche (F-CAR), Québec doctoral fellowship, and University of Toronto Open Fellowship.

Works Cited

Bourdieu, Pierre. 1986. "The Forms of Capital." In *Handbook of Theory and Research for the Sociology of Education*, edited by John G. Richardson, 241–58. New York: Greenwood Press.

Cardinal, Harold. 1969. *The Unjust Society*. Edmonton: Hurtig.

Dosman, Edgar. 1972. *Indians: The Urban Dilemma*. Toronto: McClelland and Stewart.

Forte, Maximilian. 1998. "Renewed Indigeneity in the Local–Global Continuum and the Political Economy of Tradition: The Case of Trinidad's Caribs and the Caribbean Organization of Indigenous Peoples." In *Proceedings of the 24th Annual Third World Conference*. Chicago: Third World Conference Foundation.

Friedman, Jonathan. 1999. "Indigenous Struggles and the Discreet Charm of the Bourgeoisie." *Australian Journal of Anthropology* 10: 1–14.

Gajic, Barbara. 1997. "Jim Mason: The Kind of Reward You Put in Your Heart." In *The Meeting Place: Aboriginal Life in Toronto*, edited by Frances Sanderson and Heather Howard-Bobiwash, 97–105. Toronto: Native Canadian Centre of Toronto.

Gupta, Akhil, and James Ferguson. 1992. "Beyond Culture: Space, Identity, and the Politics of Difference." *Cultural Anthropology* 7 (1): 6–23.

———, eds. 1999 [1997]. *Culture, Power and Place; Explorations in Critical Anthropology*. Durham: Duke University Press.

Harper, Vern. 1974. *Following the Red Path, the Native People's Caravan, 1974.* Toronto: NC Press.

Hastrup, Kirstin, and Karen Fog Olwig. 1997. Introduction. In *Siting Culture: The Shifting Anthropological Subject*, edited by Kirstin Hastrup and Karen Fog Olwig, 1–14. London: Routledge.

Howard-Bobiwash, Heather. 1999. "'Like Her Lips to My Ear': Reading Anishnaabekweg Lives and Cultural Continuity in the City." In *Feminist Fields: Ethnographic Insights*, edited by Rae Bridgman, Sally Cole, and Heather Howard-Bobiwash, 117–36. Peterborough: Broadview Press.

———. 2003. "Women's Class Strategies as Activism in Native Community Building in Toronto, 1950–1975." In *Keeping the Campfires Going: Urban American Indian Women's Activism*, edited by Susan Applegate Krouse and Heather Howard-Bobiwash. Special Issue of *American Indian Quarterly* 27 (3–4).

Howard, Heather A. 2004. "Dreamcatchers in the City: An Ethnohistory of Social Action, Gender, and Class in Native Community Production in Toronto." Unpublished Ph.D. dissertation, Department of Anthropology, University of Toronto.

———. Forthcoming "How Did Native Women Use Strategic Alliances with Non-Native Reformists to Organize Native Community in Post–WW II Toronto?" Document Project, Women and Social Movements.

Lee, Richard B. 2003. "Indigenous Rights and the Politics of Identity in Post-Apartheid South Africa." In *At the Risk of Being Heard: Identity, Indigenous Rights and Post-Colonial States*, edited by Bart Dean and Jerome Levi, 80–111. Ann Arbor: University of Michigan Press.

Lobo, Susan. 2009. "Urban Clan Mothers: Key Households in Cities." In *Keeping the Campfires Going: Native Women's Activism in Urban Areas*, edited by Susan Applegate Krouse and Heather Howard-Bobiwash, 1–21. Lincoln: University of Nebraska Press.

Kirby, Kathleen. 1996. *Indifferent Boundaries: Spatial Concepts of Human Subjectivity*. London: Guilford Press.

NAFC (National Association of Friendship Centres). 1997. History and Background. Mandate-NAFC-1997. http://www.nafc-aboriginal.com.

Nagel, Joane. 1996. *American Indian Ethnic Renewal: Red Power and the Resurgence of Identity and Culture*. New York: Oxford University Press.

Nagler, Mark. 1970. *Indians in the City: A Study of the Urbanization of Indians in Toronto*. Ottawa: Canadian Research Centre for Anthropology, Saint Paul University.

Native Canadian Centre of Toronto. 2002. In the Spirit of Unity: A Synopsis of Programs and Services Available to the Urban Aboriginal Population in the Greater Toronto Area. Toronto: Native Canadian Centre of Toronto.

Native Canadian Oral History Project. 1983. "Vern Harper in an Interview with Alex Cywink." Tape #OHT83031, Spadina Rd. Library, Toronto.

Niezen, Ronald. 2003. *The Origins of Indigenism*. Berkeley: University of California Press.

Obonsawin, Roger. 1987. "The Native Canadian Centre of Toronto: 25 Years of Community Service, 25 Years of Growth." *Boozhoo* 1 (4): 24–29.

Obonsawin, Roger, and Heather Howard-Bobiwash. 1997. "The Native Canadian Centre of Toronto: The Meeting Place for Aboriginal People for 35 Years." In *The Meeting Place: Aboriginal Life in Toronto*, edited by Frances Sanderson and Heather Howard-Bobiwash, 25–59. Toronto: Native Canadian Centre of Toronto.

Pelletier, Wilfrid, and Ted Poole. 1974. *No Foreign Land: The Biography of a North American Indian*. New York: Pantheon Books.

Peters, Evelyn. 1996. "'Urban' and 'Aboriginal': An Impossible Contradiction?" In *City Lives and City Forms: Critical Research and Canadian Urbanism*, edited by Jon Caufield and Linda Peake, 47–62. Toronto: University of Toronto Press.

Redbird, Duke, and Marty Dunn. 1971. *Red on White: The Biography of Duke Redbird*. Toronto: New Press.

Ryan, Joan. 1978. *Wall of Words: The Betrayal of the Urban Indian*. Toronto: PMA Books.

Sanderson, Frances, and Heather Howard-Bobiwash, eds. 1997. *The Meeting Place: Aboriginal Life in Toronto*. Toronto: Native Canadian Centre of Toronto.

Toronto Telegram. 1966. Photo caption: "Governor General Roland Michener, with Mrs. Michener, Swings Sheldon Driver High in the Air ..." 29 November.

Toronto Star. 1963. "Indian Centre: Does It Reach Those Who Need It?" 4 December.

Toronto Star. ca. 1963. "Indian Centre Does Not Support Militants." *Toronto Star*.

Toronto Star. 1966. "Indian Centre Is Erasing 'Beads and Buckskin' Image." Cover of Family Section. Unknown title, clipping file, Toronto Native Community History Project.

Treat, James. 2003. *Around the Sacred Fire: Native Religious Activism in the Red Power Era*. New York: Palgrave Macmillan.

Vanderburgh, R.M. 1977. *I Am Nokomis, Too: The Biography of Verna Patronella Johnson*. Don Mills, ON: General Publishing.

———. 1980. "Women and the Politics of Culture: Class and Gender Conflicts in the Toronto Native Community." *Canadian Woman Studies* 2 (1): 82–83.

Weaver, Sally. 1993. "First Nations Women and Government Policy, 1970–1992: Discrimination and Conflict." In *Changing Patterns: Women in Canada*, edited by Sandra Burt, Lorraine Code, and Lindsay Dorney. Toronto: McClelland and Stewart.

7

Neoliberalism and the Urban Aboriginal Experience
A Casino Rama Case Study

Darrel Manitowabi

The following is a case study of the experiences of Aboriginal migrants in the small city of Orillia, in south-central Ontario. On 31 July 1996, Casino Rama opened on the nearby Rama-Mnjikaning First Nation (formerly known as Rama), initiating an Aboriginal migration to the region. During 2002 and 2004, I conducted fieldwork in the city of Orillia and on the Rama-Mnjikaning First Nation to understand the holistic impact of Casino Rama. The casino is the province's only Aboriginal commercial casino and is purported to be the largest single-site employer of Canadian Aboriginals, with seven hundred employed (Casino Rama 2005).[1] Colonial membership structures preserved in the Indian Act require that these Aboriginal workers reside in the nearby cities of Orillia and Barrie, Ontario, although they are employed on a reserve.[2]

My objective is to contribute to the greater understanding of the urban Aboriginal experience and the effects of neoliberalism in Canada. Previous studies on Aboriginals in urban settings have focused either on social networks (e.g., Guillemin 1975) and socio-economic class (e.g., Dosman 1972; Brody 1971), or both, combined with culture, gender, and Aboriginal/non-Aboriginal relations (e.g., Howard 2004). My analysis combines elements of these previous studies with an emphasis on social networks and neoliberalism. This analysis is unique, however, since most urban Aboriginals in Orillia represent a contemporary movement and the migration occurred with the purpose of acquiring employment at two reserve-based localities (Casino Rama and within Rama-Mnjikaning's administration). This chapter argues that the urban Aboriginal experience is conditioned by the interactions of Aboriginal symbolic capital and neoliberalism. I will subsequently expand on the meaning of these terms in the context of my fieldwork, which will compare and contrast Aboriginal experiences at Casino Rama and Rama-Mnjikaning.

Background

Given the dire economic situation of most First Nations in Canada, the monetary success and expansion of Indigenous casinos in the United States made such opportunities attractive to them. As a result, in the early 1990s the Chiefs of Ontario considered establishing a casino on a First Nation.[3] The chiefs determined strategically that rather than have multiple, competing reserve-based casinos, one casino should be established on an Ontario First Nation, which would benefit all First Nations in terms of employment and revenue (Casino Rama Revenue Agreement 2000).[4]

The New Democratic provincial government of the time had been considering opening new casinos in Ontario when it learned of the Chiefs of Ontario's intentions. Dialogue then took place between the province and the Chiefs that centred on creating catchment areas so that the new provincial and First Nation casinos would not compete with one another. In 1993, the province and the chiefs formally agreed that one casino would be developed on an Ontario First Nation and that its revenue would be shared by all Ontario First Nations (Casino Rama Revenue Agreement 2000; Campbell 1999, 20). At that point, the Chiefs of Ontario invited all Ontario First Nations to submit proposals to host the casino; of the fourteen submitted, the chiefs selected Rama-Mnjikaning because of location, their experience with tourism, and community support for the project (Campbell 1999, 22; Casino Rama Revenue Agreement 2000). Casino Rama opened on 31 July 1996.

As part of their successful casino bid, Rama-Mnjikaning proposed "to ensure that the First Nations Casino ... provides increasingly progressive economic opportunities to the First Nations of Ontario both within and external to the operation" (Campbell 1999, 22). Thus, since the beginning, Casino Rama has maintained a commitment to provide employment opportunities to First Nations in Ontario. In 2002 it was reported that the total workforce was 3,500 and at that time, 750 were Aboriginal (Wassegijig 2002). Aside from the casino itself, the Rama-Mnjikaning administration employs three hundred people, mostly band members; however, because of the complexities of operations, non-Aboriginals and Aboriginal non-members are employed as well.

Urban Aboriginals in Orillia

Aboriginal migrants seeking employment at Casino Rama are not able to find accommodation on Rama-Mnjikaning, except for a limited number of rental opportunities. Further, only those who are considered band members can acquire permanent housing on the reserve. For a person to be considered a band member in Rama-Mnjikaning, at least one of his/her parents must be an existing band member. Those who marry into the community can apply to the chief and council to become band members (see, for example, Frideres 2001: 24–31).

Given these restrictions, many Aboriginal migrants seek rental accommodations off-reserve. Since Orillia is the closest urban centre (a fifteen-minute drive away), the majority of migrants rent apartments in the city and commute to Rama-Mnjikaning. A lesser number seek rentals in Barrie, a thirty-minute drive south of Orillia. A daily complimentary shuttle service transports workers from Orillia to Casino Rama.

According to Statistics Canada, the total population of Orillia in 2001 was 29,121, with 860 identified as Aboriginal (see Table 1 for a population description). Most of this population was recent, since 780 reported that they had moved to Orillia within the last five years (Statistics Canada 2005a). Based on the demographics in Table 1, it appears that there is a sizeable young Aboriginal community in Orillia (in fact, there are more Aboriginals in Orillia than in Rama-Mnjikaning).[5] Because Casino Rama opened in 1996, the bulk of this population probably moved to Orillia to seek employment. Based on the information tabulated by Statistics Canada and my fieldwork experience, the Orillia urban Aboriginal population does not experience the poverty documented in other studies (e.g., Royal Commission on Aboriginal Peoples 1996, Vol. 4).

From my experiences in the Ontario cities of Sudbury, Hamilton, and Toronto, it is often possible to find segments of the Aboriginal community at the local Aboriginal friendship centre, but although 860 Aboriginals live in Orillia, finding them as a community can be a difficult task. Orillia does not have a friendship centre, but has a Native Women's Group, similar to a friendship centre since it offers social and cultural programming to all urban Aboriginal people in Orillia. Historically, friendship centres in Ontario have met the cultural, social, and recreational needs of urban Aboriginals and have acted to establish an urban Aboriginal presence in culturally diverse urban centres (Royal Commission on Aboriginal Peoples, Vol. 4, 565). Furthermore, friendship centres have acted as mechanisms of community building while maintaining Aboriginal culture and identity (Howard, chapter 6 this volume).

Table 1: Demographic Characteristics of the Orillia Urban Aboriginal Community in Comparison to the City of Orillia and Province of Ontario, 2001

Characteristic	Aboriginal	Orillia	Ontario
Population	860	29,121	11,410,046
Registered Indian	560	—	—
Métis	150	—	—
Inuit	0	—	—
Median age	24.8	39.7	37.2
Education			
Less than high school (%)	25	20.7	13.2
High school (%)	9.5	36.2	33.7
Some post-secondary (%)	11.9	9.4	7.9
Trades, college certificate (%)	50	22.5	19.5
University degree (%)	2.4	11.5	25.7
Average earnings ($)	23,757	28,234	35,185
Unemployment rate (%)	7.5	6.3	6.1

Source: Statistics Canada 2001a, 2001b.
Note: The Aboriginal education range is "25 years of age and over," while the education figures for Orillia and Ontario are based on the age interval "20–34" because Statistics Canada provides different age ranges for both groups. I consider the Orillia and Ontario age range comparable, since the Aboriginal median age is young. The high percentage of Aboriginal college/trade certificates seems to be a result of the training required at the casino such as for blackjack dealers. Georgian College and a private training firm provide casino training.

Although not technically a friendship centre, the Women's Group operates like one. For instance, activities at the Women's Group include language classes, youth nights, socials, and arts and craft classes; it also houses an Aboriginal psychologist who provides counselling services. The activities of the Native Women's Group are not restricted to women, and I participated in men's circles and various family social events held throughout the year. Furthermore, the City of Orillia and businesses in Orillia recognize the contributions of the Women's Group and have donated food and materials for activities. While I was at the Native Women's Group, there was little or no participation from casino workers; indeed, the men's circles I participated in had on average only four attendees, and this activity was eventually cancelled due to low participation. Most of the programming that my family took part in had low participation, with the exception of major community meals and socials such as those held at Halloween or Christmas.

While living in Orillia, I observed urban Aboriginals daily, either at the grocery store, at the local shopping mall, or while dining at a restaurant. Further, I witnessed groups of urban Aboriginals participating in recreational activities such as volleyball or hockey, spending time with their families, or socializing at one or more of the city bars. It was common for urban Aboriginals to maintain links with their home communities by spending their off-work time commuting to home reserves. This is consistent with RCAP's (1996, Vol. 4, 535) observation that Aboriginal urbanization "tends to include frequent returns to their home communities."

For many Aboriginal migrants, extensions of home community kinship and/or friendship networks exist in Orillia even before they arrive; thus in most cases the Aboriginal migrant arrives with existing social networks and eventually establishes new friendships at the casino and Rama-Mnjikaning. As opposed to finding urban Aboriginal migrants in physical places of social and cultural activity such as a friendship centre, therefore, it appears that the Aboriginal migrant presence in Orillia exists through social networks that have either been established at the workplace or represent a continuation from home reserves. It is common, for instance, for a group of friends or extended family to rent a house in Orillia collectively.

Although for the most part the composition of such Aboriginal social groups is "Aboriginal only," this is not always the case. In some instances, I observed friendships with non-Aboriginal casino employees representing hybrid social groups. Further, since groups work at similar times and have the same days off, social activities between friends take place at similar times. During the time I was in Orillia, one of the bars sponsored a well-attended "casino night" early in the week, which was targeted at casino workers since weekends off are rare unless one works in the casino administration.

Despite the fact that Aboriginal casino migrants work at Rama-Mnjikaning, most of them have no involvement or interaction with the reserve community. The activities and services at Rama-Mnjikaning are provided for band members; hence, most are unable to take advantage of participating in the community. The only times that Aboriginal casino employees participate in Rama-Mnjikaning are at one of the two pow-wows held annually or at the annual Aboriginal men's hockey tournament. I observed Aboriginal casino employees dancing or socializing at the powwow, and a group of males formed a Casino Rama men's hockey team that participated in the tournament, while others played on their home reserve's hockey team.

Positions in the Rama-Mnjikaning administration provide another source of employment for non-member Aboriginals. In such instances, the intensity of social interaction with band members has led to a greater participation in the community. Rama-Mnjikaning further distinguishes between Aboriginal non-member casino workers and those who work in administration by permitting children of non-member Aboriginal administration workers to attend the First Nation school and/or daycare. One non-member Aboriginal employee summed up the situation best: "I feel like a complete outsider here. Systematically government policies don't give me a residency here somehow but yet I participate fully in everything community-wise, so it's a little irony in that with these attachments to government policies artificial lines are drawn, where, I'm sure in other communities you find yourself in a matter of time you sort of evolve into a belonging or fellowship."[6]

It is apparent from the above narrative that it can be a challenge for the non-member Aboriginal migrant to participate in the Rama-Mnjikaning community; however, there is a certain amount of personal choice involved in whether non-members participate in Rama-Mnjikaning or Orillia social circles. I observed, for instance, that Aboriginal migrant employees may send their children to Rama-Mnjikaning's daycare, establishing a social link through those children to the Rama-Mnjikaning community, yet live in Orillia and socialize with networks of fellow Aboriginal migrants.

The composition of urban Aboriginals is also ever-changing. Based on insights from my fieldwork and from statistics (see Table 1), Aboriginal work experience and formal education are, on average, lower than that of Orillia and Ontario. On average, most occupy part-time entry-level positions, usually during the graveyard shift (midnight to 8 a.m.) and on a short-term contract (there is no union at the casino). Based on discussions with casino workers, this type of part-time employment is directed at those with little work experience and educational background. For employees in this circumstance, the transition to stable employment is challenging. Based on interviews, employees recited workplace regulations associated with working at the casino. Such stipulations include a regulated personal appearance such as "looking professional" and courteous conduct such as "smiling," and "speaking professionally" to patrons. Furthermore, employees spoke of a ten-point system in place to manage the performance of employees. Any violation of the terms of employment at the casino such as being late, not showing up for work, or improper conduct in the workplace counts as a point, and the accumulation of ten points can lead to employment termination. After six months of no absences and not being late, the employee status is reset to zero.

This type of employment regulation has proved difficult for many Aboriginals with little previous work experience and has often led to employment termination. I observed that the casino as a whole has a high turnover rate, with a corresponding high turnover rate in urban Aboriginals; for instance, two Aboriginal migrants boarded with me during my two-year stay in Orillia and each lasted about a year. In addition, landlords are hesitant to rent to migrants due to the unpredictability of their employment. Twenty of my interviewees and acquaintances in Orillia no longer worked at the casino when I left in 2004.

On the other hand, the situation is different for the non-member Aboriginal Rama-Mnjikaning administration workers. Most arrive with sufficient work experience and education; as a result, most occupy highly skilled positions within the administration (e.g., police officers, managers, policy advisors). These employees have a lower employment turnover rate and there is thus a consistent presence in this segment of urban Aboriginals.

Symbolic Capital, Neoliberalism and the Urban Aboriginal Experience

Why do a portion of Aboriginals face challenges adjusting to employment at the casino? To answer this question I draw upon Bourdieu's (1998a) notion of symbolic capital and the critique of neoliberalism (e.g., Harvey 2007; Teeple 1995). According to Bourdieu, symbolic capital refers to "any property (any form of capital whether physical, economic, cultural, and social) when it is perceived by social agents endowed with categories of perception which cause them to know it and to recognize it, to give it value" (1998a, 47). The volume of capital differentiates social groups; for instance, an unskilled labourer has less capital (e.g., education and economic prestige) than a business executive (ibid., 5).[7] For Bourdieu and Wacquant, symbolic capital is operationalized within a "field" that they define as "a network, or a configuration, of objective relations between positions. These positions are objectively defined, in their existence and in the determinations they impose upon their occupants, agents or institutions, by their present and potential situation (situs) in the structure of the distribution of species of power (or capital)" (Bourdieu and Wacquant 1992, 97).[8] In the case of Casino Rama, it is possible to envisage the casino as the field, while education and work experience function as forms of symbolic capital that distinguish employment positioning.

The concept of neoliberalism can be traced to the period before the 1980s, when the relationship between the wealthy and poor was expressed by the terms "modernization" and "dependency." Beginning in the 1980s and 1990s, non-government agencies such as the World Bank and International Monetary Fund wanted to improve the position of the poor. They envisioned that a liberalization of the market was necessary to solve the problem of poverty (Harvey 2007; Babb 2005; Teeple 1995).

In Canada, Ontario emerged as the leader in neoliberal economic reforms during the recession of the 1980s. This economic circumstance proved disastrous for David Peterson's Liberal government, leading to the election of the New Democratic Party, led by Bob Rae. As part of his platform, Rae promised an "Agenda for the People" inclusive of a social charter (embedded social rights), Aboriginal self-government, and economic unification with Canada (Graefe 2002; Rachlis and Wolfe 1997, 35). Unfortunately, economic conditions in Ontario prevented Rae from delivering his agenda. The unemployment rate in Ontario hit a high of 10 percent in 1992 (Walkom 1994, 99), and the NDP became desperate for an economic stimulus. This is evident in the following statement Rae made on 5 April 1993: "Unless we reduce operating costs through restructuring and reforming government departments and programs and through agreements with public sector employers and employees, we will no longer be able to afford the level of public investment Ontario needs in jobs, training, and capital to meet the economic challenges in the 1990s" (cited in Rachlis and Wolfe 1997, 353).

Despite Rae's early criticism of casinos in 1990, the desperate economic conditions seemed to change his mind regarding the economic potential of casinos in Ontario. In 1992, the NDP developed a policy paper on gaming and with little public input established a casino in 1994 in Windsor, Ontario (Walkom 1994, 82, 110–11). Concurrent with Rae's commitment to Aboriginal self-government, the NDP government initiated negotiations with Ontario First Nations to explore casinos and gaming authorities, eventually leading to the creation of Casino Rama (ibid.).

The Confluence of Aboriginal Capital, Neoliberalism, and Urbanity

For most Aboriginal communities, unemployment remains a persistent problem (see, for example, Wotherspoon and Satzewich 2000; Elias 1996); thus, Casino Rama represents an opportunity for potential employment. The legacy of colonially induced unemployment (ibid.) compared with the statistics on the lower levels of education of Orillia urban

Aboriginals (see Table 1) suggests that the educational and economic capital of Aboriginals is less than that of non-Aboriginals. The following statement from an Aboriginal employee illustrates this point: "My first impression was that it was gonna be a Native casino like, it was on a reservation [sic] and they say, employ a lot of Natives, but there's a lot of Natives that start below and then they got to make their way up but there's also the white men that start off at the top and we don't really get the chance to get the experience to get there unless we take their courses [formal Western education] and even though we have experience."[9]

There are a minority of Aboriginal migrants with sufficient symbolic capital in the form of work experience and education who hold desirable positions within the casino, such as supervisors; however, for the majority, insufficient symbolic capital suppresses desirable employment opportunities.

Situating Aboriginal symbolic capital with neoliberalism, I have argued elsewhere (Manitowabi 2007) that Casino Rama is both a provincial strategy to control the proliferation of Aboriginal casinos (e.g., the deal for one casino) and a neoliberal solution to Aboriginal poverty by permitting Aboriginal participation in the economy.[10] The latter is particularly favourable to governments, since it reduces social welfare costs associated with unemployment. The neoliberal model, however, promotes corporatization, privatization, maximum growth, and individual productivity as logical social behaviour (ibid.). The problem with this logic, according to Bourdieu (1998b, 98), is that "the ultimate basis of this economic order placed under the banner of individual freedom is indeed the *structural violence* of unemployment, of insecure employment and the *fear* provoked by the threat of losing employment [italics in original]."[11] This economic order applies to the field of Casino Rama, since most employees (Aboriginal and non-Aboriginal) begin on a short-term contract. Conformity to expectations of individual productivity at the casino is "rewarded" with long-term employment while non-conformity results in termination of employment. In essence, Bourdieu suggests, this type of employment operates as a type of social Darwinism.

Situated within the broader political context, it is important to note that these recent urban Aboriginal experiences exist in relation to power since the Aboriginal control of Casino Rama is an illusion. The casino is purported to be the "largest employer of First Nations" (Casino Rama 2005). This statement masks the reality that the majority of Aboriginal employment positions are contractually limited, entry-level positions with a high turnover rate. With the exception of the few who have sufficient work experience and education, the harsh reality is that most Aboriginal casino employees arrive with a sense of optimism but are forced to return to their communities, since the casino does not accommodate Aboriginals in the way it is marketed. Furthermore, the casino is labelled as "Aboriginal" (Casino Rama 2005), but the reality is that the majority of employees are non-Aboriginal (78.6 percent as of 2002), it is managed by Penn National Gaming of Pennsylvania, and the rules for casino operations are defined by the Ontario Lottery and Gaming Corporation. The irony of the false marketing of Casino Rama as Aboriginal was perhaps best articulated by an Aboriginal casino employee: "It's weird living in the white world, even though I'm working on the rez."[12]

Aside from symbolic capital and the challenges of casino neoliberalism, social relations between Aboriginals and non-Aboriginals present an additional obstacle for long-term employment. In some cases, animosity exists between some non-Aboriginal supervisors and Aboriginal employees because of income tax exemptions for Aboriginals working on a reserve, meaning that sometimes Aboriginal employees make more money than their non-Aboriginal supervisors. Such employees often feel indirectly socially distanced, since non-Aboriginal superiors and co-workers are periodically overheard commenting on "special privileges" for Aboriginal employees. An Orillia newspaper has suggested that some Aboriginal casino employees face workplace discrimination and unjust firings. In one story, a humiliated Aboriginal claimed that "white people always come first before the native people" (Moro 2006). In another, a fired casino Aboriginal claimed he was stereotyped as "lazy" by a non-Aboriginal supervisor and commented that Aboriginal advancement at the casino is the exception and not the rule (McKim 2005).

Despite the fact that the majority cannot adapt to the casino, new Aboriginal migrants continually arrive to replace those who have left, meaning that although the Aboriginal employee changes, the Aboriginal migrant experience remains relatively constant. Most Aboriginal migrants arrive with similar experiences on their home First Nations that have forced them to seek economic opportunities such as those provided by the casino; however, symbolic capital continues to condition their experiences at the casino. The lack of economic opportunities on First Nations results in a corresponding lack of job experience and skills that are needed to adapt to the casino.

On the other hand, there are Aboriginals without much education and work experience who have persisted at the casino despite the obstacles. Based on information from personal interviews I note that it is common for those lacking experience or education to work the graveyard shift on a part-time contract. After about a year, however, it is possible to apply for desirable full-time positions. Although such instances occur, they appear to be the exception rather than the rule (McKim 2005).

Time has allowed the successful minority of Aboriginal migrants to establish social networks in Orillia and, in some cases, in Rama-Mnjikaning. While in the field, I participated in both networks, at times interacting with Aboriginal migrants in Orillia and at other times participating in social events in Rama-Mnjikaning. This was also the case of one Aboriginal family with one member who has worked in the casino administration since it opened. This individual was one of the few who participated regularly at the Orillia Native Women's Group and in the Rama-Mnjikaning community. His prolonged residency in Orillia established participation in one locality, and his prolonged social interaction at his workplace in Rama-Mnjikaning with band members allowed for participation in Rama-Mnjikaning. Most Aboriginal migrants, however, do not have access to participation in this set of social relations, and are therefore excluded from Rama-Mnjikaning and restricted to Orillia.

Conclusion

Three preliminary interpretations emerge from insights from my fieldwork experience. The first is that Casino Rama exists as a neoliberal solution to First Nations unemployment, in turn causing an Aboriginal migration to Orillia. Second, the urban Aboriginal experience is characterized by social networks of kin, friendships, and co-workers. Third, symbolic capital influences the urban Aboriginal experience in Orillia and in Rama-Mnjikaning, since those Aboriginals with sufficient education and work experience tend to adapt successfully to their new work environment and urban locality. In effect, Casino Rama appears not to benefit the economically disadvantaged populations that neoliberalism is intended to benefit.

Despite these interpretations, it is important to note that this is a preliminary understanding of the urban Aboriginal experience resulting from Casino Rama. It is possible that more Aboriginal migrants will secure permanent employment at the casino and raise families in Orillia, planting the seeds for an enhanced future urban Aboriginal presence. It is further possible that future generations of established urban Aboriginal families in Orillia will contribute to and strengthen the cultural and social activities of the Orillia Native Women's Group, as other urban Aboriginals have done elsewhere (RCAP 1996; Howard 2004). Until that time, however, it will remain a challenge for urban Aboriginal casino migrants to succeed at Ontario's only Aboriginal commercial casino and establish a greater urban Aboriginal presence in Orillia.

Notes

I am thankful for the casino workers who took the time to participate in this study. I am also grateful for the funding provided by an Ontario Problem Gambling Research Centre Doctoral Fellowship (2002) and a University of Toronto Lorna Marshall Doctoral Fellowship in Social and Cultural Anthropology (2003). Versions of this paper have been presented at various conferences. Specific to this chapter, I have benefited from discussions with Heather Howard-Bobiwash, Craig Proulx, and from the comments of an anonymous reviewer. The perspectives contained in this chapter are, however, my own.

1 The Mississaugas of Scugog have a charity casino on their First Nation called the Great Blue Heron Charity Casino. The First Nation is east of Rama-Mnjikaning, near Port Perry, northeast of Toronto. As well, the Anishinabe of Wauzhushk Onigum First Nation operate a charity casino named the Golden Eagle Casino in Kenora, Ontario.

2 Frideres (2001, 22–46) details the evolution of the Indian Act inclusive of excerpts and commentary. For instance, the act determines the identity of "Indians" and residency on reserves.

3 The Chiefs of Ontario is a political organization that represents Ontario's 134 First Nations' interests at the regional, provincial, and national level (see http://www .chiefs-of-Ontario.org).

4 There are numerous publications on Indigenous casinos in the United States; for recent anthropological accounts see Cattelino (2008) and Darian-Smith (2004). For a survey of the Canadian experience, see Belanger (2006).

5 In 2001, the on-reserve population of Rama-Mnjikaning was 597 (Statistics Canada 2005c).

6 Information from my field notes, 2004.

7 This theory has affinities with Marxism and political economy, though Bourdieu distinguishes his position since it is not strictly economic but incorporates symbolism, agency, and cultural practice (see Bourdieu 1990, 122–34).

8 Bourdieu and Wacquant compare the concept of field to a game because agents follow rules and compete with one another. The capital an agent possesses determines success within a field (see Bourdieu and Wacquant 1992, 98).

9 Quote from transcribed interview, 2003.

10 For a study of neoliberal policies at the First Nations reserve level, see Slowey (2008).

11 Symbolic violence refers to how "the dominated perceive the dominant through the categories that the relation of domination has produced and which are thus identical to the interests of the dominant" (Bourdieu 1998a, 121).

12 Quote from transcribed interview, 2003.

Works Cited

Babb, Sarah. 2005. "The Social Consequences of Structural Adjustment: Recent Evidence and Current Debates." *Annual Review of Sociology* 31: 199–222.

Belanger, Yale D. 2006. *Gambling with the Future: The Evolution of Aboriginal Gaming in Canada*. Saskatoon: Purich Publishing.

Bourdieu, Pierre. 1990. *The Logic of Practice*. Stanford: Stanford University Press.

———. 1998a. *Practical Reason: On the Theory of Action*. Stanford: Stanford University Press.

————. 1998b *Acts of Resistance against the Tyranny of the Market*. New York: New Press.

Bourdieu, Pierre, and Loic Wacquant. 1992. *An Invitation to Reflexive Sociology*. Chicago: University of Chicago Press.

Brody, Hugh. 1971. *Indians on Skid Row*. Ottawa: Information Canada.

Campbell, Karen. 1999. "Community Life and Governance: Early Experiences of Mnjikaning First Nation with Casino Rama." Master's of Social Work thesis. Winnipeg: University of Manitoba.

Casino Rama. 2005. About Casino Rama. http://www.casinorama.com/aboutcr .aspx.

Casino Rama Revenue Agreement. 2000. "Casino Rama Revenue Agreement. An Agreement Made on the 9th Day of June, 2000 Between Her Majesty the Queen in Right of Ontario, and Ontario Lottery Gaming Corporation, and Ontario First Nations Limited Partnership and Mnjikaning First Nation Limited Partnership." http://www.ofnlp.org/revenue_agreement.html.

Cattelino, Jessica. 2008. *High Stakes: Florida Seminole Gaming and Sovereignty*. Durham, NC: Duke University Press.

Darian-Smith, Eve. 2004. *New Capitalists: Law, Politics and Identity Surrounding Casino Gaming on Native American Land*. Toronto: Nelson.

Dosman, Edgar J. 1972. *Indians: The Urban Dilemma*. Toronto: McClelland and Stewart.

Elias, Peter. 1996. "Worklessness and Social Pathologies in Aboriginal Communities." *Human Organization* 55 (1): 13–24.

Frideres, James S. 2001 *Aboriginal Peoples in Canada: Contemporary Conflicts*. Sixth edition. Toronto: Prentice-Hall.

Graefe, Peter. 2002 *Striking a New Balance: Neoliberalism, The Provinces and Intergovernmental Relations in Canada, 1985–2002*. Ph.D. thesis. Montreal: Université de Montreal.

Guillemin, Jeanne. 1975. *Urban Renegades: The Cultural Strategy of American Indians*. New York: Columbia University Press.

Harvey, David. 2007 [2005]. *A Brief History of Neoliberalism*. Toronto: Oxford University Press.

Howard, Heather A. 2004. "Dreamcatchers in the City: An Ethnohistory of Social Action, Gender, and Class in Native Community Production in Toronto." Ph.D. thesis. Toronto: University of Toronto.

Manitowabi, Darrel. 2007. *From Fish Weirs to Casino: Negotiating Neoliberalism at Mnjikaning*. Ph.D. thesis. Toronto: University of Toronto.

McKim, Colin. 2005. "Racism Alleged at Casino." *Orillia Packet and Times* 8 January 2005, electronic edition. http://www.orilliapacket.com.

Moro, Teviah. 2006. "Protestors Charged." *Orillia Packet and Times* 23 March 2006, electronic edition. http://www.orilliapacket.com.

Rachlis, C., and D. Wolfe. 1997. "An Insiders' View of the NDP Government of Ontario: The Politics of Permanent Opposition Meets the Economics of Permanent Recession." In *Government and Politics of Ontario*, edited by G. White, 331–64. Toronto: University of Toronto Press.

Royal Commission on Aboriginal Peoples. 1996. Report of the Royal Commission on Aboriginal Peoples. Six volumes. Ottawa: Minister of Supply and Services Canada.

Slowey, Gabrielle. 2008. *Navigating Neoliberalism: Self-Determination and the Mikisew Cree First Nation*. Vancouver: University of British Columbia Press.

Statistics Canada. 2005a. 2001 Aboriginal Population Profile—Orillia, Ontario. http://www12.statcan.ca/english/profil01/AP01/Index.cfm?Lang=E.

Statistics Canada. 2005b. 2001 Community Profile—Orillia, Ontario (City). http://www12.statcan.ca/english/profil01/CP01/Index.cfm?Lang=E.

Statistics Canada. 2005c. 2001 Community Profile—Mnjikaning First Nation 32 (Rama First Nation 32). http://www12.statcan.ca/english/Profil01/CP01/Search/SearchForm_Results.cfm?Lang=E.

Teeple, Gary. 1995. *Globalization and the Decline of Social Reform*. Toronto: Garamond Press.

Wassegijig, Kevin. 2002. Funding for Cultural Events: Casino Rama. Presentation at the Business of Cultural Industries Conference, Toronto, Ontario. 28 November.

Walkom, Thomas. 1994. *Rae Days*. Toronto: Key Porter Books

Wotherspoon, Terry, and Vic Satzewich. 2000. *First Nations Race, Class, and Gender Relations*. Regina, SK: Canadian Plains Research Center.

8
Challenges to and Successes in
Urban Aboriginal Education in Canada
A Case Study of Wiingashk Secondary School

Sadie Donovan

Aboriginal education in Canada has been and continues to be fraught with power imbalances and colonial agendas. The formidable and pervasive legacy of colonialism in contributing to the continued under-achievement of Aboriginal students in Canadian school systems cannot be overemphasized. Throughout the tumultuous history of Euro-Cana-dian/Aboriginal relations, educational policy has been driven by paternal-ism, prejudice, and political expediency (Axelrod 1999; Bear Nicholas 2001). The residential, day, and industrial school systems have arguably been the most effective colonial apparatuses of First Nations' subjugation. Throughout the history of these institutions, the assaults launched against Aboriginal cultures have been sustained and pervasive. The loss of tradi-tional lands, enfranchisement, internalized colonialism, cultural and linguis-tic genocide, and community divisiveness are but a few of the detrimental consequences of federal education policy (Kirkness 1998; Miller 1996; Milloy 1999; St. Denis 2007).

In the 1960s, Aboriginal leaders spoke out against these oppressive policies, denouncing the Canadian state for the history of abuse and neg-lect that Aboriginal peoples had suffered at their hands (Cardinal 1969). Since then, a number of improvements have been made to First Nations education, such as a greater number of band-operated schools and the development of culturally inclusive curriculum (Abele, Dittburner, and Graham 2000; Barman, Hébert, and McCaskill 1987). Much more needs to be done in order for education equity for Aboriginal peoples to be fully realized, however (Brant-Castellano 1999; Calliou 1999). For urban

Aboriginal communities in particular, assertions of jurisdiction and control over education are often enacted within a political landscape that largely excludes their needs. Despite the invisibility of urban Aboriginal aspirations in education policy discussions, however, urban communities are taking action with the resources available to them.

This chapter highlights the complex issues facing urban Aboriginal students today by focusing on Wiingashk Alternative Secondary School, a program based out of N'Amerind Friendship Centre in the city of London, Ontario, where I conducted my master's research. This program works to redress the damage caused to Aboriginal students by mainstream systems, primarily through the use of holistic educational strategies and culturally sensitive staff who value and validate the experiences of their students.[1] My assessment of Wiingashk is contextualized and supported by a brief review of the complexities of urban Aboriginal educational jurisdiction and an examination of contemporary urban Aboriginality in Canada. From there, I move to consider the myriad of factors that impede urban Aboriginal student success, including the various "risk" factors attributed to them by policy-makers and administrators, and demonstrate how Wiingashk works to empower youth in an exemplary manner.

The Politics of Control: Urban Aboriginal Jurisdiction and Control over Education

In Canada, assertions of jurisdiction and control over education that urban Aboriginal peoples make are enacted within a political landscape that consistently excludes their needs.[2] This stems directly from the fact that they are *urban* Aboriginal peoples who, as such, are ineligible for the social benefits associated with on-reserve Status Indians.[3] The systematic exclusion of urban Native groups from discussions pertaining to educational needs can be traced to the late 1960s and early 1970s, when Status Indian interest groups began to vocalize their perceptions of the role the government should take in their affairs.

In 1969, the federal government released the White Paper, a document that sought to absorb Aboriginal peoples into mainstream society by eliminating all "special treatment" and, consequently, any need of an education strategy tailored to Aboriginal peoples (Canada 1969). The National Indian Brotherhood's (NIB) response, *Indian Control of Indian Education* (1972), argued that Aboriginal peoples had the right to administer their own educational programs. The NIB defined the mandate of Aboriginal education as "salvaging Aboriginal languages, cultures, and societies, and of transmitting those cultures, with their unique understanding ... and distinctive worldviews" (Battiste 1995, vii–ix). The NIB succeeded in turning federal policy on its head. In 1973, the federal government adopted NIB's proposal, in principle, as national policy and initiated the process of Aboriginal control by regionally funding Aboriginal culture and education training centres throughout Canada (ibid., ix).

During these early discussions about jurisdiction and control over Aboriginal education issues, the major stakeholders—the NIB and the federal government—concerned themselves with the educational affairs of Status Indians. Talks focusing on this legalized Indigenous category continued to dominate Aboriginal education policy discussions through the 1970s and into the 1980s. In 1988, the Assembly of First Nations (AFN), formerly the NIB, released a report titled *Tradition and Education: Towards a Vision of Our Future* that demanded greater control and jurisdiction over the education of their children. As with *Indian Control of Indian Education* in 1972, the primary focus of *Tradition and Education* was the educational issues of Status and Treaty First Nations peoples. When the NIB reconstituted itself as the Assembly of First Nations in 1982, it continued to exclusively serve the needs of the Status Indian, on-reserve community, thereby negating any education issues relating to Non-Status, or Status Indian, off-reserve, urban Aboriginal peoples.[4] As a result, the conversations concerning control of Aboriginal education continued to be confined to Status Indian and federal government players. This altered slightly with the release of the *Royal Commission on Aboriginal Peoples* in 1996. Despite this shift, however, Status Indian issues continued to take precedence, particularly with respect to educational needs and jurisdiction.

Urban Aboriginal groups, like the N'Amerind Friendship Centre in London, Ontario, struggle within this predominantly one-sided landscape for funding, representation, acceptance, and visibility; yet, urban Aboriginal people are a steadily growing demographic within census metropolitan areas (or CMAs). As such, their needs must be included in discussions of "jurisdiction" and "control" with respect to education if these concepts are going to become anything more than rhetorical statements.

Contemporary Realities: An Examination of Urban Aboriginality in Canada

Within the last sixty years, Aboriginal urbanization has increased significantly. In 1901 only 5.1 percent of Aboriginal peoples lived in urban areas. Although by 1950 this number had increased minimally to 6.7 percent, it climbed sharply in the 1970s and 1980s when it reached approximately

35 percent (Peters 2005, 340). During the 1960s, studies such as the Hawthorn Report (1966) attempted to explain the surge of Aboriginal migration by contending that Aboriginal peoples no longer wanted to live on reserves due to depressed social and economic conditions (Peters 2005, 341). Though this surprised policy-makers at the time, the out-migration of large numbers of Aboriginal people off-reserve seemed inevitable. In the mid-twentieth century, population growth was supported by the extension of provincial standards in health, social assistance, and education on reserves. The restrictions on mobility created by the 1951 *Indian Act* were also removed, further allowing for outward migration into provincial spaces (Podlasly 2002, 4). The increased contact with urban society and the high expectations that these services generated (coupled with rapid population growth) prompted on-reserve Aboriginal peoples to move to urban areas in search of better resources (Peters 2005, 341; see also Darnell, chapter 3 this volume).

The search for resources such as education and better economic opportunities still prompts large numbers of Aboriginal people to move to cities.[5] According to the 2001 census, approximately 49.1 percent of Aboriginal people currently live in urban areas, while 31 percent of Aboriginal peoples identify as living on-reserve, and 20 percent live in off-reserve rural areas (Richards and Vining 2004, 5). Despite the large number of urban Aboriginal peoples, the number of programs and services that effectively serve this demographic remain scarce. Silver and colleagues (2006, 17) maintain that the move Aboriginal people make from the reserve to the city is frequently a move from one marginalized community to another. In an educational context, the marginalization experienced by urban Aboriginal people can be even more pronounced depending on whether one is considered a Status or Non-Status Indian (Silver et al. 2006, 12).

The federal government is responsible for delivering social services to Status Indians on reserve as defined by the *Indian Act*. As such, urban Aboriginal people are, by and large, ineligible for any social benefits beyond those issued to all residents of a province. Although the federal government maintains that urban Status and Non-Status Aboriginal peoples are the responsibility of provincial governments, provincial governments contend that all Aboriginal people are the responsibility of the federal government (Silver et al. 2006). Major Aboriginal organizations, like the Assembly of Manitoba Chiefs, have also seen their responsibilities being confined to First Nations people on-reserve. In short, urban Aboriginal people are denied support from government and other leading Native organizations because they are seen as the responsibility of "somebody else" (Silver et al. 2006, 12).[6]

Legislative wrangling surrounding who is technically responsible—the provincial or federal government—for supporting urban Aboriginal peoples is a major stumbling block to the growth of economically thriving urban communities. The need for effective social support becomes even more urgent when one considers that the urban Aboriginal population is considerably younger than the non-Aboriginal population. At a national level, the majority of the urban Aboriginal population is below the age of twenty-five. According to Statistics Canada, Aboriginal children aged zero to fourteen account for 40 percent of the urban Aboriginal population in most census metropolitan areas (CMAs) (StatsCan 2005). In addition, the national Aboriginal population aged fifteen to twenty-four has more than doubled between 1981 and 2001, with most of this demographic located in large metropolitan centres like Saskatoon, Edmonton, and Regina. The demographic shift to a younger population is significant, particularly because in fifteen years, urban Aboriginal populations will make up a large part of CMAs. In Saskatoon, for example, one out of every six children is Aboriginal (ibid.). These demographics attest to the urgency of developing culturally relevant and meaningful programs for urban Aboriginal youth, who, in the near future, are going to be significant contributors to the urban economy (Richards and Vining 2004, 2). Furthermore, their ability to thrive in these settings depends on their ability to succeed in secondary and post-secondary institutions, as anyone who enters the workforce with limited formal education has few good job opportunities (ibid.). In Manitoba and Saskatchewan, for example, where Aboriginal people will comprise 17 percent of the total workforce in the next decade and a half, education represents the economic future of the two provinces (Silver et al. 2006, 15).

While retention and graduation rates have improved among urban Aboriginal populations, an educational gap still remains between Aboriginal and non-Aboriginal youth in urban settings (Richards and Vining 2004). The fact that Aboriginal students are marginalized within education systems and often come from low socio-economic backgrounds predisposes them to be labelled "at risk" by educational policy-makers and school administrators (see my section below for a more detailed commentary on the concept of "at risk" and how it applies to urban Aboriginal youth). These contemporary acts of segregation are undergirded by human-capital arguments, which contend that the purpose of schooling is to prepare students for the workforce. Repo (2006b, 19) argues that a lack of federal involvement in public education systems has created an ideological vacuum that business organizations are happy to fill. "The most serious problem with this … [is that it is creating] a monoculture in education, where all other aspects of 'schooling' a new generation are being put on a back-burner—if not on life support" (ibid.). The resultant outcome is that provincial school systems are operating as businesses with hierarchical management structures. Repo metaphorically equates principals to CEOs and teachers as harassed middlemen with little decision-making power and the mandate to create a generation of "internationally competitive worker-bees" (2006b, 20). Added to that is standardized testing, which ensures that "competitive spirit is fostered throughout schools, and that those who are hindmost are properly shamed. The kudos go to the swift, but for those students who do not shine in the pressure-cooker atmosphere of pencil-and-paper testing, there are always the 'applied courses'" (ibid.). Essentially, "the student has metamorphosed to a product and quality control from above has become a major preoccupation" (Repo 2006a, 20). The "quality control" that Repo refers to is manifested in streaming policies, which gear students to either "academic" or "practical" courses. Often, Aboriginal students round out the group of those who seem best suited for practical labour. Concepts of cultural deficiency, which maintain that Aboriginal cultures do not see success in education as important, have also contributed to the streaming of Aboriginal students into less rigorous and stimulating education programs (Allison and Paquette 1991). As a result, many fail or drop out.

Such obstacles in education create the conditions for the achievement gap that exists between Aboriginal and non-Aboriginal populations. Statistics Canada reports that the educational gap between Aboriginal and non-Aboriginal peoples actually widened from 1981 to 2001. Aboriginal men aged twenty to twenty-four, for example, are less likely to have completed high school than non-Aboriginal men of the same age group. Aboriginal men are also more likely to drop out of school than Aboriginal women (StatsCan 2005). Overall, the number of Aboriginal students that drop out of mainstream education systems is staggering. Chalifoux and Johnson (2003, 66) report that many proposed government reforms have not been implemented; as a result, an alarming seven of ten First Nations youth drop out of school. In 2000, the Report of the Auditor General concluded that, at the rate Aboriginal students are currently dropping out, it will take at least twenty years for them to reach economic parity with other Canadians (Canada 2000, 13). These startling figures clearly indicate that the needs of Aboriginal youth are not being met in mainstream systems.

Falling into Categories of Risk: A Profile of Wiingashk Secondary Students

Like many Aboriginal youth, students who attend Wiingashk have been defined as "at risk" by educational policy-makers and school administrators. There are many definitions of what constitutes an at-risk youth, however. For example, at-risk students are usually youth who are poor, are ethnic minorities, and/or have to deal with socio-economic and familial problems including inadequate housing, child abuse, and divided households (Evans 1995, 48). Other scholars have added that individual concerns such as boredom, loneliness, and peer groups influence whether or not a student is considered "at risk" (Schissel and Wortherspoon 2001, 3). Other risk variables include teen pregnancy, poor academic achievement, negative attitudes of teachers and administrators toward certain categories of students, and negative opinions of parents toward schools (Van der Woerd and Cox 2003, 210).

Policy-makers and administrators label students who are disengaged with the school system as being "at risk." Typically, disengagement is manifested in poor attendance, poor academic achievement, and instances of unruly behaviour, such as disrespect toward teachers and school codes of conduct. Essentially, students who exhibit this type of behaviour are deemed to be at risk of dropping out of the educational system altogether.[7] Indeed many of them do. In an effort to reengage these students in education and learning, schools have created alternative education programs designed to serve these populations. Wiingashk is an example of this type of program, albeit one with a focus on the needs of Aboriginal youth.

The disengagement of Aboriginal students from school is of particular concern to educational policy-makers because the numbers of Aboriginal students that drop out is much higher than those of their non-Aboriginal peers. In Ontario, 42 percent of the Aboriginal population aged fifteen and over has less than a high school diploma compared to 30 percent of non-Aboriginal people. Furthermore, only 6 percent of Aboriginal students have completed a university degree compared to 18 percent of their non-Aboriginal peers (Ontario Ministry of Education 2007, 35). Nationally, the numbers are even grimmer. Across Canada, only 23 percent of Aboriginal people have a high school diploma (ibid.). As a result, large numbers of Aboriginal students are designated "at risk" because they are in danger of dropping out of the school system and becoming another statistic.

At Wiingashk, students fall into many of the above identified categories. Additionally, this specific group of students is highly transient, which only exacerbates their at-risk status, as frequent moving impedes their ability to access resources available to them or to be counted among those students in need of services in the first place. Of the nine students that I interviewed, three were from out of province, four were affiliated with local reserves, and two were originally from elsewhere in Ontario.[8] Many had experienced a great deal of movement, either between provinces and cities, or between the city and their home reserve. Brittany, for example, moved between cities, dividing her time between her mother's home and her father's home:[9]

> SD: So where are you from originally? Are you from London?
>
> Brittany: I was born in X, Ontario. I stayed there for kindergarten and grade two and then I moved to London 'til grade three to half of grade six and then I moved back to X with my mom and dad and then back with my dad. Yeah, after grade six I moved back with my dad.
>
> SD: But you live with your mom now?
>
> Brittany: Yeah.

Two brothers attending Wiingashk experienced the highest mobility. Matt, the older of the brothers, had moved from "Saskatchewan, to BC, to Spokane, to Washington, down to Saskatchewan, then I went back to Cranbrook, BC, and then I went back to Alberta, Crow's Nest, then I went back to Saskatchewan, stayed there for three years, and then I came here [to London]." Matt had moved from Saskatchewan to London when he was twelve in order to live with his father. Dave joined his older brother a year later, and for the last seven years, both brothers have resided in London.

These accounts represent the different degrees of mobility that characterize the Wiingashk students. In most cases, the high degree of movement is partially explained by the fact that all of the students, save one, come from a divided household and either split their time between parents or have stayed exclusively with one parent while losing contact with the other.

In addition to being highly transient, students at Wiingashk are labelled "at risk" for a variety of other reasons, including truancy and individual issues. Many of the students reported not attending school as the main reason for why they had been referred to an alternative program. Personal struggles that Shayenne was dealing with affected her ability to participate in school. According to her,

I dropped out 'cause of some personal problems. And I almost felt like I was going to have a nervous breakdown or something. I couldn't handle going to school so I just quit. So I didn't go to school and I was out all summer and I decided to come back to school so I came here, to Wiingashk … I was struggling last year in school, 'cause—not this past summer but the summer before—two weeks before I had to go back to school, my cousin died. He was only seventeen when he died; he died in a car accident. It was really hard on me and I couldn't concentrate in school. And I know people say, "Oh that's not an excuse," but it really hurt … I think last year was the worst year of my life. I used to have an alcohol problem too, but I fixed it. I didn't quit, but I got a handle on it.

For Dave, an encounter with racist remarks prompted him to lash out in anger and resulted in his dismissal from the mainstream school system. As he shared with me, "I'd say the reason for me not graduating high school is because I held kids hostage because I was having a bad day, and I warned the whole school, but I guess they didn't take me seriously. So I ended up barricading kids in the library and holding them hostage in there … I warned them not to piss me off, but the 'white kids' decided to call me a wagon burner … so at that point in time, I beat up the one kid and held the rest hostage."

Other students reported a general disconnect from the school system. According to Jared, "I just didn't feel like I had to be there but now I do … I just didn't think school was that important. That was like grade nine and ten, and I just stopped." Matt became disengaged with the school system because he was not stimulated by what he was being taught: "Most of the stuff is usually pretty boring for me … I just fly through this stuff, so I get bored and I stop doing it."

As the testimonies have shown, students at Wiingashk are faced with a variety of challenges that impede their performance in mainstream school systems. Many of the students are extremely mobile, which makes it hard for them to settle in one particular place. Most of the students are from divided families, which gives them added familial responsibilities. A number of other factors, both in school and at home, also contribute to disengagement. The death of Shayenne's cousin and her struggles with alcohol inhibited her ability to participate in school. In Dave's case, racist remarks directed at him by white students led him to rebel. For both Jared and Matt, a lack of stimulation from within the system itself led to their apathy. In these respects, the students at Wiingashk assume many of the characteristics that policy-makers attribute to at-risk students: they come from low socio-economic backgrounds, they have to deal with individual concerns such as personal issues with drugs and alcohol, they frequently move between different provinces, cities, and households, and, they are considered low academic achievers. In the eyes of policy-makers and school administrators, these youth are "textbook cases." Simplistically attaching categories of risk to students like the ones at Wiingashk fails, however, to consider the overarching social and ideological conditions that create these categories of risk in the first place. A holistic approach, such as the one used at Wiingashk, helps staff to foster Aboriginal youth by focusing on unity, continuity, and interconnectedness.

Identifying a Philosophy of Student Success: An Examination of Holistic Education

N'Amerind's education initiative is grounded in a holistic understanding and approach to education. A holistic approach focuses on the spiritual, mental, physical, emotional, and social needs of students. Aboriginal approaches move away from linear models of Western thought, preferring to conceive of education as a medicine wheel, with all directions being of equal importance and interconnected (Battiste 1995; Hampton 1995).[10] As the cultural worker at the school, Glen MacDougall, defines it, "life, from day zero 'til you end is all about understanding what's around you. And there is never an end to your learning. Every day is something new. And it's not like modern-day concept where I go from kindergarten to university and then I'm done" (personal communication). The essential point to be taken from this statement is that learning does not have a beginning or an end. It is a continuous, ongoing process, not one that can be arbitrarily and hierarchically divided into grades or degrees. The Native education counsellor, Dorothy French, adds that the aim of Aboriginal education is to be able to impart to youth a sense of who they are as Aboriginal people. She iterates that not only do Aboriginal students have to be versed in mainstream knowledge, but "you have the additional responsibility of knowing who you are and your culture, because you have to be effective enough to take that information and make it work for you. So in essence, I would call the students and those who continue on ... warriors in development, because they have to live in both worlds. They have to know when to differentiate" (personal communication).

Contemporary Aboriginal youth, then, must be taught through approaches and in milieux that foster and respect their cultures. Currently, this approach is lacking in the majority of contemporary education systems. While many public school systems have incorporated Native languages and Native studies courses, they are, by and large, not essential parts of the curriculum; moreover, although a school may list an

Aboriginal course on paper, it does not mean that it will actually be offered. Often, course offerings vary depending on who is available to teach and how many students are interested in taking the course (Donovan 2007). To date, there has not been a cohesive movement within education systems across Canada to effectively infuse Aboriginal perspectives into core curriculum or the very dynamic of schools themselves. Schools are still culturally and cognitively imperialist in that they discredit and deny Aboriginal knowledge bases and values (Battiste 1998, 20). As a result, Aboriginal students feel alienated and disengage themselves from the system.

A number of scholars (Bouvier and Karlenzig 2006; Ismail and Cazden 2005; Wilson and Wilson 2002) have commented on the need for educational institutions to bring about more meaningful change. According to Bouvier and Karlenzig (2006, 17), educational strategies must move away from additive approaches and toward more qualitative and transformative ways of teaching and learning. This involves acknowledging that Indigenous peoples' world views, social structures, and pedagogy are legitimate forms of knowledge and can offer a further dimension to the Western experience of schooling. Further, Antone (2000) asserts that because education is a primary socializing agent, programs that promote a positive Aboriginal identity need to be developed, particularly bilingual/bicultural types of education that allow Aboriginal students to function in both Indigenous and non-Indigenous communities. Because additive approaches to curriculum have proven ineffective, N'Amerind staff members feel as though students would be best served by providing them with a holistic education that allows them to compete in mainstream society while instilling in them a strong and confident sense of who they are as Aboriginal people. During my fieldwork, I witnessed the success of this approach with the students firsthand.

Strategies of Success: Wiingashk and the Creation of Warriors in Development

During the academic year 2006–2007 when I worked with N'Amerind staff and students, Wiingashk students experienced both academic and personal success. A differentiation is made in order to correspond to the discrepancy between administrative and community definitions. The reality is that in contemporary times, success as defined by contemporary culture is the one that has the most social clout. Academic success provides students with skills that make them marketable in a job economy; consequently, for Aboriginal communities searching for economic equity and sustainability, academic success is indeed important. The staff at N'Amerind acknowledged this. What is unique about N'Amerind's approach, however, is that they consider students as entire persons and also define success in those terms. According to French,

> success is to stay true to who you are as an Aboriginal person. But you have to be able to succeed in mainstream. You have to make yourself valuable so you're going to get employed. But then you can still go and know your ceremonies, know your language, and know your social structure, because that's who we are. And we're not a dying race, despite what perception has. We are continuing and we're building and getting stronger and bigger. (personal communication)

French's statement illustrates the importance of being a valuable contributor to both mainstream and Aboriginal communities. This multidimensional perspective stems from her Aboriginal heritage whereby the

> whole social structure as Aboriginal people is built on family ... when you look at the way Aboriginal people view [success], it takes everybody to succeed in that family. So you take parents matched with the babies and the youth are matched with the seniors. We need to look at how do we give our youth back what their roles and responsibilities are ... our youth are not successful in mainstream systems, and I know that. So in order to help them succeed, my role at Wiingashk is to expose them while they're here to as much of their Aboriginal ceremonies, celebrations and people as possible and to connect them within their community. (personal communication)

While industrial capitalist societies emphasize the individual and her accomplishments, many Aboriginal communities are centred upon relationships. The crux is that, for Aboriginal people, "success" is defined by and dependent on how effectively one can navigate within a Eurocentric framework. Therefore, it is integral that Aboriginal students are able to navigate their way in mainstream society, albeit grounded in the knowledge of who they are as Aboriginal people and their responsibilities to their communities (French, personal communication).

Judging from the success that the Wiingashk students achieved, academic and otherwise, in the semester I was involved, a holistic conception of success had proven effective. Academically speaking, the alternative school teacher, Paul Milton,[11] commented that this group of students'

> success rates were off the charts in comparison to past years. It depends how you grade success: Do you grade success by how long you can engage a student to keep coming to school to keep them interested, to provide a place that they're comfortable enough to come to and work at? Or do you

do it strictly by credits? It's usually a combination of the two. And we had our core of students, so I'd say about eighty percent of our enrollment for the term, were regular. Now regular doesn't necessarily mean a hundred percent attendance, but I'd say more than eighty percent attendance. So successful in those terms because they started coming to school again and successful in terms that everyone that stayed is going to get at least two credits—their Native Studies and usually one academic credit. If you compare that to years past this program has gone through in particular, that's pretty good. [If you can show that] the kids are coming to school again, that kids that weren't going to school before and they are now, and they're achieving, then you've succeeded in re-engaging that student in education. (personal communication)

As evidenced in Milton's statement, the students at Wiingashk were successful in both academic credits obtained and reengagement with the education process. As a consequence of the academic and personal success that students have had at Wiingashk, the program was in high demand for the second semester. Milton noted that the "students had success here, told other students about it, and the word spread that this was a good place to come. So it's a popular choice right now" (personal communication).

A critical component to the success that students have at Wiingashk is the fact that it is operated out of the N'Amerind Friendship Centre, which acts as the hub of the urban Aboriginal community in London. Schissel and Wortherspoon (2001, 7) maintain that successful educational programs are connected to public services and local community initiatives in a holistic manner. This allows them to be able to deliver a variety of services to students, thus transforming schools into community centres. Although new to the program as of this year, Milton also attested to the importance of having the school at the friendship centre. In his words, "I think having it here at this centre provides a good opportunity for them to stay comfortable and allow the centre to promote itself as more of a community ... it's also effective that the kids can use the resources in the centre. There's a criminal justice department, there's drug and alcohol abuse [services]; there's a lot of [resources] that they can become familiar with in case they ever need it, and they will also have the support of the Aboriginal community" (personal communication).

In addition to the insights provided by staff members, interviews conducted with the current students also help to identify the reasons why Wiingashk is successful. Many students who had become disengaged with mainstream institutions enjoyed the alternative program. Overall, three variables attributable to Wiingashk's success can be garnered from the student interviews, namely (1) that it is operated within the friendship centre, (2) that it includes a cultural component, and (3) that it is led by a culturally sensitive and respectful teacher.

Many students reported liking the fact that the school was located at the friendship centre. For example, Jared found it easier to focus and liked the fact that he was "among my own people." Dave told me that, although different alternative programs were available to him, he "took this one up because it's all Natives here." Matt also decided to come to Wiingashk because "it's a Native school." He metaphorically described it as a family, implying a sense of feeling as though one was part of a tight-knit community.

In addition to the locale, the students also liked the cultural component that was integrated into the program. Every Monday and Tuesday after-noon, Glen MacDougall passes on traditional teachings to the students in order to reconnect and familiarize them with their Aboriginal heritage. Since 1998, MacDougall has been part of the Wiingashk alternative pro-gram, and his enthusiasm and love for the students has made him an influ-ential and empathetic mentor. The caring and compassionate spirit that he brings to the program has affected the students in positive ways. Jared told me that "[Glen] teaches me stuff I didn't know about before ... It's good to know stuff about my heritage." Dave enthusiastically stated that, "I love the teachings ... I didn't have any background of my own view of my ancestors before I came here." He added that, in the mainstream, he felt as though he was not allowed to express his Aboriginality without being reprimanded. "They didn't want [us] to speak in our language or even practising it at the school. They were more or less trying to transition us to the 'white' culture." Like Jared and Dave, Shayenne came to Wiingashk because she desired to know more about her own heritage. According to her, "I heard ... you get traditional teachings and I don't really know much about that ... I wasn't brought up traditionally... Plus it's good to know what it's like and what's out there and what kinds of medicines there are ... everything's interesting."

A third and critical factor to the success of the program is that it has been led by a culturally sensitive and respectful teacher. Staff at N'Amerind repeatedly informed me that a teacher who recognizes the value of their culture is a critical component of success. The current teacher, Mr. Milton, epitomizes this quality. As such, he received glowing reviews from both staff and students alike. Although he did not have a great deal of experi-ence teaching Native students in the past, Milton approached his position as "a learning opportunity for me to understand the Native community." Milton's openness and readiness to learn has made him accessible to the students. According to MacDougall, "I got to take my hat off to Paul. Like he's really respectful to them ... I think he's an awesome teacher."

Students also felt the same. Like many students at Wiingashk, Jared was at risk of dropping out of school altogether because he had become disconnected with the mainstream system. Jared expressed to me that in the mainstream system, he felt as though he had to do a lot of things on his own. At Wiingashk, he appreciated the help that Milton offered. "[In the mainstream system, the teachers] tell you to something and you gotta do it, but with [Mr. Milton], like he tells you to do it, and if you don't want to do it or can't do it, he'll help you out with it. But these other teachers, they just like tell you to do it and expect you to do it." In this quote, Jared reveals that frustration with the curriculum can manifest in the student withdrawing from the process altogether. Though teachers may perceive this as defiance against their authority and not offer to help, in fact, it is something else altogether. The ability of Milton to recognize this and approach the students accordingly is what has made him so effective. Derek liked the fact that Mr. Milton didn't "nag" or "single you out." Essentially, Milton was respected by the students because he, in turn, respected them. This reciprocal dynamic has helped to foster a strong learning community at Wiingashk.

As seen in the above testimonies, the success that Wiingashk is currently having is attributable to a number of crucial factors: (1) it is located within an Aboriginal community centre, thereby strengthening community ties between students previously disconnected from it; (2) it includes traditional teachings that reacquaint students with their Aboriginal heritage; and (3) it is led by a teacher that values and respects the students for who they are as Aboriginal people. These factors have culminated in making Wiingashk the thriving learning environment that it is today.

Conclusions

Although urban Aboriginal people are a fast-growing demographic in cities across Canada, the reserve-centric perspective maintained by all levels of government excludes their educational aspirations. The legislative jockeying over who is responsible for urban Aboriginal education is further compounded by the ever-growing and youthful nature of urban Aboriginal populations. In Ontario, for example, more than 70 percent of the Aboriginal population lives off-reserve (Ontario Ministry of Education 2007). A large percentage of those are urban youth who face pervasive challenges to their education in traditional Western schooling systems, which are exacerbated by societal attitudes at large. Cultural deficit thinking, transience, and overt and institutional forms of racism all coalesce to make schooling an uphill battle for Aboriginal youth.

While it is of little wonder that students become disillusioned with a system that is, for all intents and purposes, exclusionary, urban Aboriginal communities are working to redress the damage caused by mainstream systems using the resources available to them. The rich interview excerpts of both staff and students at N'Amerind reveal that programs like Wiingashk Alternative Secondary School are vital to the success of urban youth.

At its core, education is not a privilege; it is an inherent right. As such, Aboriginal peoples have a right to an education that is nurturing and empowering. Provincial education systems sharply contrast with Aboriginal ways of knowing and interpreting the world by championing competitiveness, individual achievement, and compartmentalized thinking. Dave (student at Wiingashk), when referring to learning about his Aboriginal heritage, poignantly stated, "I feel it's better to learn about your people than not to learn about them because if it's your history, if it's your background, you always have a right to learn about it." In accordance with this right to educational equity, educational instruction, undergirded by holistic principles, must become the norm, not the option. If federal and provincial governments are genuine about improving academic achievements of Aboriginal students, urban initiatives, like Wiingashk, must be given serious consideration, as they are vital pathways to achieving success.

Notes

1 This chapter is a synopsis of research conducted during my master's degree concerning the urban Aboriginal community of London, Ontario, Canada, between the summers of 2006 and 2007. The thesis was structured as a collaborative action ethnography (Erickson, 2006) and served a dual purpose: to fulfill the requirements of my master's degree and to serve as a reference document for the London Aboriginal community as they advocated for the creation of an Aboriginal immersion public school.

2 See Donovan, Sadie (2007).

3 Although the chapter distinguishes between "urban Aboriginal people" and Status Indians, I acknowledge that the majority of urban Aboriginal peoples are Status; however, the differentiation parallels federal government policy, which strips Status Indians of the majority of their social benefits once they relocate off-reserve. Because of this, I use "urban Aboriginal people" to refer to both Status and Non-Status Indians living off-reserve. Though the two groups are differentiated by government policy, they are often treated similarly in urban settings.

4 The Native Council of Canada has also gone through a period of reconstitution. When they separated from the NIB in 1968, the NCC represented Non-Status Aboriginal people and Métis; however, the divergent interests of the two groups

caused internal tensions. In 1983, prairie Métis broke away to form the Métis National Council. In 1994, the NCC changed its name to the Congress of Aboriginal Peoples (CAP) and now comprises an uneasy alliance of urban and off-reserve Aboriginal people, non-prairie Métis, Non-Status, and C-31 Aboriginal people. Like the AFN, CAP receives funding from the Department of Indian Affairs because they changed their mandate to include representation of Status off-reserve Aboriginal people. This puts them in direct competition with the AFN, who also claim to represent Status off-reserve First Nations peoples. CAP argues that because the AFN is reserve-based, it cannot provide services to off-reserve Native people (Sawchuk 1998, 37–38). The AFN does not acknowledge CAP as a legitimate urban representative, however. This parallels the position of the National Association of Friendship Centres (NAFC), which represents 117 friendship centres in Canada. The AFN argues that CAP blames them for all wrongdoings against Native people, and that this takes the heat off the government (NAFC board minutes, February 2007).

5 Darnell argues that the urban–rural migrations of Aboriginal people are adapted from traditional subsistence patterns, whereby people move around a territory in search of exploitable resources. For a further discussion of these "nomadic legacies," refer to Darnell (chapter 3, this volume; also 2003) and Darnell and Manzano-Munguia (2004).

6 With the exception of the NAFC and provincial urban organizations like the OFIFC.

7 Dei (1995) has critiqued the term "dropout" because it ignores the larger societal forces that impede student performance in schools. He argues instead that minoritized students are "pushed out" of mainstream systems. While his critique is relevant and necessary to note, space does not allow me to enter into an examination of risk discourse. As such, I will continue to use the term "dropout" for purposes of clarification.

8 Differences by gender will not be a variable examined in this chapter. Of the nine participants, four were girls and five were boys; thus, there were not predominant numbers of either boys or girls, and both sexes responded similarly to the same questions. When asked what they liked about Wiingashk, for example, all students, regardless of gender, told me that they like being able to work at their own pace. Other questions were similarly responded to.

9 Names of students have been changed to protect anonymity. When asked if they wanted to use an alias, many N'Amerind staff responded that they would prefer their real names. Their wishes have been respected accordingly in this chapter.

10 In noting how important holistic education and notions of relationships are to the N'Amerind community and their educational philosophy, it must also be said that establishing a "common identity" is complex and often difficult in urban settings. As Ward and Bouvier maintain (2001, 5) "class differences, access to resources, and education differentially shape Aboriginal people's experiences in urban centers." Lawrence (2004) also adds that access to resources is also compounded by the degree to which one "looks Indian" or not. Further, as the life histories of the Wiingashk students attest to, many urban Aboriginal peoples come from various tribal backgrounds across Canada and the United States; therefore, finding a common sense of "community" or "relationship" in urban centres is highly nuanced and multifarious.

11 A pseudonym.

Works Cited

Abele, Frances, Carolyn Dittburner, and Katherine Graham. 2000. "Towards a Shared Understanding in the Policy Discussion about Aboriginal Education." In *Aboriginal Education: Fulfilling the Promise*, edited by Marlene Brant Castellano, Lynne Davis, and Louise Lahache, 3–24. Vancouver: University of British Columbia Press.

Aboriginal Peoples Survey. 2001. "Initial Findings: Well-Being of the Non-Reserve Aboriginal Population." Statistics Canada Catalogue # 89-589-XIE. http://www.statcan.ca/english/freepub/89-589-XIE/school.htm.

Allison, Derek John, and Jerry Paquette. 1991. *Reform and Relevance in Schooling: Destreaming and the Common Curriculum.* Toronto: OISE Press.

Antone, Eileen. 2000. "Empowering Aboriginal Voice in Aboriginal Education." *Canadian Journal of Native Education* 24 (2): 92–101.

Assembly of First Nations. 1988. *Tradition and Education: Towards a Vision of our Future,* vol. 1. Ottawa: Assembly of First Nations.

Axelrod, Paul. 1999. *The Promise of Schooling: Education in Canada, 1800–1914.* Toronto: University of Toronto Press.

Barman, Jean, Yvonne Hébert, and Don McCaskill, eds. 1987. *Indian Education in Canada, Volume 2: The Challenge.* Vancouver: University of British Columbia Press.

Battiste, Marie. 1998. "Enabling the Autumn Seed: Toward a Decolonized Approach to Aboriginal Knowledge, Language, and Education." *Canadian Journal of Native Education* 22 (1): 16–27.

———. 1995. "Introduction." In *First Nations Education in Canada: The Circle Unfolds,* edited by Marie Battiste and Jean Barman, vii–xx. Vancouver: University of British Columbia Press.

Bear-Nicholas, Andrea. 2001. "Canada's Colonial Mission: The Great White Bird." In *Aboriginal Education in Canada: A Study in Decolonization,* edited by K.P. Binda and S. Calliou, 9–33. Mississauga, ON: Canadian Educators' Press.

Bouvier, Rita, and Bruce Karlenzig. 2006. "Accountability and Aboriginal Education: Dilemmas, Promises, and Challenges." *Our Schools, Our Selves* 15 (3): 15–33.

Bouvier, Rita. 2001. "Good Community Schools Are Sites of Educational Activism." In *Resting Lightly on Mother Earth: The Aboriginal Experience in Urban Educational Settings,* edited by Angela Ward and Rita Bouvier, 49–62. Calgary: Detselig Enterprises.

Brant Castellano, Marlene. 1999. "Renewing the Relationship: A Perspective on the Impact of the Royal Commission on Aboriginal Peoples." In *Aboriginal Self-Government in Canada,* edited by John Hylton, 92–111. Saskatoon: Purich Publishing.

Brant Castellano, Marlene, Lynne Davis, and Louise Lahache, eds. 2000. *Aboriginal Education: Fulfilling the Promise.* Vancouver: University of British Columbia Press.

Calliou, Shari-Lynn. 1999. "Sunrise: Activism and Self-Determination in First Nations Education (1972–1998)." In *Aboriginal Self-Government in Canada,* edited by John Hylton, 157–88. Saskatoon: Purich Publishing.

Canada. 2000. *Report of the Auditor General of Canada.*

Canada. 1969. *Statement of the Government of Canada of Indian Policy 1969.* Ottawa: Queen's Printer.

Cardinal, Harold. 1969. *The Unjust Society.* Vancouver: Douglas & McIntyre.

Chalifoux, Thelma, and Janis Johnson. 2003. *Urban Aboriginal Youth: An Action Plan for Change.* Ottawa: Standing Senate Committee on Aboriginal Peoples.

Darnell, Regna. 2003. "The Persistence of Nomadic Habits in Urban–Rural Migration: Towards a Qualitative Demography." In *Papers of the Thirty-Fifth Algonquian Conference*, edited by H.C. Wolfart, 75–89. Winnipeg: University of Manitoba Press.

Darnell, Regna, and Maria Cristina Manzano Munguia. 2004. "Nomadic Legacies and Urban Algonquian Residence." In *Papers of the Thirty-Sixth Algonquian Conference*, edited by H.C. Wolfart, 173–86. Winnipeg: University of Manitoba Press.

Dei, George J. Sefa. 1995. *Drop Out or Push Out? The Dynamics of Black Students' Disengagement from School: A Report.* University of Toronto/OISE, Department of Sociology of Education. Toronto: Ontario Institute for Studies in Education.

Donovan, Sadie. 2007. "Validating a Claim for Aboriginal Immersion in Canada: A Case Study of Wiingashk Alternative Secondary School." Unpublished master's thesis. University of Western Ontario. London, Ontario, Canada.

Erickson, Frederick. 2006. "Studying Side by Side: Collaborative Action Ethnography in Educational Research." In *Innovations in Educational Ethnography: Theory, Methods, and Results*, edited by George Spindler and Lorie Hammond, 235–57. Mahwah, NJ: Lawrence Erlbaum Associates

Evans, P. 1995. "Children and Youth 'At-Risk.'" In *Organisation for Economic Co-operation and Development Centre for Education Research and Innovation, Our Children at Risk*, 13–50. Paris: Organisation for Economic Co-operation and Development.

Hampton, Eber. 1995. "Towards a Redefinition of Indian Education." In *First Nations Education in Canada: The Circle Unfolds*, edited by Marie Battiste and Jean Barman, 5–46. Vancouver: University of British Columbia Press.

Hawthorn, H.B., ed. 1966–67. *A Survey of the Contemporary Indians of Canada: A Report on Economic, Political, Educational Needs and Policies.* 2 vols. Ottawa: Indian Affairs Branch.

Ismail, Masturah, and Courtney Cazden. 2005. "Struggles for Indigenous Education and Self-Determination: Culture, Context, and Collaboration." *Anthropology and Education Quarterly* 36 (1): 88–92.

Kirkness, Verna. 1998. "Our Peoples' Education: Cut the Shackles; Cut the Crap; Cut the Mustard." *Canadian Journal of Native Education* 22 (1): 10–15.

Lawrence, Bonita. 2004. *"Real" Indians and Others: Mixed-Blood Urban Native Peoples and Indigenous Nationhood.* Vancouver: University of British Columbia Press.

Miller, J.R. 1996. *Shingwauk's Vision: A History of Native Residential Schools.* Toronto: University of Toronto Press.

Milloy, John S. 1999. *A National Crime: The Canadian Government and the Residential School System 1879–1986.* Winnipeg: University of Manitoba Press.

National Indian Brotherhood. 1972. *Indian Control of Indian Education.* Ottawa: National Indian Brotherhood.

Ontario Ministry of Education. 2007. *Ontario First Nation, Metis, and Inuit Education Policy Framework.* Ottawa: Aboriginal Education Office, Ministry of Education.

Peters, Evelyn. 2005. "Indigeneity and Marginalization: Planning for and with Urban Aboriginal Communities in Canada." *Progress in Planning* 63: 327–404.

———. 1996. "'Urban' and 'Aboriginal': An Impossible Contradiction?" In *City Lives and City Forms: Critical Research and Canadian Urbanism*, edited by Jon Caulfield and Linda Peake. Toronto: University of Toronto Press.

Podlasly, Mark. 2002. *Canada's Domestic Expatriates: The Urban Aboriginal Population.* http://www.gingergroup.org/resources/Podlasly.pdf.

Repo, Satu. 2006a. "The Contested Terrain of Public Education." *Our Schools, Our Selves* 15 (2): 19–22.

Repo, Satu. 2006b. "The Elephant in the Schoolhouse." *Our Schools, Our Selves* 16 (1): 19–22.

Richards, John, and Aidan Vining. 2004. "Aboriginal Off-Reserve Education: Time for Action." C.D. Howe Institute *Commentary* 198 (April).

Sawchuk, Joe. 1998. *The Dynamics of Native Politics: The Alberta Métis Experience.* Saskatoon: Purich Publishing.

Schissel, Bernard, and Terry Wortherspoon. 2001. "The Business of Placing Canadian Children and Youth 'At-Risk.'" *Canadian Journal of Education* 26 (3): 321–39.

Silver, Jim, Kathy Mallet, Janice Greene, and Freeman Simard. 2002. *Aboriginal Education in Winnipeg Inner City High Schools.* Manitoba: Canadian Centre for Policy Alternatives.

Statistics Canada. 2005. "Aboriginal Peoples in Canada's Urban Area— Narrowing the Education Gap." http://www.statcan.ca/english/freepub/81-004 -XIE/2005003/aborig.htm#top.

St. Denis, Verna. 2007. "Aboriginal Education and Anti-Racist Education: Building Alliances across Cultural and Racial Identity" *Canadian Journal of Education* 30 (4): 1068–92.

Van der Woerd, Kimberly, and David Cox. 2003. "Educational Status and Its Association with Risk and Protective Factors for First Nations Youth." *Canadian Journal of Native Education* 27 (2): 208–22.

Ward, Angela, and Rita Bouvier. 2001. "Introduction." In *Resting Lightly on Mother Earth: The Aboriginal Experience in Urban Educational Settings*, edited by Angela Ward and Rita Bouvier, 5–17. Calgary: Detselig Enterprises.

Wilson, S. 1994. "Honouring Spiritual Knowledge." *Canadian Journal of Native Education* 21 (suppl.): 61–69.

Wilson, Kathi, and Evelyn Peters. 2005. "'You can make a place for it': Remapping Urban First Nations Spaces of Identity." *Environment and Planning D: Society and Space* 23 (3): 395–413.

Wilson, Stan, and Peggy Wilson. 2002. "Editorial: First Nations Education in Mainstream Systems." *Canadian Journal of Native Education* 26 (2): 67–68.

9

A Critical Discourse Analysis of John Stackhouse's
"Welcome to Harlem on the Prairies"

Craig Proulx

Although the majority of Aboriginal people now live in cities (Statistics Canada 2005),[1] there are few analyses of their newspaper representations. Two notable exceptions are Warry (2007), who discusses the neo-conservative bias of Canada's national newspapers with passing reference to the mainstream media's representations of Aboriginal peoples in cities, and Furniss (2001), who provides a deft critical discourse analysis of local and regional reportage on Aboriginal and non-Aboriginal relations in a small town (Williams Lake, B.C.) Journalistic feature articles that approximate an ethnographic approach and focus on Aboriginal peoples in cities are also rare. Canada's Apartheid, the multi-part series on Aboriginal and non-Aboriginal relations by John Stackhouse (*The Globe and Mail* 2001) is one of those rarities. His introduction and part one, "Welcome to Harlem on the Prairies," pay particular attention to Aboriginal peoples living in Saskatoon, Saskatchewan. Stackhouse problematizes non-Aboriginal racism toward Aboriginal peoples through a series of vignettes, personal histories, and interviews involving Aboriginal and non-Aboriginal peoples.

The introduction to Canada's Apartheid, begins with an acknowledgement of how Canadians "tolerate systematic racism" toward Aboriginal peoples and how "we accept a quiet apartheid[2] that segregates, and thus weakens, native and non-native society." Stackhouse also points out Canadians' "lack of will" to deal with this "most enduring crisis." The aim of the whole series of articles, as stated in the introduction, is to allow the readers to "judge" whether Aboriginal and non-Aboriginal cultural incommensurabilities can be "peacefully" bridged and closer ties forged. Stackhouse presents himself as an unbiased presenter of a snapshot of a night of policing on 20th Street in Saskatoon. The articles also aim to "give the nation's most difficult relationship a reality check" (Stackhouse 2001a).

I analyze Stackhouse's representations of urban Aboriginal peoples in "Welcome to Harlem on the Prairies" (Stackhouse 2001b), part one of Canada's Apartheid, by using critical discourse analysis (CDA) to show that the lexical choices made, and the semantic strategies used, by Stackhouse do not provide the means to achieve the goals he sets out. Coupled with his overall strategy of decontextualization, Stackhouse ensures, contrary to his stated purposes, that readers do not have the objectivity/agency to make a clear "judgment" about urban Aboriginal life in Saskatoon. Through critical discourse analysis I reveal underlying non-Aboriginal discourses about Saskatoon's "Harlem on the Prairies." I will show that Stackhouse represents the Aboriginal inhabitants of 20th Street in a simplistic, stereotypical, non-agentative, and non-contextual-ized manner unreflective of the diversity of Aboriginal experience in cities. Stackhouse's discursive strategies reveal his embeddedness in discrimina-tory discourses that have structured Aboriginal and non-Aboriginal rela-tions over the past century and earlier (see Harding 2006).[3] I engage in a fine-grained micro-analysis of selected parts of this multipart series to illustrate this embeddedness. My familiarity, resulting from anthropolog-ical field work in Toronto, with the non-Aboriginal discriminatory dis-courses of Aboriginal primitiveness, dysfunction, incapacity, addiction, identity, leadership corruption, and assumptions of how Aboriginal peo-ples in cities are out of place enables me to "recognize important features and patterns in advance" in this sample (Wood and Kroger 2000, 80). This one sample, therefore, provides sufficient material to ground my arguments. As Wood and Kroger (2000, 81) make clear, discourse analysts have no need to apologize for small numbers of participants or texts— "bigger is not necessarily better." Lastly, it is important to note that I am interested in how the above types of discourse circulate within this sample and not in attacking the person who produces it (78).

Racism and the Press

Szuchewycz (2000, 499) maintains that "the ideological characteristics of newspaper discourse have been particularly well documented" (e.g., Fowler 1991; Hall 1982; Kress & Hodge 1979; Trew 1979a, 1979b). Mass media plays a major part in "the construction and reproduction of dominant ideologies of sexism, classism, and racism" as it "frames and contextualizes news events and thus provide readers with a specific 'definition of the situation.'" It is important to note, then, that the media are shaped by the wider society, and that the media also play a vital role in shaping the social and cultural discursive practices of the wider society. Elites tend to control the definition of the situation, or "the power to define" (Proulx 2003), through the control of media, political, corporate, academic, and legal discourses. It is through this control that "the particular ideologies and social cognitions underlying everyday racism are reproduced and reinforced" (van Dijk 1993 in Szuchewycz 2000, 499). Newspaper professionals presume that their audience share common values, interests, and concerns and, therefore, they select what to report based upon their audience's common-sense knowledge and values (Furniss 2001, 5).[4] A dominant popular consensus is formed, maintained, and reproduced through the definition of the situation circulated by the media (Szuchewycz 2000, 499). This consensus masks structural divisions, inequalities, or differences in perspective among groups in society (Furniss 2001, 5). Consciously or unconsciously, the language used to communicate to readers is shaped by this consensus. This form of language is the newspaper's "public idiom," its version of the "rhetoric, imagery and underlying common stock of knowledge which forms the basis of the reciprocity of producer/reader" (Hall et al. 1978, 61). By closely analyzing the lexical and semantic content of the Stackhouse article I will foreground central mechanisms by which dominant beliefs and values are implicitly communicated[5] (Furniss 2001, 5). Newspapers today decry overt racism in explicit terms, and I note above how Stackhouse does this in his introduction. I will show how Stackhouse, as a representative of and representor for the conservative business-oriented *Globe and Mail* newspaper, through a purportedly unbiased examination of life on 20th Street, reproduces the dominant and largely covert racist definition of the situation about Aboriginal peoples in Canada historically held by non-Aboriginal elites and inculcated in non-elites.

Critical Discourse Analysis (CDA): A Brief Overview

Critical discourse analysis is a complex praxis privileging language as a central part of human life interconnected with other elements of social life (Fairclough 2003, 2). CDA does not reduce all life to language, nor does it say that "everything is discourse" (ibid.). However, critical discourse does not merely reflect social processes and structures, but affirms, consolidates and, in this way, reproduces existing social structures" (Teo 2000, 11).

Discourse is socially constituted and socially constitutive. Discourse is therefore social action. Language is studied because it is the primary instrument through which ideology is transmitted, enacted, and reproduced (Foucault 1972; Pecheux 1982 in Teo 2000, 11). Critical discourse analysts start at the micro level of linguistic structures and progress through discourse strategies in their interactional and wider social contexts; in this way they "unlock the ideologies and recover the social meanings expressed in discourse" (Teo 2000, 11). A goal of CDA is "to unpack the ideological underpinnings of discourse that have become so naturalized over time that we begin to treat them as common, acceptable, and natural features of discourse. In other words, ideology has become common belief or even 'common sense.' Adopting 'critical' goals would then enable us to 'elucidate such naturalizations, and make clear social determinations and effects of discourse which are characteristically opaque to participants'" (Fairclough 1985, 739 in Teo 2000, 12).

This chapter aims to reveal the ideological underpinnings of Canada's Apartheid (Stackhouse 2001a, 2001b) thereby denaturalizing the "common sense" at the base of Canadian racism toward Aboriginal peoples. I begin by examining Stackhouse's lexical choices.

Lexical Choice in "Welcome to Harlem on the Prairies"

Texts are "elements of social events" and also have "causal effects" in the constitution of social reality (Fairclough 2003, 8). Texts have "causal effects upon, and contribute to changes in, people (beliefs, attitudes, etc.), actions, social relations, and the material world" (ibid.). Fairclough (1995, 104) maintains that "texts do not mirror reality; they constitute it and this depends on the social positions and interests of those who produce them." Word choice is central to representation in all texts. The conscious choice of particular words over other words makes analysis of these lexical choices imperative. Analyzing representative strategies in texts thus necessitates looking at "what is included and what is excluded, what is made explicit or left implicit, what is foregrounded and what is backgrounded, what is thematized and what is unthematized, what process types and categories are drawn upon to represent events and so on" (ibid.). I will analyze Stackhouse's "social motivations for particular choices" and "the relations of domination" and ideologies that structure these choices.

Stackhouse's lexical choices for the Aboriginal peoples of 20th Street, his inclusions and exclusions and what he foregrounds and backgrounds, are revealing on a number of levels. First, Stackhouse uses stereotypical categories for many of the inhabitants of 20th Street. Second, the Aboriginal "representatives" of 20th Street are spoken for in certain ways and are not allowed to speak for themselves. Relatedly, Aboriginal mental processes are excluded while non-Aboriginal mental processes are foregrounded in detail. Lastly, by and large, Aboriginal peoples are unnamed, or if they are named, they tend to be linked to stereotypical images of "Indians." This is in opposition to how the two police officers and other non-Aboriginal peoples are represented.

In "Welcome to Harlem on the Prairies," Stackhouse begins the section The Stereotypes of 20th Street by averring that "of course, native stereotypes are to 20th Street what neon signs are to Las Vegas." He lists them as the "provincially owned liquor store, with its windows barricaded like an inner-city bank"; the provincial welfare office is painted as "the west side's main economic force and, in a horrible irony, the source of most of the liquor store's cash" (Stackhouse 2001b). These word choices are meant to demonstrate to the readers that Stackhouse is sensitive to these stereotypes of Aboriginal peoples as drunken, lazy, welfare bums who are associated with certain stereotypical places and actions. By choosing these particular words he presents himself as an enlightened individual who alerts his readers to the sources of some of their own generalizations of Aboriginal peoples. It is meant to appear that Stackhouse takes the moral high ground in recognizing how stereotypes continue to govern how Aboriginal peoples are understood and treated in Canada.

By explicitly referring to these stereotypes, however, he deflects attention from his own reinforcement of these stereotypes and others throughout the article. With the exception of Louttit, two Aboriginal political leaders, one Aboriginal judge, and one Aboriginal social action agency member, all Aboriginal peoples are described variously in these words: "intoxicated mother, hardened hair spray drinkers, derelict uncle, bodies full of intoxicants that would kill most people, shirtless man lying on the pavement splattered in blood, prostitutes, gang leader, drug dealer, two parents passed out with their baby clothed only in diaper, crying, Keith is the face of all those statistics on native justice, and victims." As I point out in Reclaiming Aboriginal Justice, Community, and Identity (2003, 7), these stereotypes are "interpretative repertoires" that provide a useful conceptual tool to understand the "implementation of discourses in ... actual settings" and a way of "understanding the content of discourse and how that content is organized" (Wetherell and Potter 1992, 90). Wetherell and Potter define interpretative repertoires as "discernible clusters of terms, descriptions, and figures of speech often assembled around metaphors or vivid images ... we can talk of these things as systems of signification and as the building blocks used for manufacturing versions of actions, self and social structures in talk. They are some of the resources for making evaluations, constructing factual versions and performing particular actions" (ibid.).

Here is an example of how word choice reveals underlying interpretative repertoires: In the section To Serve and Protect, Stackhouse describes "The Indian Beat—a square mile of reckless inebriation." Here, non-Aboriginal interactional ethics that state that individuals must be abstemious and not drink in public are used to negatively stigmatize Aboriginal peoples (Proulx 2003: 50). Guillemin (1975) discusses the public performances of socializing Micmacs in Boston and the risks they take through alcohol. She also discusses the dominant society's point of view on drinking as an action to be undertaken in private or in controlled situations with approving and participating friends: "Since the police and other keepers of the peace in urban and reservation areas have the same values as the rulers of American society, they perceive public inebriation as an ultimate degradation, a fall from civilization. They judge Indians who drink publicly even more harshly than the individual white, because Indians as a group seem to have been born uncivilized with no shame about their categorical degradation" (191–95).

Cunneen (1992), an Australian criminologist, also discusses the racist nature of policing and the police "preoccupation with containing and controlling Aboriginal people's behaviours, languages, and interactions in public space" (in Williams-Mozley 1998). I maintain that this same interpretative repertoire on Aboriginal drinking is illustrated throughout Stackhouse's article. Note the word *reckless* in the above example. It would appear that not only are all the Indians on the Indian Beat inebriated, they are *recklessly* inebriated. Perhaps being drunk would be acceptable if you were drunk in a non-reckless, responsible, controlled, and non-violent manner. It is implied that this is how non-Aboriginal peoples drink and that the Aboriginal peoples of 20th Street are not capable of this. The image implies that the entire street is filled with drunken, out-of-control Indians. No non-Aboriginal alcoholics are shown to contribute to this square mile of inebriation, even though, if one goes to any "skid row," one is likely to see drunks from a variety of different groups.

Stackhouse's vivid images plug into an extant vocabulary for describing and defining Aboriginal peoples in Canada (Warry 2007; Harding 2006; Furniss 2001, 9). This vocabulary is a predominant non-Aboriginal system of signification that is often utilized in everyday talk (Proulx 2003; Furniss

2001, 9) and is taken up in newspaper texts that covertly speak to readers of how *they* (Aboriginal peoples) *are* and how *they are not us*, without explicitly stating that this is the case. These texts allow non-Aboriginal peoples to construct their *selves* in binary opposition to Aboriginal peoples. Stackhouse's word choices show Aboriginal peoples as emotional, violent, savage, and inferior. This allows non-Aboriginal peoples to define themselves as reasonable, law-abiding, civilized, and superior. As Harding (2006) points out these binaries have been used by elites, the press, and the general non-Aboriginal public to construct Aboriginal people negatively, thereby allowing non-Aboriginal peoples to deprive Aboriginal peoples of land, rights, and financial livelihoods since the mid-1800s.

If one looks at how Stackhouse describes the actions of Aboriginal peoples on 20th Street versus the actions of the two police officers this *us-versus-them* binary becomes more clear. Aboriginal peoples are described variously in the following ways: "drink hair spray," "violate parole and break curfew," "spit at the police," "ram police vehicles and gun down police dogs," "they can't cope with the city," "Judy is drunk often and leaves her kids alone to go out to party with no food in the house," "drinking and watching TV all day," "lies on mattress in a puddle of his own urine and feces," "passed out on kitchen floor," and "door left wide open with the baby on the floor." Activities of the two cops, in contrast, apart from their enforcement duties dealing with uncivilized, savage, abusive, drunken and violent Aboriginal lawlessness, include: "Helping into ambulance, raises horses and rodeoing, lobby for a detox centre, visits [victimized Aboriginal] women in hospital, avoid confrontation, coaches 13-year-old [Aboriginal] daughter on how to put her intoxicated mother to bed, visits Bobby Johnson engages in small talk, checks for fire hazards and food, called Child Protection." The categorical degradation and abnormality of the Other is contrasted with the categorical respectability and normality of these agents of the state and by implication all other non-Aboriginal peoples. The stereotypes that Stackhouse uses throughout his article, then, all reprise and reinforce the interpretative repertoires underpinning the racism that permeates non-Aboriginal society.

While it might be expected that *some* of the denizens of a Harlem-like ghetto would be dysfunctional, psychologically damaged, addicted, marginalized, powerless, violent, and criminal; not all of the inhabitants of Saskatoon would be so. Silver et al. (2006) and Robertson and Culhane (2005) show how socially created and maintained disciplinary/surveillance spaces such as 20th Street (Razack 2002, 10–11) contain many individuals and families who are poor, hard-working, and raising families under onerous conditions but who are not dysfunctional in the manner presented above. This is one of the central exclusions in Stackhouse's article, which reinforces a strong racist undercurrent in non-Aboriginal attitudes toward Aboriginal peoples. Non-Aboriginal people continue to see Aboriginal peoples, particularly in cities, as only being able to occupy the above stereotypical categories. As one of my Aboriginal fieldwork informants in Toronto once said to me: "The drunken Indian is ten feet tall, but a sober one is invisible. No one notices all the ones that they pass that are on their way to work, on their way home, on their way to committees, whatever. No one notices those ones, but everybody notices the one that is drunk on the street" (Proulx 2003, 50).

Klein (2002, E1) points out that Stackhouse's depictions "didn't reflect the reality of most aboriginals and non-aboriginals in the city" and that there are other Aboriginal peoples in Saskatoon: "We have to remember, this is a city where the chair of the Chamber of Commerce is an aboriginal person, the chair of the board of police commissioners is an aboriginal woman, where 10% of the student population (at the University of Saskatoon) are aboriginal people and students hold significant positions of power."

Apart from a brief mention of the "Saskatoon Tribal Council," an organization that advocates for urban Aboriginal interests and runs many social programs for Aboriginal peoples in Saskatoon, no other urban Aboriginal agencies are mentioned. The fact that the Saskatoon Indian and Métis Friendship Centre—open since 1963, located a mere two blocks from 20th Street, and operating many urban social programs—is not mentioned is a significant exclusion. Stackhouse's exclusion of all those organizations and agencies continues to render them invisible and perpetuates the idea in the minds of readers that there are only drunken, addicted, sexually and physically abusive, violent, and criminal Aboriginal peoples in cities. Stackhouse's argumentative ploy of associating Aboriginal peoples with violence and criminality is one that has "been used historically to discredit Aboriginal peoples and causes in news discourse" and reinforces Aboriginal peoples as "alien, unknowable and ultimately a threat to civil order" (Harding 2006, 221).

Not only does Stackhouse exclude mention of other *types* of Aboriginal peoples on 20th Street, he also selectively incorporates the *voices* that are allowed to define life on 20th Street. Only relatively influential Aboriginal (two Aboriginal politicians, an Aboriginal judge, and an Aboriginal social action agency member) and powerful non-Aboriginal people (two police officers, a non-Aboriginal police liaison officer, and the mayor of Saskatoon) are allowed to speak. Stackhouse does not give voice to any of the people who actually live on 20th Street beyond those who are drunk, abusive, violent, or bad parents. Even these negatively portrayed *types* are only allowed to speak in terms of demonstrating how they are not *us* (non-Aboriginal). What they are allowed to say ("What ya doin', fuckin pigs?" "Get out of here, you white motherfuckers." "Bobby mumbles a few words." "I'm going to fuckin' kill you.") only contributes to the representation of their categorical degradation, relegating them to the category of Other.

Representational strategies of visibility/inclusion/voice and invisibility/exclusion/silence insure that a very limited section of 20th Street's population is shown and heard, thereby robbing the Aboriginal residents, both dysfunctional/visible and functional/invisible, of the agency to represent themselves according to their needs and concerns. Culhane (2003, 595) based on Goode and Maskovsky (2001), in discussing the invisibility of Aboriginal women preyed on by a serial killer or killers in the Downtown Eastside of Vancouver, says that these forms of visibility and invisibility are "constitutive of a 'regime of disappearance.'" This term "describe[s] a neo-liberal mode of governance that selectively marginalizes and/or erases categories of people through strategies of representation that include silences, blind spots, and displacements that have both material and symbolic effects."

Stackhouse creates a "densely woven veil or regime of disappearance" for the peoples of 20th Street in three ways: first, through a preference for exotic and spectacular representation of drugs, sex, violence, and crime rather than the ordinary and mundane brutality of everyday poverty; second, through the "pathologizing of poverty"; and, third, through the exclusion of the "resistance practiced and visions of change articulated by subjects of these discourses" (Culhane 2003, 595). I maintain that the marginalizations, erasures, and silencing of categories of people reflect Stackhouse's conscious or unconscious embeddedness within the above stereotypical discourses that have structured non-Aboriginal understandings of Aboriginal peoples over time, as Harding (2006) has effectively demonstrated. Stackhouse's exclusion of any poor but healthy and hardworking Aboriginal peoples perpetuates a continuing process of wilful national blindness wherein the "recognition of the burden of social suffering carried by Aboriginal people in this neighborhood—and in Canada as a whole—elicits profound discomfort within a liberal, democratic nation-state like Canada, evidencing as it does the continuing effects of settler colonialism, its ideological and material foundations, and its ongoing reproduction" (Culhane 2003, 595).[6]

Mental Processes

Related to the issue of voice and agency is the portrayal, or lack thereof, of mental processes among the peoples of 20th Street. Mental processes "represent the inner world of news participants," and how these inner states are represented can tell much about who Stackhouse attributes agency to and who he does not (Pietikäinen 2003, 602). Stackhouse consistently allows the non-Aboriginal actors within the article to give voice to their inner thoughts and feelings. The police are allowed to speak about what they thought of where they grew up and the positive and negative influences that this entailed. They speak of their "frustration" and "anger" with those Aboriginal offenders who do not respect themselves (due to drug and alcohol abuse) and do not respect others with whom they have relationships (spousal, parental). This is contrasted with their thoughts and expressions of love for their own children and hobbies. The police are also allowed to express their inner thoughts on their dissatisfaction with the "revolving door" justice system, and how Aboriginal irresponsibility to themselves and others justifies their racism toward "individual Indians" but not the whole race. The police are represented as complex and human through their thought processes.

On the other hand, the inhabitants of 20th Street (twenty Aboriginal individuals and numerous anonymous Aboriginal groups) are, with four exceptions, not allowed to express anything of their mental processes. Hair Spray Jerry the girlfriend beater, with whom Stackhouse chooses to open "Welcome to Harlem on the Prairies," is not allowed to express why he drinks hairspray or beats Diane or why he ended up in this state. He is not allowed to tell readers what he thinks of the police twisting his arm to subdue him. This lack of representation of his thought processes renders him un-sentient and inhuman. But the police are allowed to express their mental processes of their encounter with Jerry: "The scene makes their blood boil." In other examples, Native groups (anonymous) merely "believe" that the justice system treats them in a discriminatory manner in comparison to non-Aboriginals. But the non-Aboriginal police liaison officer Craig Nyirfa (identified) is allowed to "*understand* the problem" of Aboriginal peoples being treated differently for alcohol offences than non-natives. The mayor is allowed to "remember his policing days," speak of police "frustrations" leading to infamous starlight tours,[7] and, when asked if starlight tours should happen, replies, "I don't think so. Will it happen again? I would hope not." The mayor is allowed to "think" and "hope," yet no Aboriginal person gets to impart what s/he thinks about his/her frustrations or hopes on this issue or any other. Additionally,

Stackhouse employs a mitigation strategy by allowing the mayor and the other police in this section to speak about their thoughts on starlight tours and their "frustrations" with Aboriginal offenders. None of the inhabitants of 20th Street are given the opportunity to discuss what they think of starlight tours or the non-Aboriginal mitigation of them. Overall, the exclusion of representations of the mental processes of many of the Aboriginal peoples of 20th Street robs them of agency and contributes to the idea that they are non-cognitive, irrational, impulsive, and dangerous while simultaneously portraying non-Aboriginals in a dichotomous, cognitive, rational, considered, and helpful manner.

Stackhouse often uses phrases such "some indians," "aboriginal groups," "native groups," "native politicians," "many natives," "fucking Indians," "native men," "an entire family," and "an aboriginal population." These anonymizing phrases are used strategically first to lump "all" Aboriginal peoples into special-interest groups who threaten the political, economic, and social status quo and/or to create undifferentiated groups of "them" as opposed to the non-Aboriginal "us." The lack of explicit names for these groups means no context is provided as to exactly who (e.g., specific Aboriginal social action agencies, academics, social workers) is making these statements. The lack of attribution contributes to the sense that these groups are simply complainers who lack any legitimacy in the eyes of non-Aboriginal readers. In The Stereotypes of 20th Street, the section in which Aboriginal involvement in finding solutions to the problems of 20th Street is criticized, Stackhouse chooses this anonymous construction: "Louttit is angry at his society, and his people. 'You hear native groups say, We need this or that. Yeah, we need them to come down here and do something.'" There are two lexical choices of interest here. Stackhouse, in "Louttit is angry at *his* society, and *his* people" [my italics] reinforces a continuing ignorance among non-Aboriginals that there is only *one* Aboriginal society or people when in fact there are *many* across Canada. Second, the "native groups" are unnamed and are portrayed, as native groups often are in the press, as selfish whiners who think they are entitled to help from the non-Aboriginal state but are unwilling to "do something" about it. These "groups" are spoken for by Louttit, who, although he is part Aboriginal, is also, as a police officer, an agent of the state. No specific context is given about who these groups are or their mandates, policies, and solutions. Instead of assigning responsibility to non-Aboriginal elites and federal-versus-provincial jurisdictional squabbling, Louttit blames the victims and condemns an unspecified and undemocratic Aboriginal leadership ("we need elected leadership") for failing to "take care of our problems." There is no discussion of the structural inequities resulting from continuing colonialism (for example, government provision of substandard education, which leads to reduced employability, lower income, under-housing, or homelessness). This example illustrates how lexical choices foreground certain ideas and relegate to the background or exclude others. It also shows the technique of "selective incorporation" in the way Aboriginal voices are only "incorporated in ways that largely support the dominant frame" (Harding 2006, 225).

It is interesting how Stackhouse uses Loutitt's status as a "part-Aboriginal" to legitimize his discourse as an "insider." This enables Stackhouse to voice conservative views without saying them directly. By having the insider Loutitt blame "his" own people Stackhouse legitimizes the widely held non-Aboriginal stereotype that all Aboriginal leaders are corrupt, lazy, irresponsible, and bad managers of the largesse showered upon Aboriginal peoples by the Canadian state (Furniss 2001, 19).[8] Additionally, Loutitt's hybridity is used to construct him as a successfully assimilated Aboriginal person. By not being a "full" Aboriginal he is not susceptible, according to non-Aboriginal peoples, to the usual sources, of Aboriginal Otherness as discussed above. Loutitt is, therefore, a "good guy" whose views can be trusted.[9]

Context: Shaping Public Consciousness/Opinion through Exclusions

Fairclough (1995, 50) maintains that we need to go beyond the "immediate situation of the communicative event (the 'context' of the situation)" in any text to focus on the "wider social and cultural context" in which the text is embedded. The "wider conceptual matrix must be attended to because it shapes discursive practices in important ways and is itself cumulatively shaped by them" (ibid.). A major part of the wider conceptual mix in Aboriginal and non-Aboriginal relations in Canada is racism and its material consequences, as Stackhouse points out. Here I focus on elements of the historical and cultural context of Aboriginal and non-Aboriginal relations and how Stackhouse's decontextualization goes against his stated aims of providing information—"a reality check"—to allow readers to "judge" whether Aboriginal and non-Aboriginal cultural incommensurabilities can be "peacefully" bridged and closer ties forged. Indeed, the exclusion of necessary information about the political, legal, and social context that has such a negative impact on the lives of Aboriginal peoples in Canada leads readers to blame Aboriginal victims for their own situations and allows non-Aboriginal Canadians to deny that they have any role in the creation and maintenance of these negative symbolic and material relations. I recognize that newspaper articles are only given a certain amount of space to make their points, so some context must necessarily be excluded; however, given Stackhouse's aims, at least some substantive discussion of the legal and political context surrounding Aboriginal and non-Aboriginal relations should have been made explicit in the article. In the next section I examine one of many instances where the exclusion of context occurs.

Aboriginal Justice

Given that this article is structured around a night of policing, the mitigation of police use of starlight tours, and told predominantly through non-Aboriginal and elite Aboriginal criticisms of the justice system, it is curious that so little context is provided about the causes of the problems with the justice system.[10] The following are samples of text wherein decontextualization of the wider social, legal, and cultural context promotes a form of ignorance that serves to reinforce the division that Stackhouse is purportedly trying to reconcile.

First, Stackhouse provides no context for Aboriginal overrepresentation in the justice system. The article states, "But there seems to be no end to the friction between a largely non-native judicial system and aboriginal people, who account for about one-fifth of the local population but more than half of those arrested on a typical night" (2001b). More Aboriginal people are arrested even though they only constitute a fraction of the overall population. What is excluded here is any discussion of over-policing. Williams-Mozley (1998) provides a definition and an excellent discussion of the non-Aboriginal denial of this process through equality discourse in the Australian context:

> At its most basic level, the concept is taken to mean both the extent of police intervention and the nature of that intervention. It is used here to describe the incessant surveillance and intervention by police with respect to Aboriginal peoples' use and occupancy of public space. Despite police protestations over time which claim that the law is applied equally and impartially to all, research clearly shows that no other group or class of people within Australian society is subject to the same inordinate degree of scrutiny and supervision. The fact that Aboriginal people's use and occupancy of public space is the object of over-policing can be determined from their continuous history of over-representation in arrest rates for trivial or minor offences against "good order."

The problem of over-policing has been documented in Canada as a serious problem for Aboriginal peoples (RCAP 1996, 35–39; Quigley 1994, 273–74) and has recently been linked to racial profiling (Murray 2003), yet Stackhouse does not refer to police over-surveillance and intervention in the lopsided ratio of Aboriginal to non-Aboriginal arrests. Without some mention of this issue and other overrepresentation factors such as sentencing disparities[11] (LaPrairie 1999), Stackhouse leaves readers with "a common misconception that the problems that render too many Aboriginal communities inherently more criminogenic than non-Aboriginal communities are essentially 'of their own making'" and therefore not the responsibility of non-Aboriginal stakeholders (Dickson-Gilmore and LaPrairie 2005, 53). Indeed, Stackhouse makes a comment that illustrates this misconception on the part of non-Aboriginal peoples, thereby reinforcing it: "With Canada's highest crime rate last year, many residents blame an aboriginal population that they say can't cope with the transition from isolated reserves to a multicultural city, where universal laws and an independent police and courts are supposed to prevail" (2001b).

Not only are Aboriginal victims being blamed for their criminogenic behaviours they are *all* ("an aboriginal population") also portrayed as being unable to cope with the move to city life. Harding (2006, 210) notes that this rhetorical strategy "blames problems that people of color experience, as a result of institutionalized racist policies and practices, on their inability or unwillingness to adapt to the ways of the dominant society." Again, there is an exclusion of Aboriginal peoples who "cope" well with city life, who lead lives of public service, for example, as discussed above. Throughout Stackhouse's representation of 20th Street the pervasive "blame the victim" mentality among non-Aboriginal peoples is conditioned by "democratic racism," which operates under this set of assumptions:

> If equal opportunity and social equality are assumed to exist, than the lack of success on the part of a minority population must be attributed to some other set of conditions. One explanation used by the dominant culture is the notion that certain minority communities themselves are culturally deficient (e.g., lacking intellectual prowess; more prone to aggressive behavior or other forms of deviant behaviour). In this form of the dominant discourse, it is assumed that certain communities (e.g., African Canadian) [Aboriginal peoples] lack the motivation, education or skills to participate fully in the workplace, educational system and other areas of Canadian society. Alternatively, it is argued that the failure of certain groups to succeed and to be integrated into the mainstream dominant culture is largely due to

recalcitrant members of these groups refusing to adapt their traditional, different cultural values and norms to fit into Canadian society, and making unreasonable demands of the host society. (Henry and Tator 2000, 294)

The previous Stackhouse quote also contains a covert criticism of special treatment for Aboriginal peoples in the justice system. Stackhouse says that "universal laws and an independent police and courts are *supposed* to prevail" (emphasis added). In Canada the discourse of equality is cherished. All peoples regardless of race are *supposed* to be treated equally. Affirmative action of any sort, for many non-Aboriginal people in Canada, goes against equality protections and leads them to complain that affirmative actions for Aboriginal peoples are "race-based."[12] Restorative justice as mandated in the Criminal Code of Canada subsection 718.2(e) is perceived to go against "universal law," which accords equal treatment to all, thereby protecting against sentencing disparity. As Haslip (2000) points out, "Despite the Supreme Court of Canada's rationale for different sentences for offenders committing the same offence, the reality is that section 718.2(e) will be perceived by both judges and the general public as creating a two-tiered justice system or a 'race-based justice' system whereby subsection 718.2(e) becomes a 'get out of jail free' card for Aboriginal peoples."[13] In the Division among the Chiefs section of the article, Stackhouse is more explicit in presenting negative views on restorative justice, saying, "But the concept has sparked more skeptics [anonymous and not attributed] than supporters [anonymous and not attributed]— Louttit says that, in his experience, repeat offenders plead for sentencing circles and community-based rehabilitation only so they can get back to a life of crime and violence as quickly as possible" (2001b). Stackhouse ignores evidence of successful community justice (Green 1998; Sivell-Ferri 1997; Proulx 2003). Instead, he reinforces the common race-based and "get out of jail free card" public assumptions by using a part-Aboriginal police officer's unspecified "experience" of restorative justice to denigrate it. Harding (2006), discussing decontextualizing strategies, says that "by reporting on issues critical to aboriginal people, which often have long historical antecedents that are little understood or known by the public in a decontextualized fashion, the news media may discourage the public from supporting vital initiatives in the areas of treaty-making, residential schools and self-government" (230–31).

I suggest that Stackhouse's lack of context on the history and causes of overrepresentation, along with his representation of Louttit's decontextualized negative views on new justice initiatives, aids in discouraging the public from supporting vital new justice initiatives that could reduce overrepresentation and play a role in building self-government. The lack of context on the causes of Aboriginal overrepresentation in the justice system *disables* readers' abilities to effectively judge why "there seems to be no end to the friction between a largely non-native judicial system and aboriginal people" (2001b).

At the same time, the lack of context *enables* readers to blame Aboriginal peoples by pandering to the unspoken assumptions already held by many non-Aboriginal Canadians. When Stackhouse's lexical choices—his implicit denial of the agency of Aboriginal people on 20th Street through regimes of disappearance, lack of voice and thought processes, and decontextualization of justice for Aboriginal peoples—are examined through this lens it is clear that Stackhouse, consciously or subconsciously, operates under the assumptions of democratic racism. Overall, then, the power of the wider social and conceptual matrix embodied in justice discourse, in the discourse of democratic racism, and in equality discourse shapes the text, the "immediate situation of the communicative event," and this event, in turn, shapes the "wider social and cultural context" within which the text is embedded (Fairclough 1995, 50).

The Division among the Chiefs

Stackhouse's representation of controversies surrounding the problems confronting Aboriginal and non-Aboriginal peoples, as exemplified in his 20th Street example, is problematic. It fits within the shaping of non-Aboriginal discourses on the factionalization in Aboriginal leadership, concerns about the legitimacy and accountability of Aboriginal leaders who represent Aboriginal interests, and incrementalism versus "radical" Aboriginal approaches to solving their problems across a host of domains. All of these discourses continue to, often negatively, shape media representations of Aboriginal peoples, policy, and practice today (e.g., Ibbitson 2006, A4; Curry 2006a, A5; *The Globe and Mail* 2005, A14; Gibson 2005, A13).

Stackhouse represents two chiefs—George Lafond, the "elected chief" of the Saskatoon Tribal Council (STC) and Lawrence Joseph, "vice-chairman" of the Federation of Saskatchewan Indian Nations (FSIN)—their definitions of the situation, and their proposed solutions to them. I want to be very clear here. I am *not* critiquing the ideas or positions of these two individuals. I am analyzing how Stackhouse represents them and how this representation also goes against his stated aims. How Stackhouse describes each chief, contextualizes their past histories and positions, what he allows them to say, the amount of space given to each to present their positions, and the extent to which direct quotations are used versus paraphrasing (indirect speech) all combine to manage the readers' perceptions and their definition of the situation, and links them to the wider discourses outlined above.

Chief Lafond

Over a number of paragraphs Lafond is described and contextualized as the "elected" chief of the STC, who is "not cut from the same cloth of most native leaders in Saskatchewan." He is a "pinstriped native who drives a Jeep, lives in a largely white neighbourhood on the east side of the river" to whom John Diefenbaker was a "boyhood hero." He is described as a "Red Tory." He sees "the divisions stem from both the province's economic decline and Ottawa's preference[14] to deal with natives on their reserves, rather than in cities." He worries that no group has yet brought the two solitudes together and is quoted as saying "What I fear is that if you vacate the middle ground, extremists will fill it." Lafond is then paraphrased: "If the middle ground is to be reclaimed, he believes more new money will be needed. He ... would like to see the justice system reformed" and "he says, police should stop treating self-inflicted abuse—most commonly drinking and drugs—as crimes that merit formal charges. They also should break the cycle of jail, parole and re-arrest, he says, by trying new ways to rehabilitate offenders" (Stackhouse 2001b).

In the controversy over restorative justice discussed above, Lafond is represented as being "aware of such beliefs, among natives and whites. He has struggled to maintain a conciliatory line through the recent wave of troubles [starlight tour controversy]. He believes that his council's relationship with the police kept the city from exploding last year when the Darrell Night case went public. He also believes that it is changing the police force for the better."

Lawrence Joseph

Stackhouse begins his representation of Joseph by stating that "Lawrence Joseph disagrees." He then goes on to say in two paragraphs:

> If Lafond is a conciliator, Joseph, vice-chairman of the Federation of Saskatchewan Indian Nations, is a hard-liner, the Al Sharpton of Saskatoon politics, a minority leader who seems to want to inflame racial divisions every time controversy emerges. Confrontation, and at times conflict, are his tools.
>
> To him, just about every problem for his province's natives is the result of a white conspiracy, and just about every offer made to natives is not good

enough. He talks of "token Indians" and "piecemeal" measures, and cultural-sensitivity programs that he considers "a joke." (Of the police force, he says: "You can't teach an old dog new tricks.") (Stackhouse, 2001b)

Stackhouse concludes his representation of Joseph immediately following these paragraphs, in the first line of the next section, Changing the Face of Saskatoon's Force: "Despite Joseph's tirades, which many police officers believe led to their chief being fired, the force says it has tried to change its personnel and its culture."

Analysis of Division among the Chiefs

The description of each of the chiefs is telling in a number of ways. First, Lafond is given a great deal of positive description. He is a "conciliator, an elected chief, who is not cut from the same cloth of most native leaders" and he is a Red Tory. Joseph, on the other hand is described, in only two paragraphs, mostly in negative terms. Stackhouse does not say whether or not he was elected as he does with Lafond. This immediately begins the process of undermining the legitimacy of Joseph as a leader. Joseph is a "hard-liner, the Al Sharpton of politics" and he is a "minority leader" who "inflames racial divisions." Lafond is presented favourably while Joseph is demonized. Lafond is legitimate and represents an implied majority position while Joseph is illegitimate and represents only a small "minority." Henry and Tator (2002, 18) point out that "opponents can be marginalized by defining them as being 'radicals,' special interest groups, or spokespeople who do not represent anyone but themselves." The overwrought and inflammatory description of Joseph as opposed to the measured and reassuring description of Lafond is a standard way to marginalize a person whose positions and views are threatening to the status quo of incremental change over substantive and radical change. Stackhouse uses a rhetorical tactic of debasement supported by semantic strategies of exaggeration and dramatic contrast through judgmental adjectives (Harding 2006, 209) to deprive Joseph of legitimacy without having to state explicitly that Lafond's ideas and background are safer and more preferable for non-Aboriginals. Stackhouse, rather than trying to find common ground to heal divisions by providing measured descriptions of each chief, instead reinforces the divisions between the two chiefs, implicitly reinforcing a widely held non-Aboriginal view that there is only factionalization among Aboriginal leaders and little possibility of consensus. This also leads to the idea that if Aboriginal peoples can't agree on how to deal with their own concerns then non-Aboriginal peoples will have to continue to do it for them.

In terms of contextualizing the positions of each chief, Lafond is represented as a well-rounded figure, and he is given the space to discuss a wide variety of his views on Aboriginal problems and solutions as well as his views on Aboriginal/non-Aboriginal relations. Lafond is represented as claiming the middle ground in all controversies in order to forestall extremism. He is also allowed to claim success in keeping the city from exploding due to his conciliatory approach and his council's relationship with the police.

Joseph, on the other hand, is given little space to contextualize himself. He is a cardboard cut-out or merely a straw man erected to prove Lafond's sensibility and credibility. Stackhouse says that "Lawrence Joseph disagrees" with Lafond's assessment of a better and changing relationship with Saskatoon's police force yet provides him no space to say exactly why he disagrees or to present his proposals for change. Indeed, Stackhouse continues his demonization of Joseph through contextualizing him as an "inflame[er] of racial divisions" who only uses "confrontation" as a tool to deal with the "white conspiracy" at the heart of all Aboriginal problems. The term "white conspiracy" is, to my mind, a derogatory term that casts doubt on the realities of settler colonialism and its continuing effects. Many non-Aboriginal peoples desperately want to believe that colonialism has ended and are willing to go to great lengths to deny their continuing complicity in it or, at the very least, to minimize it (Proulx 2003, 3). If Joseph consistently cites colonialism as a root cause for Aboriginal oppression and marginalization in Canada, then calling colonialism a "white conspiracy" is an effective way to render it fictional and imagined. Joseph, then, becomes an isolated individual under the influence of a delusion. Stackhouse also presents Joseph as another one of those natives to whom "just about every offer made [by non-Aboriginal stakeholders] to natives is not good enough," as discussed above. Joseph is represented as being ungrateful for all the wonderful things that non-Aboriginal peoples have provided that are actually, in many cases, merely stop-gap, incrementalist[15] measures (Peach 2004; Prince 2002). Hence, any criticisms that Joseph makes of the incrementalist approaches to Aboriginal problems favoured by governments ("piecemeal measures and cultural sensitivity programs that he considers a joke") are framed in dismissive terms excluding any of the substantive ideas that Joseph may have presented. He is not allowed space to offer his alternative ideas.

Stackhouse takes great pains to legitimize Lafond as an "expert" with a cool head on the controversial issues. Stackhouse directly quotes Lafond with context on numerous occasions; for example, "what I fear is that if you vacate the middle ground," Lafond says, "extremists will fill it." Direct quotes are used to give this threat "a semblance of 'facticity' and authenticity" (Teo 2000, 18). Not only is he allowed to speak directly to the readers, this expert is also allowed to place in their minds the *fact* of a *threatening* extreme Aboriginal activism. This is a very obvious attempt to link *isolated and uncommon forms* of Aboriginal activism, for example, Oka, to Aboriginal peoples who are dissatisfied with incrementalism and red-faces-in-white-places (indigenization) policy and practice and want more substantive but non-violent change. This form of linkage continues in the media. John Miller (2005) shows, for example, how print media consistently linked the non-violent protest at Ipperwash with violent protests at Oka and Gustafsen Lake in order to create the basis for a moral panic among non-Aboriginals about the use of guns and violence to over-throw the Canadian way of life.

Joseph, on the other hand, is fully quoted only once through a folk say-ing: "You can't teach an old dog new tricks." Joseph is speaking of the police force that Lafond claims to have changed for the better. Otherwise, Joseph's opinions are reduced to paraphrased sound bites denuded of the context necessary to understand the complexity of Joseph's critique of the police. For example, Joseph is paraphrased: "He talks of token Indians ..." This can be taken two ways. First, it could be a fragment of a larger dis-cussion on how some Aboriginal peoples who work for the state, or have the state's ear, think that they have more input into policy and decision making than they really do. In fact these Aboriginal peoples are seen as "token Indians" by many Aboriginal and non-Aboriginals in this context. They are there to add a veneer of cultural sensitivity and to make it look like the state is actually listening to Aboriginal concerns. Second, it could be a discussion of how police forces are moving forward with indigeniza-tion by hiring a few "token Indians" to give a red tinge to a white force. Louttit could be seen in this context. Stackhouse's paraphrasing provides none of the complex context necessary for Joseph's positions to be under-stood by the readers. Indeed, Stackhouse writes off Joseph's positions as "Joseph's tirades," thereby further denigrating and marginalizing the "hard-liner" that opposes the position of conciliation, accommodation, and incrementalism that Stackhouse supports through his detailed repre-sentation of Lafond.

In Division among the Chiefs, Stackhouse continues to go against his stated aims. Rather than provide a reasoned and fully contextualized dia-logue between two Aboriginal leaders who disagree on the state of Aboriginal and non-Aboriginal relations and pathways for change that could "peacefully bridge" different worlds, Stackhouse's representational strategies reinforce existing divisions. By demonizing, delegitimizing, decontextualizing, and selectively editing Joseph, he deprives readers of a "reality check" and the ability to "judge" a different path than the middle road advocated by Lafond and implicitly supported by Stackhouse and *The Globe and Mail*. Through his use of inflammatory language about the potential threat presented by Joseph's ideas, Stackhouse preys on non-Aboriginal fears of *uppity Indians* who would upset the status quo. No bridge is provided here; only an ever-widening abyss.

Conclusion

Critical discourse analysis is a useful tool for revealing interpretative repertoires/ideologies underpinning representation in texts. John Stackhouse outlines what seems to be an emancipatory project to foreground non-Aboriginal racism against Aboriginal peoples and to find ways to bridge the gaps that separate these two groups through informational exchange. The critical discourse analysis presented here, however, shows that Stackhouse's representations achieve the opposite. His stereotypical lexical choices, exclusions of non-stereotypical Aboriginal peoples, voices, and thought processes, his reinforcement of the assumptions of democratic racism, semantic strategies of marginalization, decontextualization, delegitimization, and demonization in representing non-status quo positions all combine to create informational gulfs rather than bridges. These strategies disable rather than enable rational judgment. The reader is left with the idea that there is only one path to follow and that this is the path of the conservative status quo. Different pathways for change, when they are presented at all, are portrayed as threatening the status quo. Rather than presenting a new picture of Aboriginal peoples in cities, Stackhouse, by and large, simply reproduces misconceptions of Aboriginal city life as *only* dysfunctional, fragmented, anomic, and violent. While this is a part of Aboriginal life in cities it is not the only part. As more recent analyses have shown (Buddle 2005; Lawrence 2004; Peters 2004; Proulx 2003; Howard-Bobiwash 2003; Jackson 2002; Lobo and Peters 2001) Aboriginal life in cities is functional, community-oriented, socially conscious, and creative on numerous individual and institutional levels. That a major national newspaper would continue to reinforce the older, stereotypical view reveals the depth and persistence of Canada's Apartheid.

Notes

1 Critical Discourse Analysis (CDA) of newspaper representations/discourses on minorities and Aboriginal peoples around the world is a growing field of scholarly interest that focuses primarily on reserve, reservation, and rural populations (Harding 2006; Pietikainen 2003; Henry and Tator 2002; Hutchinson 2002; Furniss 2001; Szuchewtcz 2000; Teo 2000; Avison and Meadows 2000; Bird 1999). Until the above academics started to focus on this domain through CDA, most of the previous work was based on content analysis, which Furniss maintains (2001, 33n18) resulted in an "essentially static model" because it only assessed the "relative frequency of various categories of news reporting about Aboriginal people" (ibid.). Content analysis did not capture fine-grained textual changes or "changes in the broader social, political, and cultural contexts in which their readers are situated" (ibid.). Some examples of articles using content analysis are Skea (1993–94), Grenier (1994), Miller (1993), and Singer (1982).

2 Warry (2007, 75) is critical of Stackhouse's seizure of the powerful apartheid label and its subtle promotion of neo-conservative political agendas that suggest that Aboriginal peoples can only be successful if they leave the reserves, give up their traditions, and assimilate/integrate into the urban non-Aboriginal world.

3 While Warry (2007, 75–76) critically touches on Stackhouse's involvement in neo-conservative ideologies on Aboriginal issues, including Stackhouse's concentration on individual pathologies and hopelessness and his focus on the nepotism, corruption, and lack of accountability of Aboriginal leaders, ideas that pander to widely held non-Aboriginal Canadian biases, Warry does not engage in fine-grained analysis of Stackhouse. This paper does engage in a fine-grained analysis of these and other issues within Stackhouse.

4 Warry (2007, 76) says, "The power of political commentary is that it comes pre-formulated and often tailored to our built-in biases and political orientations. It is meant to spark debate and to present multiple summations of complex issues. In the process, unfortunately, it over-simplifies and falls too easily onto complex stereotypes and common sense solutions."

5 I do not mean to imply that all readers are dupes of elite ideologies in every instance.

6 Warry (2007, 76) points to how Stackhouse builds "his representations on the personal stories of individuals. He never seriously engages larger issues of colonialism and post-colonialism. As a result, when Stackhouse concentrates on well-known social pathologies on and off reserve, including addictions and family violence, we are left with images of hopelessness and are never asked to examine mainstream political indifference and responsibility."

7 "Starlight tours" is the name Aboriginal peoples give to the police practice of taking troublesome, often drunk, Aboriginal people to the edge of town and leaving them there to find their way home. Often they are left without coats and shoes. In winter this practice is particularly dangerous and has resulted in deaths by freezing of Aboriginal people. Two Saskatoon police officers were charged in the Darrel Night starlight tour case. This case is discussed in the Stackhouse article under analysis.

8 Warry (2007, 76) charges that Stackhouse "falls prey to a blaming mentality" when referring to Aboriginal leadership and critiques Stackhouse for suggesting that "too many Aboriginal leaders have 'retrograde attitudes' that keep their people in second-class status." Rather than focusing on the work that Aboriginal leaders and peoples have done on Aboriginal rights and treaty rights, among others, Stackhouse "instead focuses on the 'rampant corruption and nepotism' of leaders."

9 I thank Heather Howard-Bobiwash for alerting me to how Stackhouse uses the insider Loutitt.

10 For example, "Widespread bias and racism against Aboriginal peoples within Canada translates into systemic discrimination within the criminal justice system further serving to alienate Aboriginal peoples. This systemic discrimination is felt by Aboriginal peoples in a number of ways including more charges being laid against Aboriginal people than non-Aboriginal people. In addition, Aboriginal people spend less time with defence counsel than do non-Aboriginal people. This, in turn, results in both more and longer prison terms for Aboriginal offenders than non-Aboriginal offenders and bail is refused more frequently to Aboriginal accused than non-Aboriginal accused" (Haslip 2000).

11 Quigley (1994, 275–76) notes that "socioeconomic factors such as employment status, level of education, family situation, etc., appear on the surface as neutral criteria. They are considered as such by the legal system. Yet they can conceal an extremely strong bias in the sentencing process. Convicted persons with steady employment and stability in their lives, or at least prospects of the same, are much less likely to be sent to jail for offences that are borderline imprisonment offences. The unemployed, transients, the poorly educated are all better candidates for imprisonment. When the social, political and economic aspects of our society place Aboriginal people disproportionately within the ranks of the latter, our society literally sentences more of them to jail. This is systemic discrimination."

12 For example, Prime Minister Stephen Harper described the Fraser River salmon fishery in British Columbia, where the Federal Fisheries Department provides Aboriginal-only openings to fish commercially, as race-based (Curry 2006b: A8). Indian Affairs Minister Jim Prentice, in attempting to calm the storm raised by Mr. Harper and to indicate policy change for the non-Aboriginal fishers, said, "We are supportive of a policy of equality of access to the commercial fishery" (ibid.). *The Globe and Mail*, in an editorial on the controversy, supported the government by saying, "In pledging to let all commercial fishermen fish at the same time, the government is on solid ground (*The Globe and Mail* 2006, A12). It is noteworthy that the prime minister, the minister of Indian Affairs, and *The Globe and Mail* ignore the fact that non-Aboriginal fishers, for many years previous to this fishery policy change, had more opportunities to fish than Aboriginal peoples in what was a colonially based exclusion of Aboriginal fishers. This was, in fact, a race-based fishery based on non-Aboriginal dominance tacitly supported by government and police. The affirmative action to redress this imbalance is decried as offending equality discourse when, in fact, equality discourse is being used to hide offences to non-Aboriginal historical advantage and entitlement. See also Gibson (2005, A13) for a right-wing discussion of how Canada has an Aboriginal "program administration based on race."

13 See also J. Rudin (1999, A13).

14 The Canadian constitution assigns a range of exclusive legislative powers to the federal and provincial orders of government. Section 91-24 of the constitution deals with the division of federal and provincial powers and clearly places the jurisdiction and responsibility for Aboriginal peoples with the federal government. It is interesting that Stackhouse describes this constitutional issue as a mere "preference," thereby minimizing federal/provincial jurisdictional squabbling, a central problem for urban Aboriginal peoples in terms of who is responsible for providing funding and services.

15 "As a decision-making strategy, incrementalism is generally thought of as a response to there being a lack of sufficient information to make fully rational decisions, or where the technical complexity of non-incremental change is overwhelming ... But it may also represent a way forward when non-incremental change is likely to arouse value conflicts that are difficult to manage. Incrementalism, or stepped change, eases systems and dampens opposition, while signaling longer-run intentions. As an analytical device incrementalism generates a short-term response to a perceived need for change, while avoiding the need to engage in more deep-seated analysis" (Stewart 2006: 189–90).

Works Cited

Avison, S., and M. Meadows. 2000. "Speaking and Hearing: Aboriginal Newspapers and the Public Sphere in Canada and Australia." *Canadian Journal of Communication* 25 (3). http://www.cjc-online.ca/viewarticle.php?id=586.

Bird, Elizabeth S. 1999. "Gendered Construction of the American Indian in Popular Media." *Journal of Communication* 49 (3): 61–83.

Buddle, Kathleen. 2005. "Aboriginal Cultural Capital Creation and Radio Production in Urban Ontario." *Canadian Journal of Communication* 30 (1): 7–40.

Culhane, Dara. 2003. "The Spirit Lives within Us: Aboriginal Women in Downtown Eastside Vancouver Emerging into Visibility." *American Indian Quarterly* 27, 3/4 (Summer/Fall): 593–606.

Cunneen, C. (1992). "Policing in Aboriginal Communities." In *Aboriginal Perspectives on Criminal Justice*, edited by C. Cunneen. Sydney: Institute of Criminology.

Curry, Bill. 2006a. "Native Suit Alleges Mismanagement." *The Globe and Mail.* 8 July: A5.

———. 2006b. "No Race-Based Commercial Fishery, Minister Says." *The Globe and Mail.* 14 July: A8.

Dickson-Gilmore, Jane, and Carol LaPrairie. 2005. *Will the Circle Be Unbroken? Aboriginal Communities, Restorative Justice, and the Challenges of Conflict and Change.* Toronto: University of Toronto Press.

Fairclough, Norman. 1985. "Critical and Descriptive Goals in Discourse Analysis." *Journal of Pragmatics* 9: 739–63.

———. 1995. *Media Discourse.* London and New York: Edward Arnold.

———. 2003. *Analyzing Discourse: Textual Analysis and Social Research.* London and New York: Routledge.

Foucault, Michel. 1972. *Archaeology of Knowledge.* London: Tavistock Publications.

Fowler, Roger. 1991. *Language in the News.* New York: Routledge.

Furniss, Elizabeth. 2001. "Aboriginal Justice, the Media, and the Symbolic Management of Aboriginal/Euro-Canadian Relations." *American Indian Culture and Research Journal* 25: 21–36.

Gibson, Gordon. 2005. "Canada's Apartheid Wall." *The Globe and Mail.* 15 July: A13.

The Globe and Mail. 2005. "For Accountability on Native Reserves." 24 October: A14.

Goode, Judith, and Jeff Maskovsky, eds. 2001. *The New Poverty Studies: The Ethnography of Power, Politics and Impoverished Peoples in the United States.* New York: New York University Press.

Green, Ross Gordon. 1998. *Justice in Aboriginal Communities: Sentencing Alternatives.* Saskatoon: Purich Publishing.

Grenier, Marc. 1994. "Native Indians in the English-Canadian Press." *Media, Culture and Society* 16: 313–36.

Guillemin, Jeanne. 1975. *Urban Renegades: The Cultural Strategy of American Indians.* New York and London: Columbia University Press.

Hall, Stuart. 1982. "The Rediscovery of 'Ideology': Return of the Repressed in Media Studies." In *Culture, Society and the Media*, edited by Michael Gurevitch, Tony Bennett, James Curran, and Janet Woollacott, 56–90. New York: Methuen.

Hall, S., C. Critcher, T. Jefferson, J. Clarke, and B. Roberts. 1978. *Policing the Crisis: Mugging, the State, and Law and Order.* London: Macmillan.

Harding, Robert. 2006. "Historical Representations of Aboriginal People in Canadian News Media." *Discourse and Society* 17 (2): 205–35.

Haslip, Susan. 2000. "Aboriginal Sentencing Reform in Canada—Prospects for Success: Standing Tall with Both Feet Planted Firmly in the Air." *E Law* 7 (1). http://www.murdoch.edu.au/elaw/issues/v7n1/haslip71_text.html.

Henry, F., and C. Tator. 2000. "The Theory and Practice of Democratic Racism in Canada." In *Perspectives on Ethnicity in Canada: A Reader*, edited by Madeline A. Kalbach and Warren E. Kalbach, 285–302. Toronto: Harcourt Canada.

———. 2002. *Discourses of Domination: Racial Bias in the Canadian English-Language Press.* Toronto: University of Toronto Press.

Howard-Bobiwash, Heather. 2003. "Women's Class Strategies as Activism in Native Community Building in Toronto 1950–1975." *American Indian Quarterly* 27 (3/4): 566–82.

Hutchinson, Michael. 2002. "Guilty until Proven Innocent: Perception Is Reality." *Aboriginal Times*, 9–15.

Ibbitson, John. 2006. "Aboriginal Poverty and Enormous Challenge." *The Globe and Mail*, 20 September: A4.

Jackson, Deborah Davis. 2002. *Our Elders Lived It: American Indian Identity in the City.* DeKalb: Northern Illinois University Press.

Klein, Gerry. 2002. "Meet the Neighbours: They're Still Parallel Universes but the Worlds of Aboriginals and Whites Are Moving Closer." *Saskatoon Star Phoenix*, 30 November: E1.

Kress, Gunther, and Robert Hodge. 1979. *Language as Ideology.* London: Routledge & Kegan Paul.

LaPrairie, Carol. 1999. "Sentencing Aboriginal Offenders: Some Critical Issues." In *Making Sense of Sentencing*, edited by Julian V. Roberts and David P. Cole, 173–85. Toronto: University of Toronto Press.

Lawrence, Bonita. 2004. *"Real" Indians and Others: Mixed-Blood Urban Native People and Indigenous Nationhood.* University of British Columbia Press.

Lobo, Susan, and Kurt Peters, eds. 2001. *American Indians and the Urban Experience.* New York: Altamira Press.

Miller, Bruce G. 1993. "The Press, the Boldt Decision and Indian–White Relations." *American Indian Culture and Research Journal* 17 (Summer): 99–119.

Miller, John. 2005. "Ipperwash and the Media: A Critical Analysis of How the Story Was Covered." Draft report submitted to Aboriginal Legal Services of Toronto. http://www.attorneygeneral.jus.gov.on.ca/inquiries/ipperwash/policy _part/projects/pdf/ALST_Ipperwash_and_media.pdf.

Murray, Kimberly R. 2003. "Race Relations Draft Report." Aboriginal Legal Services of Toronto. http://aboriginallegal.ca/docs/JWG.htm.

Peach, Ian. 2004. "The Charter of Rights and Off-Reserve First Nations People: A Way to Fill the Public Policy Vacuum?" The Saskatchewan Institute of Public Policy, University of Regina, Public Policy Paper 24. http://www.uregina.ca/ sipp/documents/pdf/PPP24%20I_Peach.pdf#search=%22incrementalism%20in %20Aboriginal%20policy%22.

Pecheux, M. 1982. *Language, Semantics and Ideology: Stating the Obvious.* Trans. H. Nagpal. London: Macmillan.

Peters, Evelyn. 2004. "Three Myths about Aboriginals in Cities." Canadian Federation for the Humanities and Social Sciences, Breakfast on the Hill, Ottawa, Ontario, 25 March. http://fedcan.ca/images/File/PDF/BOH/breakfast -peters0304.pdf.

Pietikainen, Sari. 2003. "Indigenous Identity in Print: Representations of the Sami in News Discourse." *Discourse and Society* 14 (5): 581–609.

Prince, M. J. 2002. "The Return of Directed Incrementalism: Innovating Social Policy in Canada." In *How Ottawa Spends 2002–2003: The Security Aftermath and National Priorities*, edited by G. B. Doern, 176–95. Toronto: Oxford University Press.

Proulx, Craig. 2003. *Reclaiming Aboriginal Justice, Community and Identity.* Saskatoon: Purich Publishing.

Quigley, Tim. 1994. "Some Issues in Sentencing of Aboriginal Offenders." In *Continuing Poundmaker and Riel's Quest: Presentations Made at a Conference on Aboriginal Peoples and Justice*, edited by Richard Gosse, James Youngblood Henderson, and Roger Carter, 269–300. Saskatoon: Purich Publishing.

Razack, Sherene. 2002. *Race, Space and the Law: Unmapping a White Settler Society.* Toronto: Between the Lines.

Robertson, Leslie and Dara Culhane, eds. 2005. *Hide in Plain Sight: Reflections of Life in Downtown Eastside Vancouver.* Vancouver: Talonbooks.

Royal Commission on Aboriginal Peoples. 1996. *Bridging the Cultural Divide: A Report on Aboriginal People and Criminal Justice in Canada.* Ottawa: Minister of Supply and Services Canada.

Rudin, Jonathan. 1999. "Aboriginal Offenders and the Criminal Code: There Is a Good Reason Why the Sentencing Provisions Refer Specifically to Natives." Commentary, *The Globe and Mail*, 9 February, A13

Sivell-Ferri, Christine. 1997. *The Four Circles of Hollow Water.* Ottawa: Supply and Services Canada. Cat. no. JS5-1/15-1997E.

Silver, Jim, et al. 2006. *In Their Own Voices: Building Urban Aboriginal Communities.* Halifax: Fernwood.

Singer, Benjamin D. 1982. "Minorities and the Media: A Content Analysis of Native Canadians in the Daily Press." *The Canadian Review of Sociology and Anthropology* 19 (3): 348–59.

Skea, Warren H. 1993. "The Canadian Newspaper Industry's Portrayal of the Oka Crisis." *Native Studies Review* 9 (1): 15–31.

Statistics Canada. 2005. "Study: Aboriginal People Living in Metropolitan Areas." *The Daily.* 23 June. http://www.statcan.ca/Daily/English/050623/d050623b.htm.

Stackhouse, John. 2001a. "Introduction." Canada's Apartheid. *The Globe and Mail*, 3 November, F1. http://v1.theglobeandmail.com/series/apartheid/stories/introduction.html.

————. 2001b. "Welcome to Harlem on the Prairies." Canada's Apartheid. *The Globe and Mail*, 3 November: F2. http://v1.theglobeandmail.com/series/apartheid/stories/20011103-1.html.

Stewart, Jenny. 2006. "Value Conflict and Policy Change." *Review of Policy Research*. 23 (1): 183–95.

Szuchewycz, Bohdan. 2000. "Re-Pressing Racism: The Denial of Racism in the Canadian Press." *Canadian Journal of Communications* 25 (4): 497–514.

Teo, Peter. 2000. "Racism in the News: A Critical Discourse Analysis of News Reporting in Two Australian Newspapers." *Discourse and Society* 11 (1): 7–49.

————. 2006. "The Fraser Fishery Rules." 15 July: A12.

Trew, Tony. 1979a. "Theory and Ideology at Work." In *Language and Control*, edited by Roger Fowler, Bob Hodge, Gunther Kress, and Tony Trew, 94–116. London: Routledge & Kegan Paul.

————. 1979b. "'What the Papers Say': Linguistic Variation and Ideological Difference." In *Language and Control*, edited by Roger Fowler, Bob Hodge, Gunther Kress, and Tony Trew, 117–56. London: Routledge & Kegan Paul.

van Dijk, Teun A. 1993. *Elite Discourse and Racism*. Newbury Park, CA: Sage.

Warry, Wayne. 2007. *Ending Denial: Understanding Aboriginal Issues*. Peterborough, ON: Broadview Press.

Wetherell, M., and J. Potter. 1992. *Mapping the Language of Racism: Discourse and the Legitimation of Exploitation*. New York: Columbia University Press.

Williams-Mozley, John. 1998. *Explanations of Police Racism*. Oodgeroo Unit Indigenous Guest Speaker & Research Forum, 30 October. Queensland University of Technology. http://www.oodgeroo.qut.edu.au/academic _resources/academicpape/explanations.jsp.

Wood, Linda A., and Rolf O. Kroger. 2000. *Doing Discourse Analysis: Methods for Studying Action in Talk and Text*. Thousand Oaks, London, and New Delhi: Sage Publications.

10
Urban Aboriginal Gangs
and Street Sociality in the Canadian West
Places, Performances, and Predicaments of Transition

Kathleen Buddle

In the shadow of Aboriginal treaty rights and land claims struggles, a different order of "turf wars" is taking shape.[1] Native gang members are engaged in mortal combat over street corners, "stables," schools, and local community centres as they vie for dominance in the street drug trade. This article addresses urban Aboriginal gang formation as a response to perceived crises of "place" among Native youth in Western Canada.

As "the nation" diminishes in analytical import, cities, regions, and other subnational entities acquire significance as relational schemes in which collective processes can be situated. And yet, phenomena such as gangs, media, and political organizations cannot be apprehended by examining the city or the reserve in isolation (Buddle 2008, 2007, 2005, 2004a).[2] Gangs are typically multi–First National, even multicultural, entities, premised on the relinquishing of any cross-cutting cultural loyalties. These are also processual and historically grounded forms of social organization that may incorporate on-reserve kin connections and other affiliates outside city boundaries when opportune. The territories gangs encompass are thus organized according to dense strategic nodes, spread over a broad region (cf. Sassen 2002, 13).

Aboriginal gangs seem to emerge under conditions characterized by tremendous competition over scarce and valued resources. For this reason, membership boundaries tend to be relatively rigid, functioning to exclude access to non-members. Still, the social organization of Native gangs is characteristically dynamic, fluid, and dialectical. In general, urban Native social collectivizing activity is often predicated on a group's ability to continually reformulate boundaries around shifting domains of difference. Ways of constituting and conceiving of group solidarity in a culturally and experientially diverse city setting thus depend on the capacities individuals have for managing a complex array of symbolic material—on their adeptness at shifting the frame and moving between varying range of foci, at forming and reforming and performing identities in different situations (Buddle 2005). In what follows, I attempt to account for the relational nature of street gang experience by addressing the complicated, nuanced, and sometimes contradictory conditions bearing on identity and community formation.

Within the social field of the gang, members will generally maintain commitments to different levels of belonging that anchor their activities in particular places. Where a youth's relatives are themselves gang members, for example, the tension between the commitment to kin and to the gang—to home and street—may be complementary. In many instances, moreover, the place one takes in the gang is analogous to one's cultural place. The politics of cultural and class hierarchies are thus articulated according to an inherited mode of absorbing change rather than being replaced by an entirely novel configuration of relations between capital, goods, and people.

In cities, the nuclear family has become the primary household unit, challenging the extended family network that persists on reserve. Without traditional supports, the urban domestic unit may lack the emotional resources to provide salient socializing spaces. That youth venture toward the street, therefore, need not necessarily entail a rejection of "family" per se but rather a striving toward a more expansive notion of kin. Gangs, as fraternal organizations, often supply the approval, support, and recognition that are otherwise lacking. The gang, additionally, may confer value on new and erstwhile undervalued types of everyday performance.

For urban Native youth, identifications with the street, gangs, and media—each in distinct ways—exist in a dialectical relationship to kin relatedness. Each provides a context for important socio-cultural work to be done. Gangs as new sites of kinship production provide for urban Aboriginal youth, without binding and guiding ties, access to an alternative order of sociability and "hard way" teachings on to "how to be human" (cf. Curtis 1998, 1237).

For boys and girls, peer groups that enable a "cutting of the apron strings" may provide the necessary psychological space for experimenting with symbolic materials, including testing and revalorizing received notions concerning urban masculinity, femininity, and morality; proper collateral and intergenerational alignment; legitimate modes of material accumulation; and correct and incorrect order and agency. It is by re-signifying and reconfiguring these and other intersecting meaning clusters that gang members are able to formulate and perform a unified image of their difference from others. These groups—often born of shared interest and experience—provide new spaces of belonging and facilitate the forging of identifications, outlooks, and behaviours among otherwise alienated youth. Thus, contemporary gangs, much like spaces of Aboriginal media production or political action (Buddle 2004b), appear to represent sites of sedition, where Aboriginal youth create alternative cultural codes and new spaces of fellowship in the city—at once tactically seizing a place for themselves and defying exclusion by "others."

Most often comprising recent arrivals to the city and individuals newly released from corrections facilities, Native youth gangs incorporate individuals in transition—from bush to street, from boy to man, from weak to fit. Gangs provide a viable means for negotiating a range of new territories and processes. Because gangs rely on a complex set of emotional and symbolic ties to internally order their members, they may be especially alluring to those who are without any connections, money, or position. Gangs seem to hail those who yearn for an answer to the demands of place. Former members concede, however, that the cost of membership is high, and few ultimately find in the gang solutions to their existential dilemmas.

Inquiring into the social formation of urban Aboriginal gangs and into the exact practices of sociality in which gang members invest, this chapter examines some of the structural factors that have contributed to the degradation of inner-city prairie neighbourhoods. Employing a social field analysis (Bourdieu 1990), I focus on a specific neighbourhood, gang node, and family, and connect these with constructs that have been refined over a long tradition of gang scholarship.[3]

Placing gangs in certain locales addresses the question about "where" gang activity generally occurs—usually in only certain parts of the city and increasingly on northern reserves. Additionally, this points out the central role of prisons in facilitating gang affiliations among Native offenders. I examine the impact of the social locations and the psychological dispositions of gang members as well as broader social mechanisms on the gang's capacity to carry out its most salient activities. I describe some of the situations and motivations that bear on the thinking and actions of gang members, outlining what appear to be patterns in gang members' complex relationships with their nuclear families, neighbourhoods, and nations. Finally, I show Aboriginal gang activity to be partly a product of historical conditions, policy impacts, structural conditions, and individuals' attempts both to make sense of and make the most of their circumstances. Beyond the themes of cultural diffusion and economic re-structuring, I wish to emphasize that the fluid quality of affiliation that characterizes socio-political collectivizing in Native circles more generally plays out in Aboriginal gang contexts in the recognition of particular tactics of the weak, "disciplinary technologies" or subtle forms of manoeuvre and resistance.

Gang Theory Overview

Gang theorists are at odds as to what socially organizes the gang or street subculture. Most agree about the existence of certain degree of political cohesiveness and adherence to a street code: namely a set of informal rules that govern interpersonal public behaviour. There are as many variations on this code, it would seem, as there are gang studies, however. In addition to the conditioning factors that pervade each geographic locale, gangs are not stable social entities and, as with all cultural fields, they change with time and in response to broader social, political, and economic circumstances. The focus on predominantly adolescent groups, moreover, whose mercurial biorhythms and ontological realities seem to change at a pace unmatched by any other age group, ensures that the many attempts to define "gang" are destined to become obsolete by the time articles delimiting their form come into print. To some extent, the notion of an Aboriginal gang is itself somewhat of a misnomer insofar as these cultural spaces increasingly incorporate non-Native members. The social and cultural influences that inform contemporary gang identities, moreover, do not necessarily emphasize the relationships between Native youth and a white mainstream but are at least partially based upon their interactions with other segments of Aboriginal communities and with other groups of impoverished or racialized youth.

Approaches to gangs as subcultures of violence (Wolfgang and Ferracuti 1967) have gradually given way to analytic frameworks that are now more holistic (Bronfenbrenner 1979), and to ethnographic methods of research (Fleisher 1998, 1995; Vigil 1988, 2002a; Sullivan 1988; Sánchez-Jankowski 1991; Venkatesh 2000). These ethnographic case studies and comparative analyses provide a rich source of information about the ethnic and racial composition of gangs (e.g., Curtis 1998; Cambell 1991; Hagedorn 1988; Moore 1978). While race, ethnicity and class have always been central to gang research, relatively recent efforts to apply feminist theory to analyses of women's participation in gangs provide important interventions into the literature, pointing out new layers of complexity in the study of gangs as domains of contest (Fontaine 2006; Nimmo 2001; Miller 1975; Campbell 1990; Spergel 1995; Curry and Decker 1998; Moore 1991; Chesney-Lind and Joe 1996).[4]

Whereas most gang studies tie gang development to social disorganization and economic deprivation, this study departs from the criminological paradigm, lending attention instead to structure, practice, consciousness, and affect. It interprets gang formation as the expression of tensions arising from individuals' (often competing) investments in different levels of social belonging and political order. Namely, I am interested in the conflict between individual autonomy and the solidarity of the nuclear family, the extended family, the multicultural neighbourhood, and the band or First Nation collective. I show that rapid culture change, migration to the city, the status ambiguity of puberty, and dislocation from the economy, the extended family, and public controls may indeed contribute to a weakening of cultural bonds and to an increasing sense of placelessness (see also Spergel 1992, 130). It is critically important to note that the reserve system is itself a relatively recently invented means of aggregating and ordering Native peoples in both geographic and symbolic space. From their inception, reserve communities have been subjected to a continuing program of disciplining projects, which have ineluctably altered the terms according to which residents confer meaning on different forms of belonging. This renders problematic any facile linking of reserves with traditionalism and social cohesion, or cities with modernity and dissolution. Instead, gang involvement is better understood as a subcultural movement from one liminal form to another. Gangs provide one opportunity for members to temporarily privilege an identification with peers until such a time when an affiliation with family or nationhood or with an interest group assumes greater significance or provides greater advantage.

Where once a sense of cultural identity or nation-consciousness may have been rooted in territory and in the complicated network of relationships with the natural environment, a ritual cycle, or through interactions with extended familial or broader clan groups; the city makes any sort of straightforward transplantation of these cultural practices virtually impossible. Often with no fixed address or with few options for affordable housing, transportation or telecommunication, for example, urban Native individuals may of necessity form more fluid friendship alliances or communal bonds with individuals with whom they are boxed in, within otherwise isolated dwellings, housing projects, and neighbourhoods. Herein, nuclear families and peer groups, more than the material space of ancestral territory, often become both their cultural foundations and their only sense of "home."

This geographic disenfranchisement may have the effect of diminishing the cultural identity or nation-consciousness of young Native people. For those who find themselves unpersuaded by the disciplining effects of traditions and extended families, and equally unaffected by city controls such as schools, police, and employers, urban gangs with their own boundaries, values, rules and styles of sociality emerge to provide structure where there is none. The gang, more than the reserve, the First Nation, or the family, achieves priority as the primary social and economic unit for those urban youth with access to a relatively limited arsenal of defensive manoeuvres and a narrowly imagined repertoire of possible lives.

I argue that while the gang may offer to resolve this crisis of place, it does not alter the broader structural constraints that generate social and political inequities and therefore does little to ameliorate the marginalization Native street gang members generally endure. Moreover, gangs seem to invest tremendous value in capitalist accumulation, in gang solidarity, and in a code of the street; hence, when gang members eventually leave gangs, they find themselves unprepared for an information-based economy, for the mundane responsibilities of family life, and for the forms of civic participation that a broader society recognizes as meaningful. I discuss some of the community-based programs that offer these individuals the tools with which to meaningfully intervene in their own lives. The programs aim to build the social capital necessary for ex-gang members to begin the long process of remaking their "selves" despite the social scarring that a criminal past generally inscribes on their minds and bodies.

Rootless Runners and the Aboriginal Gang Archive

Youth gangs have their origins in the depression era. In Canadian Indian Country, gangs probably first developed and functioned as survival units in the residential schools. The schools typically ruptured both intergenerational relations, segregating children from their parents and grandparents and familial relations, by prohibiting siblings from interacting. Offering a substandard academic education, coercing cultural replacement, and proffering no marketable skills, the schools created new spaces of liminality and classes of Native peoples who came to identify with each other on the basis of their shared sense of exclusion from both Native and non-Native circles. While Aboriginal peoples in general began flowing into

Western cities such as Winnipeg en masse in the 1960s, youth fleeing from residential schools, foster homes, and unlivable reserve circumstances have likely been making their way into cities undetected for some time. Historically, however, there has been a gap in social service records and in programming for youth aged fourteen to eighteen, who are viewed in bureaucratic terms neither as children nor as adults. Few records exist prior to the 1960s documenting their presence, movements, or fates.

Historical circumstances have provided another rationale for Native runaways. Now an elder and community activist living in Winnipeg, Ivy Chaske recounted to me the story of her many failed attempts to escape from residential school throughout the 1960s. Because the authorities would track her down through her relatives on reserve—threatening them, she says, with imprisonment should they fail to report on her where-abouts—Ivy quickly learned to make her way to urban areas. Once inside the city, anonymity provided a convenient foil. There, she studiously avoided all of her blood relations, at least inside administrative time. At night, when social workers were off the clock, youth made efforts to connect with, and to reassure, their local relations. Native social controls were still in effect during this gang era. The mothers of gang members, for example, would regularly dissuade Ivy from affiliating with their sons, reminding her of her responsibilities as a young woman in a chiefly lineage.

Ivy talks about the groups of Native youth who banded together to form fictive kin groups and survival units, stealing food and items they could pawn for money, finding hotel bars that would serve liquor to minors and landlords who would rent party rooms in vacant houses on a nightly basis, selling drugs to make ends meet, fighting often for their lives with other youth gangs, and at once avoiding the authorities at all costs. Ivy recalls that the friendship centre (founded in 1959) became an important refuge and meeting place for runaway youth and adults alike.[5]

Even today, youth in crisis often take to the streets during their adolescent years, leaving troubled foster homes or other domestic situations. Some may find refuge in group homes. Others are simply cut adrift and left entirely to their own devices. There continue to be few programs that speak directly to the needs of this demographic, despite that their numbers are growing exponentially.

Aboriginal migration into Winnipeg grew substantially in the 1970s; however, by the time Native families began moving into affordable, usually inner city, housing, post-industrialization was well under way. The low-end jobs for which Native migrants were qualified had largely disappeared (Silver 2006). Deindustrialization thus closed off the blue collar industrial and manufacturing sector—an important avenue of exit for gang youth (Venkatesh and Levitt 2000:432). At the same time, advances in media ensured that Aboriginal peoples would be exposed to messages of wealth and luxury, taunting new migrants with items and lifestyles that would remain palpably out of reach. Despite rising expectations, even among the highly skilled workers, few Aboriginal newcomers would be able to overcome the discrimination of a largely undereducated non-Native managerial class and find meaningful employment in the city. This, in combination with the social effects of more than a century of colonial policy, contributed to the under-representation of Aboriginal peoples in the Winnipeg labour force. Gangs provided participation in the informal economy, offering one solution to poverty and despair. While Canadian authorities have been monitoring Aboriginal gang activity for some time, newspaper reports and the Canadian Security and Information Services Annual Report (CSIS 2004) advises that there has been a dramatic upsurge in Aboriginal gang activity in major urban centres on the prairies where Aboriginal gangs have reached "crisis" proportions. Winnipeg is commonly referred to as the Aboriginal "gang capital" of Canada (Dohla 2003).[6] A report based on a national survey of youth gangs conducted by the Royal Canadian Mounted Police asserts that youth gangs are shifting away from a defensive territorial practices to offensive, aggressive strategies (RCMP 2006, 7). It is worth noting that crime figures, as Jean and John Comaroff contend, are often cited as a symptom of the "state of disorder" in the land. And yet, crime statistics are characteristically indeterminate insofar as they are the dual product of police and public reporting. They inevitably fluctuate in proportion to the efficacy of the legal enforcement and information services and according to the amount of trust the public places in them (2006, 219–20). It is therefore plausible that, as sociologist, Mike Davis insists, "like the Tramp scares in the nineteenth century, or the Red scares in the twentieth, the contemporary Gang scare has become an imaginary class relationship, a terrain of pseudo-knowledge and fantasy projection" (cited in Boga 1994, 486).

In direct response to the public outcry concerning the fatal gang shooting of a young non-Native man in 1997, the municipal government created the position of Gang Prevention Coordinator to oversee monthly meetings of the Inter-Agency Gang Coalition (Nimmo 2001, 3). Only when the Aboriginal gang issue became a problem for urban administrators and non-Native residents did the issue attract any serious attention from policy-makers.

To make matters worse, the alleged rise in Native crime rates has not been translated into social programs but rather into the tightening of laws concerning vagrancy, prostitution, and other legislation that increasingly circumscribes the lives of the disadvantaged. It has also provided for greater funding for corrections institutions and the Winnipeg Police Services. In 1995, the latter initiated its special Gang Unit and "gang archive." The database consists of information concerning an individual's tattoos, wearing of gang colours, and affiliations with gang members. The politics of police recognition are such, moreover, that virtually every assembly of Native youth—from those who engage in illegal property offences and violent acts, to those who rally together in support of political causes—could conceivably provide reasonable cause for police questioning.

In contradiction to the cultural dissolution thesis, the fact that urban Native youth are unanimously cast as criminal suspects may unwittingly support a nation-consciousness of sorts. Nominally viewed and often self-identified as reserve migrants, Native youth who populate cities in western Canada are marked out not only by overt signs of difference but by less obvious birthmarks, such as dress, customs, speech patterns, and dialects. Thus, even for members of third- and fourth-generation urban residents, the city may always represent a foreign place for the simple fact that they are denied full civic participation in it.

In the general public's imagination, urban space continues to register as a state of Aboriginal "out-of-placeness." Historically, because Aboriginal peoples were prohibited from participating in the private property regime and from migrating without state consent, they were effectively confined to reserves. Those reserves furthest away from southern Canadian social and economic centres attained the mark of the "traditional" and the "authentic." These are spaces where Canadians are able to image that a continuous tradition of land-based practice is plausible. Living off the land has become synonymous with in the public imagination with "real" Aboriginality.

Native peoples in Winnipeg's North End, on the other hand, assert rights based on forms of cultural difference that are difficult to articulate with the conceptual framework of modernity. Urban Indians continue to be imagined as matter "out of place." Identified as having failed to live up to formulaic renditions of "traditionalism," urban residents are structurally ambiguous, defying the morality of properly construed (marketable) cultural difference and defacing the logic of the commodity.

This is no more clearly evinced than in an advertisement placed on and then removed from a Winnipeg-based used-merchandise-exchange website (in March 2010) that offered a "free Native extraction service." Depicting Native youth as vermin-like "pesky little buggers hanging outside your home, in the back alley or on the corner," the ad writer positions Native youth as both subhuman and as belonging more properly to the wilderness. It proposes "free extraction services to relocate them to their habitat" (*Winnipeg Free Press* 2010).

Winnipeg's North End, moreover, has come to bear the added symbolic burden of comprising the city's dystopic "gangland territory." Newer intercultural black street gangs, such as the African Mafia and the Mad Cowz, and interracial gangs, such as the B-Sides, have established themselves in the city's West End, where low-income East African immigrant families are apt to settle. That race is not the primary organizing principle for these street gangs (which have incorporated Native and white members) forces theorists to consider the ways that immigration and urbanization, cultural production and consumption, colonialism and oppression, and struggles for dignity operate across ethnic, racial, cultural, regional, and temporal bounds (Alvarez 2007: 56).

As veritable containers of "social problems" these areas have become synonymous with the very notion of disorder. More often than not, the dual partitioning becomes conflated, such that urban Aboriginality and the raced underclass are uncritically coupled with chaos. The North End serves as the metaphorical antithesis to a "properly" lived civic space.

While Native street gangs are often characterized as the rootless antithesis to respectable, sedentary, traditional Native peoples and other citizens of the city, gangs are at once collective and contradictory expressions of contemporary First Nations culture and politics. Internally fractured and currently without real leaders, however, gangs lack the political consciousness and organizational expertise to engage in any form of concerted political action. Instead, they point more to an everyday style of warfare, occurring just below the surface and requiring subtle tactics and unconventional forms of resistance.

Although often conceived more as the surrendering to the sense of desolation among poor urban youth, Aboriginal youth gangs are better understood as comprising relatively diverse interpretive groups who at different moments in their "gang careers" are likely to assume differentiated positions in relation to other youth groups and to the non-Native and Native mainstreams. In general, Native street gang practice demonstrates all five of the categories of resistance that Wilson (2002) demarcates on a resistance–passivity continuum. Thus, in many respects, gang practice corresponds more with "a struggle for dignity and against its denial" (Alvarez 2007, 55) and proceeds more like the march of the "undead" than a lemming-like procession toward certain death.[7]

Comparing Canadian census data (2006), crime statistics (CCJS 2005), and policy reports (Silver 2006) reveals that Native crime rates in Winnipeg seem to have kept pace with Aboriginal urban migration rates and with the decline in jobs in skilled and unskilled labour. These figures, however, are seldom presented in conjunction. It is a critical omission that exempts social-policy-makers from moral responsibility, and shifts the blame from the conditions of a post-social welfare order onto the individuals who must endure its misfortunes.

To make matters worse, although already economically marginalized and ethnically marked as majority non-members, once they join Native gangs, individuals enter the service of larger more organizationally complex gangs such as the Bandidos or Hells Angels. "Aboriginal Gangs in Manitoba: A Preliminary Report" (Buddle, MKO, and SCO 2006) reveals that the Zig Zag Crew—an arm of the Hells Angels motorcycle club—is primarily responsible for organizing and for implementing a systematic infiltration of gang activity into the northern reserves of Manitoba.[8] Aboriginal gangs merely provide the footwork in this scheme. By distributing new and ever more dangerous drugs and exploiting Native women and youth, Native gangs—doing the dirty work for larger non-Native criminal organizations—carry forth the project of socio-cultural decay that colonizers began long ago.[9] Native gangs may therefore "represent" in a tangible form the process whereby the subaltern becomes undertaker.

When his son was shot by a Native gang member, Aboriginal Peoples Television Network's news director, Bruce Spence, surmised, "The white man has us exactly where he wants us. Our young men, who should be warriors, have lost complete sight of who they are and what they should be doing" (The Drum 2000, 40). Tactically, gangs may attempt to harness elements of state power to their advantage through a conscious mimetic inversion, which recognizes the cruelty that attends the mighting of right, and then celebrates it. Intentionally inflicting pain on and terrorizing the weakest and most alienated inhabitants of their own neighbourhoods become the gang's recognized means for objectifying the individuated pain and childhood traumas of its members. Although they successfully support survival under circumstances of extreme duress, in feeding on their own gangs nevertheless claim a pyrrhic victory.

According to the 2006 Canadian census, the Native population of Winnipeg grew to 68,380 in 2006, or nearly 10 percent of the city population, from 56,000 in 2001. Nearly half of this population is under twenty-five years of age. The Winnipeg Police Street Gang unit reports confirm that of the two thousand active gang members in Winnipeg, 70 percent are of Aboriginal descent (Constant 2006, 11). Aboriginal community organizations that regularly work with gang members estimate that while the number of Aboriginal women gang members are low, women's rate of gang affiliation through boyfriends, family, and other neighbourhood associations is as high as 80 percent among the clients they serve (Nimmo 2001, 7). Manitoba Native gang members belong to groups such as the Manitoba Warriors, Indian Posse, Redd Alert, Deuce, Nine O, Native Syndicate, North End Brotherhood, West End Boyz, and the TOL (The Over Lords) among many others. Winnipeg gangs are expanding, infiltrating northern reserves, and are becoming increasingly violent. The gangs sustain themselves primarily through the traffic of illegal drugs. They thrive as well on the avails of prostitution, extortion, money lending, illegal gambling, and insurance fraud. They have developed home bases in the northern cities The Pas, Thompson, and Flin Flon in order to distribute drugs throughout on-reserve Manitoba First Nation and Métis communities. According to the "official" crime statistics, Winnipeg currently has the highest youth violence rate in the country (CCJS 2005).

Representin' on the Range: Cowboy Indians and the Media Frontier

The street gang subcultures appear to comprise individuals who are unwilling to passively succumb to marginality, those for whom "Mcjobs" are not a viable option (despite that they generally offer better remuneration), yet those who are unable to imagine futures for themselves as professionals, tradespeople, or with long-term careers of any sort. In an effort to overcome social and political insignificance and in defiance of cultural liminality, individuals may actively reconstitute their identities by selectively combining fragments of their idiosyncratic and cultural pasts with their present realities.

Gangsta rap, hip-hop culture, film, television news coverage of gangland activities, and other forms of popular culture continue to provide powerful identifications for would-be gang members. According to former Manitoba Warrior's co-founder and president, and current anti-gang activist Brian Contois,[10] influences as diverse as Greek mythology, the *Godfather* films, biker gangs, and rap music came to bear heavily on the way he and the dozen-odd fellow founding members modelled the Warriors. Still, the digital divide that separates the Native from the non-Native population of Canada persists as a distinguishing characteristic of Aboriginal gangs. While larger biker gangs, for example, are able to make use of advances in telecommunications—using websites to post meeting dates and engaging in a variety of computer-based criminal activities—Native gangs, while making creative uses of cell phones, and prodigious contributions to the worlds of Facebook, YouTube, and Bebo, do not generally possess the capacities for cyber crime.

Already a work unit—the founding members of the Warriors were employed as bouncers at Winnipeg's Pine Creek Hotel bar—the nascent gang styled itself on other groups, such as the Outlaws biker gang, and sported logos on their vests and jackets. The Warriors and Outlaws, moreover, were structurally analogous, each having a president, vice-president, and sergeant-at-arms. As in the biker subculture, would-be members were required to complete an apprenticeship program, known as "striking." Contois concedes that when he co-formed the organization, it lacked any concrete links with Aboriginal traditions but was designed to meet certain objectives. He explains:

> I was unable to find any employment and gangs were becoming a threat to my children and my community. I felt that I needed to do something to solve these two major problems in my life so I started an organization called "The Warriors." The Warriors was founded on a code of ethics aimed at bringing some level of morality, pride, and dignity to a way of life that most poor inner-city Native men like myself had no choice but to follow. I wanted to create an alternative to the vicious gangs that were bullying our communities and seducing our children. The Warriors was only for adults and the rules of conduct were enforced to ensure that members of the organization did not act outside the code of conduct. I also wanted to create some level of employment for the adult men in my community who were suffering from despair of being unable to find jobs in mainstream society. (Contois n.d.)

Brian Contois spent the first eleven years of his life in the care of his grandmother on the Pine Creek Anishinaabe reserve. His father, a violent alcoholic, abruptly relocated Brian and his five brothers to the city. Here, without meaningful relations or familiar alliances to comfort his landing, he would come to experience differential treatment in school and routine attacks by the gangs that operated throughout Winnipeg's North End, such as the Black Aces, the Black Knights, the Logans, the Spartans, the Lords of Hell (a mixed Native, Métis, and white gang) and the Bravos, who would later become the Hells Angels. For Contois, who says "I felt something was there that wasn't there before," the city made racism palpable and mere survival a daily battle. Within his nuclear family, Brian's primary role from the ages of eleven to fourteen (when forced to move out), was to protect his mother from his father's repeated beatings. He is the only one of the six boys in his family to become a gang member. Like Contois, Ervin Chartrand's mother hailed from the Pine Creek Reserve, but Ervin and his siblings were born and raised in Winnipeg. Fellow bouncers and founding Warriors members, Chartrand and two of his brothers, Pat and Ernest, identify strongly with the Métis heritage of their father, whose premature death, Ervin says, drove their mother to alcoholism. Two other Chartrand siblings would successfully avoid gang involvement.

A study of Navajo gangs in the United States revealed that when the traditional extended family kinship structure breaks down, certain youth tend to establish a sense of connectedness by forging strong ties with television, music, and movie personalities and with popular culture in general (Mendenhall and Armstrong 2004). For gang members without positive parental influence, little knowledge of Aboriginal history, and lack of trust in community leaders, actors and hip-hop artists may provide more consistent and therefore consequential role models.

In 1992 Winnipeg, the Manitoba Warriors would come into being on the heels of its main rival, the Indian Posse. The following year, the Native Syndicate formed in the ranges of the Stony Mountain Penitentiary. Originally serving as the enforcement arm of the Manitoba Warriors, the Syndicate would eventually branch off to form an independent body. Both the Posse and the Warriors have successfully spread across Manitoba, Saskatchewan, northwestern Ontario, and Alberta. The Indian Posse, according to Contois, drew its inspiration from the American gang of the same name. It was the largest gang and most culturally "Aboriginal" in membership and activities, and sported a council form of leadership rather than the more corporate governance-by-president model. Deuce, known as the Warrior's "farm team," was composed of younger members and is more multicultural. Anecdotal information and newspaper stories indicate that American gang movies such as Colors had a strong impact on the identity of the Deuce gang. Members selectively incorporated elements of dress, gesture, and language from this film and the televised L.A riots of 1990 (*First Nations Drum* 2000). The Native Syndicate drew from mafia movies its style and is internally organized along La Cosa Nostra lines, with a boss, an underboss, and a consigliore as the three ranking positions.

The Internet provides an endless store of resources for configuring gang styles. Jessie McKay is a former Native Syndicate member and one of the first Native women to attain full membership status in a Native gang. She uses her culminated knowledge of street life to advocate for youth as a "Negative Life Style Presenter" and as the Manitoba Representative for the Congress of Aboriginal Peoples. As an outreach worker, she worked vigilantly to discourage the spontaneous displays of "Crip walking" the Native youth in her care at the Circle of Courage Safe House performed. Because the youth had appropriated these gestures from studious attention to YouTube, she was forced to rigorously monitor their computer use during program times. Despite her best efforts, high levels of FASD and psychological disorders among gang youth today, she asserts, make constant supervision and assisted-living provisions the only real avenues of exit for a growing number of gang recruits.

Brian Contois insists that the Warriors' original code of ethics and selective membership distinguished the organization from other Native and non-Native gangs. Contois's code ensured that pedophiles and other sociopaths, women, anyone under eighteen, mental incompetents, and addicts would be denied membership in the Warriors. Applicants were carefully screened for skills and character. A strong work ethic, a drivers' licence, and the capacity to manage and make money were some of the qualifications applicants were expected to possess. The Warriors accepted both Native and non-Native members. Unlike American gangs, Warriors undertook no formal initiation; instead, inductees were expected to prove their worth and move up through the gang by competently performing in its service.

Where police had failed to protect the neighbourhood, Contois asserts that the Warriors successfully invoked the threat of collective violence as a potent disincentive to the bullying behaviours of the other North End gang members who enjoyed a demographic advantage. He insists that the Warriors and the code of ethics he drafted—which was adopted widely by other gangs—had a stabilizing effect on what had been, until that point, a chaotic free-for-all. Contois maintains that ongoing difficulties in managing the increasingly defiant younger gang members made the gang as a political enterprise progressively unviable.

Despite common misgivings about Native gang members, former Indian Posse leader, Dwayne Dussome maintains that "nobody really wants to be in a gang and go around robbing and stealing from people" (*Indian Life* 1997, 1). Ervin Chartrand, former vice president of the Manitoba Warriors, reinforces the point that the factors influencing gang solidarity are frequently misrecognized: "Guys that came in had to do things ... violent things. And it's not fun. You think it's a lot of money. You see these guys driving around with fast cars, you know, gold chains, a lot of money in their pockets, girls. That doesn't last very long.... There's no happiness there, none at all."[11] Contois, McKay, Chartrand, and Dussome maintain that few would join gangs if legitimate alternatives were imaginable.

In 1997, Assembly of First Nations (AFN) Grand Chief, Phil Fontaine, approached Native gangs for information concerning how to eliminate the conditions conducive to gang formation. Brian Contois accepted the position of Special Advisor to the Assembly of Manitoba Chiefs (AMC), for which he was to draft a program to deter youth from entering gangs. Upon agreeing to collaborate, however, Contois made his position as president of the Warriors public. He was arrested shortly thereafter for possession of $325 worth of marijuana—though not before submitting his program to the AMC. On entering Stony Mountain Penitentiary, and to everyone's surprise, both Contois and Chartrand renounced their gang affiliation, avowing to commit themselves entirely to the cause of pro-youth activism. (Chartrand was arrested later, after the Manitoba Warriors become the target of an excruciatingly expensive police sting, known as "Project Northern Snow.")

An ex-member of the old guard, Contois insists that present day gangs have little honour. Where once, members adhered to the code of ethics, today chaos again prevails. Chartrand agrees. He insists that old-school gangs met to fight face to face; whereas today with the pervasiveness of shooting warfare, "you don't even see your enemies anymore." Contois attributes these cultural strains to the discrepancies between the rules and duties of first-generation or "original" and those of second- and third-generation gang members, particularly regarding drug use and child exploitation. The Warriors have since splintered into three gangs: Central Warriors, Ruthless, and Manitoba Warriors. Without the leadership to combat the oppositional "individualist" tendencies among members that are rooted in monetary gain, street commerce is eroding the organizational cohesion of these contemporary bonds of brotherhood. As on the Hobbema reserve not far from Edmonton, Alberta, where there are now more than thirteen gangs, some with as few as three members, Native gangs in Winnipeg have arrived at a critical moment in their evolution. The shift toward increasingly capitalistic social relations signals the growing unlikelihood of any sort of organized insurgent politics emerging in their midst. As low level sales operations, moreover, street gangs pose little threat to mainstream Canadian control over cash and commodities.

Contois, Chartrand, and McKay now provide educational workshops for at-risk urban youth. Not incidentally, employed through government and corrections initiatives, they once again find themselves at the mercy of capricious bureaucratic benevolence.

While media reports play up the "cowboy mentality" of Aboriginal gangs, lending undue attention to sensationalized images of gun-toting hoodlums, they do not generally account for the reasons youth join gangs, nor why gang conflicts yield fatal results. Ex-gang members attribute the increased bloodshed to the breakdown of street ethics, among other factors. In 2006, former Winnipeg gang member James Lathlin was also providing anti-gang workshops. That year, he resolved to reinvigorate old-school values with the aim of reducing street violence. Conceding that there was little hope of eliminating gangs altogether, he therefore drafted his own code of ethics—one virtually identical to Contois's original gang rules of conduct. Lathlin's strategy for communicating the code to Native gang members involved circulating the rules via the local Aboriginal media. Winnipeg based: *Thunder Voice* and *Grassroots News* newspapers, Aboriginal youth-focused *SAY Magazine*, and the Aboriginal People's Television Network national news all featured the code. These rules prohibited shooting in public areas, assaulting innocent bystanders, gang colours or flashing gang signs in the vicinity of schools, daycares or playgrounds, selling drugs to pregnant women, recruiting minors for the purposes of prostitution or other crimes to pay off drug debts, and turf building in schools or shopping areas (Owen 2006). Insiders tell me that there were a number of factors that worked to diminish Lathlin's influence in gang circles—despite the wide attention he received from media professionals—including suspicions that he had neither sufficiently extracted himself from gang life nor attained enough success in the formal economy to persuasively model change. The proposed rules, consequently, had no disciplining power.

In the city, Native peoples must negotiate a variety of administrative entities—"jumping through hoops"—to avail themselves of the basic life necessities, keeping pace with bureaucratic rhythms and mainstream political agendas. All this occurs, moreover, under the constant scrutiny of order-obsessed civilian and state governing structures. Gang members resist state surveillance and bureaucratic regulation, which effectively render all aspects of their lives "public," by penetrating the private spaces of others—through home invasions, car and identity theft, beatings, and rape.

Because it is largely other urban Aboriginal residents who are the victims of gang violence, however, Native gangs do not pose any immediate threat to the established social structure, nor do they symbolize "anarchy." The territory over which gangs battle is not ideological, but material. As Dutton rejoins, "backstreet conflicts are aimed at survival, not the articulation of principles. They are always about 'making do,' not seizing power" (1999, 74). The gang way, is therefore less an occupational choice than a temporary survival strategy.

Street Socialization

Members of Aboriginal gangs in Winnipeg seem to view gangs in contradictory ways—as integral components of the community or as neighbourhood institutions, at once performing services for and exploiting their "neighbours." Like the Mexican gang youth whose lives Zatz and Portillo document (2000, 382), Winnipeg Native youth often see themselves as protectors of the community, point to the police as troublemaking interlopers, and charge the media with failing to cover the economic problems that pervade poor non-white neighbourhoods. Gang members have also defiantly re-signified a variety of discourses and practices through which they are positioned by others in unsavoury subject positions. Juxtaposing a series of apparently contradictory principles, they dress and act tough in order to avoid trouble. They tactically pose as gangsters to protect themselves as well as to accumulate street capital. They use the public's fear of Indians to their advantage, marking themselves as "risks to security," at once performing as dangerous, industrious, and unpredictable.

What follows is an examination of "street socialization" (Vigil 1996; Bourgois 1995), a term that refers to the processes by which youth become incorporated into "street" groups such as gangs, how they come to identify with street culture, and how street values become normalized.

According to Ervin Chartrand, the gang lifestyle represented less a conscious pursuit than the logical course of his life script. At an anti-gang workshop he provided at the Nor'West Lighthouse (safehouse) in Winnipeg's North End, he explained that: "Back then, there were no community centres or people coming to your school to talk about gangs. Growing up, I didn't have any role models, only my brother … He was involved in gangs. I was ten years old when I was introduced to gangs and joined my first gang at age fourteen."

Unlike ethnic gangs, Native gang members in Manitoba may have had parents or grandparents who attended residential schools. These guardians would likely have suffered the ill effects produced through several generations of mandatory residential schooling. Inside these institutions, children were deprived of healthy parenting models and may have experienced or witnessed abuse, humiliation, and trauma. Residential schools dispossessed Native children of the very traditional teachings that function to orient behaviour and to give life meaning. Deprived of these elements of Aboriginal social capital and receiving an insufficient socialization in mainstream cultural ways, Native residential school "survivors" were abandoned to a liminal netherworld. Often to anaesthetize their pain, school survivors turned to drugs or alcohol. One gang member recalls: "When I was growing up, my little brother and I had to take care of ourselves. My dad wasn't around and my mom is an alcoholic. She would like, I don't know, she would spend all our money on booze, so me and my little brother had to take care of ourselves a lot" (Buddle, MKO, and SCO 2006, 32).

Many of the Manitoba gang members interviewed for "Aboriginal Gangs in Manitoba: A Preliminary Report" indicated that gangs offered them a sense of relationship that neither their families nor nations were able to provide. In *Patrick Ross*, Chartrand's short documentary film of a would-be-gang-member-turned-visual-artist, Ross theorizes that gang members simply "understand unity in a different way." Another gang member compares gang unity with a sort of fictive kinship: "Lots of people have that feeling like, this is my family now. You know? I never had a real family growing up. I feel real good now. Some people ... they really love the gang. They really love the gang lifestyle" (Buddle, MKO, and SCO 2006:22).

Gang members who claim to have been "born into" the gang or who associate with its members by virtue of their affiliations with relatives actively participating in gang activities may be deeply emotionally invested in the gang as well as physically connected to the territory—the material boundaries of the neighbourhood—in which gangs operate. Gang membership thus represents a gradual process of inculcation, rather than a discrete "event." Gangs recognize particular forms of intimacy and provide approval, a sense of "place" and belonging. In an urban multi–First National environment, this form of solidarity often takes precedence over collective identifications with Cree, Anishinabe or Métis Nations or with any sort of reserve-based geographic or political entities.

Gang life represents a pragmatic and rational form of urban subsistence and provides for the material necessities of a "home." In addition to high unemployment, there is a chronic shortage of affordable housing in Winnipeg. Most inner-city Aboriginal families live well below the poverty line. Fast and relatively easy money is a powerful incentive to gang involvement for youth with strong consumerist sensibilities and few marketable skills. One gang member characterized his first illegal acts as crimes of necessity—as rational and adaptive survival strategies:

> I started doing crime when I was a kid. I would go down to the corner store and steal food so my brother and I could eat. And [my mother] would get me to steal food for her too. I guess that's when I started getting into crime. It wasn't really for gangs, because I wasn't involved in gangs yet. But yeah, I had to make sure my little brother could eat. We didn't really go to school all that much, because my mom was always wanting us to do something for her. Then, when I got older, I started doing shit like boosting cars and rolling people. I guess that's when I started getting into gangs. (Buddle, MKO, and SCO 2006:24)

Sexual abuse and exploitation experiences, often by blood relatives, can lead to pent-up rage that may manifest itself in hyper-masculine (violent) behaviour among boys and self-destructive behaviour among girls. Many of the gang members interviewed disclosed having observed men abuse their female relatives over the course of their upbringing. Aboriginal gang members are highly likely to have experienced family violence and exploitation themselves. Many, moreover, are aware that they have been deprived of some very basic life necessities and harbour anger toward those whom they feel orchestrated their misery. They resent those who neglected to protect them and the system that blames them for their own misfortunes. This anger manifests itself in destructive anti-social acts and violence.[12]

There are few public spaces in cities where Native youth can congregate to engage in constructive activities outside of schools. Vigil (2003) notes that "being new to the city and separate from mainstream people and institutions limit the access, exposure, and identification that one has with the dominant culture and customs, which thus blocks avenues for integration." Unable to afford or find their way into non-Native sports and leisure groups, Native youth may begin to feel frustrated and even aggressive (when coupled with residential overcrowding). Space or "turf" thus becomes highly valued, and groups may find they must compete for places to assemble, shop, and socialize with members of the opposite sex, among other social outlets and activities. Recreation centres, bars, malls, and parks become contentious; they become potential battlegrounds for gang conflict.

Larger institutions, such as schools, rarely equitably serve poor, minority populations. This is evinced where there are deficient communication corridors or weak ties between schools and Aboriginal homes. In the classroom, the special predicament of Native students may be exacerbated when language and cultural differences interfere with learning. In addition to being underfunded, programs for students with learning disabilities tend to be premised on a normative Euro-Canadian cultural model that retrenches the alienation of non-white students. The social control mechanisms that families and schools would normally provide, therefore, are all but absent for the most marginalized segments of the Aboriginal population.

For some inner-city Aboriginal youth, attaining dominant educational, health, and even social goals is simply beyond the scope of their capabilities. Without these, they may find it difficult both to imagine themselves as employed and to attain employment. They often lack the motivation and discipline to attain work experience. They may lack family or community role models and connections to draw on when imagining what they might be capable of and generally cannot draw on connections established in the previous generation for job opportunities or for references.

With such structural barriers in place, youth may seek different opportunity paths such as illicit or illegal ventures that often entail violence (Merton 1949; Cloward and Ohlin 1960; Kornhauser 1978; Covey, Menard, and Franzese 1992; Moore 1978). It is critical to point out, however, that not everybody in such places or with such status necessarily becomes a violent gang member because of where they are and what they do. In fact, the great majority of youths in these situations avoid involving themselves in gang activities. Even they, however, must learn to negotiate the violence—structural and physical—that pervades their social spaces. Ervin Chartrand maintains that the "cycle of violence" will end when youth harness their collective strength. Youth, who are already rupturing hegemonic conceptions of kinship that are grounded in Euro-North American ideologies of individualism and the nuclear family, must contest the *practices* of the gang, though not necessarily the social entity in and of itself. Were gangs to collectively engage in constructive socio-political, or legitimate economic, activities, or "teamwork," the network units could provide a mobilizing force for social action in Aboriginal neighbourhoods. As one nine-year-old participant in the lighthouse network informs, "me and some friends have a gang called 'the Helper Posse.' We just help people."

Colonialism's cumulative effects—low education, inadequate housing, abuse and neglect, intergenerational transmission by mothers and fathers of FASD and other addictions-related disorders, the possibility of mental illness or simply poor general health, inequality, discrimination, and poverty—in conjunction with the imbalance between punitive law enforcement and preventive social welfare policies continue to push many youth into the streets.[13] Additionally, in the absence of home or school socialization, street socialization emerges, and the peer group becomes the surrogate source of support. All of these factors may lead youth to identify in contradictory ways with the street, as well as with their families and with First Nationhood. Gang members confirm that with little education, no training, and few job prospects, the economic activity of gang life seems like a rational solution to their circumstances. For these individuals, the likelihood of incarceration presents a reasonable risk.

Conclusion: Doing Time Out of Place

Out of home, and aligned with families and nations in complicated and often competing ways, Native youth in Winnipeg are increasingly finding their way into "the big house." Not coincidentally, the most common means of gang expansion is from within the Canadian penal system. When incarcerated, even for a relatively minor charge, Native youth will likely become affiliated with a gang. Generally, inmates will join under duress to avail themselves of the protection gangs provide. When released, former inmates are pressured to serve as a contact person for the gang, sell drugs, and solicit selected community members to join the gang. Whereas the American Indian Movement—with a resoundingly anti-gang orientation—formed on the streets of Minneapolis mainly by ex-cons who had learned their cultures while in prison (Compton 1997, A11), the Warriors and other Winnipeg gangs would come to use the prison population as their primary recruiting grounds.

In 2004 there were 12,653 inmates in Canadian Correctional Institutions. Of these, 17 percent were of Aboriginal descent. The majority of individuals are held in institutions in the prairie provinces. The Province of Manitoba Correctional Institutions statistics indicate that 1,300 adults and 200 youth were incarcerated in 2004. Of these, 68 percent were of Aboriginal descent.

According to a report conducted by Jim Silver, Joan Hay, and Peter Gorgen for the Canadian Centre for Policy Alternatives (2006), Aboriginal-operated community-based organizations in Winnipeg's inner city, have designed highly effective alternatives for newly released inmates, which aim to ameliorate urban Aboriginal unemployment. Urban Circle Training Centre, for example, and the people at Ogijiita Pimatiswin Inamatwin work with young Aboriginal gang members to develop on-the-job construction skills and offer job placement afterwards. Although the program is highly effective, the organizations are chronically underfunded.

Brian Contois maintains that Winnipeg Aboriginal youth are not accessing some of the traditional teachings programs, moreover, for the reason that the alleged ex-gang members operating them are in fact still active and using the government funds to bolster their ongoing recruiting or criminal activities. This is precisely what happened with Winnipeg's Paa Pii Wak safe-house project, which survived for six years on government funds as a gang-operated front for the provision of early release from prison for fellow gang members.

The inner-city-based Circle of Courage Safe House program that Jessie McKay helped to initiate provides, on the other hand, pro-youth programs, emphasizes neo-traditional teachings, endeavours to re-signify masculinity and family, and replaces errant forms of gang solidarity with more constructive versions of nation-consciousness and neighbourhood responsibility. As with those of Ervin Chartrand, and Brian Contois, the life-story-based workshops Jessie McKay provides to youth groups across Manitoba deglamorize the gangs. Spiritual advisors who engage at-risk youth tend to provide prescriptive advice, encouraging youth to develop healthy minds and bodies, and emphasize strength, hard work, and responsibility to oneself and to one's family over the gang. They encourage youth to plan for the long term rather than indulge in the immediate and draw from traditions that prize children as sacred gifts, that hold women in high esteem, and that would see the weak protected, not exploited. The testimonials Contois, Chartrand, and McKay provide, on the other hand, add to the youth's imaginative repertoires a host of prohibitive exemplars. Displaying their scars and tattoos, enumerating their health issues, and recounting their ongoing difficulties in establishing successful relationships and attaining meaningful employment, they embody the cumulative social and political consequences that gang means procure.

Contois now aligns himself with the Okijida Warriors—a traditional Anishinaabe secret society responsible for community protection. Jessie McKay transported her skills to Regina, where she now provides outreach services for the Regina Anti-Gang Strategy (RAGS). Chartrand has become a filmmaker in the Aboriginal media community. McKay and Chartrand, moreover, have linked forces with the Toronto-based group, the Seven Generations Healing Network (SGHN). This circle of Aboriginal activists updates the members of its growing network—the Peynahweechayhin Youth Empowerment Group—via a Facebook page. In addition to a proposed safe house, the group plans to inaugurate an annual "Walk of Nations" across Canada to raise awareness about Aboriginal addictions, abuse, homelessness, and incarceration. The team hopes to raise funds for the construction of a Toronto-based safe house/rehabilitation centre premised on Native healing practices.

In the meantime, young inner-city Native men and boys and an increasing number of young women in Winnipeg continue to endure family and school conflicts, cultural antagonism, and poverty. In addition, they are likely to endure personal invalidation, anomalous parenting experiences, and highly stressful gender and age-role expectations—all of which contribute to issues of devalued self-esteem. Those who are raised in a violent environment, as Barron rejoins, are likely programmed for battle (1997). They may seek out communal bonds or surrogate families in other locations, but tend to accept violence as normative in the autonomous cultural spaces they do carve out. Gangs realign relations of unity, respect, and refuge and devise their own means for deriving material benefit from these re-significations. They also offer collective strength, social recognition, and a pseudo family structure—dysfunctional though it may be—in the perceived absence of legitimate alternatives. Ultimately, with material rather than social or political goals, however, the promise of gang solidarity is elusive. At an anti-gang workshop at the Indian and Métis Friendship Centre in Winnipeg, Ervin Chartrand concedes that while he once associated the gang with family, time served in a Stony Mountain Penitentiary range proved illuminating: "I tried to sit with the brothers. They wouldn't let me sit with them. I sat at different tables with different gang members. I didn't know who to sit with ... I didn't know where I was ... It was the first time I felt alone in my life ... it was just like my mother telling me she didn't want me anymore. It hurt. That's the way I felt ... I thought these guys were my brothers. I thought they were my family. I thought they were going to protect me, to stand by me. But they didn't."

Brian Contois insists that there is no easy escape from the hard realities of doing time in a Winnipeg Aboriginal ghetto. While gangs lure youth into the false sense of having found security, a footing on the street, and a station in life: "They say they are your family; they say they're your friends, but when it comes down to it—you're just another body to them. They're there to hurt you. They make you take money from those close to you. They'll make you take the rap for things they did—and you wind up sitting in jail. And jail is no place to be" (quoted in Lindsay 2000, 11).

At the first Canadian national Aboriginal Gang Conference held in Winnipeg in October of 2008, Jessie Mckay, who is of mixed ancestry, conceded: "The whites didn't want me. The Indians didn't want me. My own mother didn't want me. The Syndicate gave me respect but took much more. I sold my soul ... I lost my kids ... and I got lost, myself."

Broader structural forces inevitably mark the terrain on which young urban Native people's life plots play out. Contradictory networks of affiliation provide gang members with the flexibility to change ground, but not to change "the" ground. Those who can merely walk on it, however, may endeavour to remark the landscape and thereby set themselves outside of society. They tell of their found position in the underworld by tattooing and cutting into their own bodies, scoring others with bullets, johns, and dope, and by spraying the built environment with a tirade of blood and graffiti. Although they succeed in making themselves seen and heard at a time when the economic, political, and social mainstreams encourage their invisibility and silence, their efforts to achieve dignity and solidarity are illusory and undermined by individualistic, and some would argue narcissistic, desires for reward sans sacrifice, and respect without reciprocation. If and when the significance of family or the culture reasserts itself—as is often the object of Aboriginal spiritual interventions—disenchantment with this style of social dissent and gang-styled solidarity may ensue. Then it is an awakening to a conception of relative values or more specifically, to the value of "all ones relations" that fuels the call for a redemptive repositioning within family folds and a reorienting toward Aboriginal aims.

Notes

1   This article was completed in 2006 and includes only minor updates in urban Aboriginal gang developments and theory after this time. I am deeply indebted to Jessie McKay, Ervin Chartrand, Nancy Flett, Brian Contois, and Ivy Chaske for their critical contributions to this research. The paper has also benefited from productive conversations with Nahanni Fontaine, Stuart Desnomie, and Lindy-Lou Flynn. I would like to thank the Southern Chiefs Organization and Manitoba Keewatinowi Okimakanak for allowing me to participate in the Manitoba Aboriginal Gangs research project and to quote from our finished report. Portions of this research were funded by a SSHRC Standard Research Grant, for which I am grateful.

2   First Nations neighbourhoods and non-Native criminal organizations along the Canadian prairies anchor multiple cross-border Aboriginal gang dynamics. Aboriginal gang activity denotes, in part, a reconfiguring of Aboriginal geographies of centrality. Gang participation offers one means for marking youth, media, and the city as central sites for articulating Aboriginality. Certainly variation exists between and within neighbourhoods; however, this has much to do with the way larger impersonal forces play into the local forms, conditions, and processes of actual neighbourhood and family contexts.

3   My intent is to bring to light a practical understanding of the circumstances that bear on street agency in one subcultural Aboriginal context and to encourage scholarly investigation into this neglected field of Canadian cultural sociology and urban anthropology. I venture a working understanding of that which constitutes a gang in this setting through a comparison of new- and old-guard gang characteristics, social capital, values, and membership practices. I draw attention to the ways the

new and the old-guard gang members distinguish themselves from each other and from the non-Aboriginal gangs operating in Manitoba.

4 Sánchez-Jankowski's (1991) comparative study of thirty-seven gangs reveals a rational approach by gang members to acquire prestige through illicit means, as reflected in the gang's intricate organizational structure, codes of conduct, and rules specifying permissible behaviour. Contrary to prevailing assumptions about gangs, he shows that drug trafficking is usually a secondary interest compared to identity construction, protecting neighbourhood territory, and recreation. Further, he posits that gangs involved in drug trafficking may only constitute a small proportion of all gangs.

Coughlin and Venkatesh (2003, 43) advise that a concern with the extent to which urban street gangs are entrepreneurially motivated is likely to orient research for the present era of gang theorists. An augmented investment in commerce activity and in revenue generation could signal a shift in interest from protecting territory and other social activities, including participation in local politics and peer support, which are generally regarded as distinguishing activities of the gang (cf. Thrasher 1963).

Other streams of emerging gang studies include the popularization and diffusion of youth culture by the media. Films such as the *Godfather* trilogy (1972, 1974, 1990), *Scarface* (1983), *Colors* (1988), *New Jack City* (1991), and *Goodfellas* (1990), along with the popularity of gansta rap and hip hop, have contributed symbolic content to the vast public repertoire of ideas from which youth experimentally select materials with which to form identifications—cultural and other (Hagedorn 1998; Klein 1995; Ro 1996; Short 1996).

5 While it is impossible to ascertain to what extent residential school escapes may have provided the impetus for the initial formation of Aboriginal youth gangs, the issue warrants fuller examination.

6 Sensationalized government reports notwithstanding, it is clear that in Manitoba, gangs are developing in the cities and migrating to reserves rather than the reverse (see Buddle and MKO, SCO 2006); thus, given that prairie reserves are often characterized by an almost *absolute* unemployment rate, gang formation must be attributable to factors more complex than mere under-employment.

7 It worth noting the irony, however, that the very rights gang members today exploit—to lawfully assemble in public and to take up residence in and to occupy cities spaces, to attend integrated bars and purchase alcohol, and to travel freely between cities and reserves—are relatively new civic entitlements, having been achieved only in the post-world-war era, when the federal and provincial governments would begin a process of repealing some of the most discriminatory clauses of the Indian Act, bringing them into conformity with human rights philosophy. Today, Native gang members can imbibe, gather, vote, hire lawyers, seek employment, and participate in traditional spiritual gatherings, enjoying greater "equality under the law," yet how they elect to valorize and to engage this repertoire of rights tends to conflict both with the First Nations and Canadian mainstreams. That many tend to wear their dysfunction defiantly on their sleeves exposes the social, cultural, intergenerational, and interpersonal ruptures that are the effects of both thoroughly invasive colonial policies seeking to de-Indigenize Indian people and newer neoliberal initiatives that punish members of the urban poor through the steady withdrawal of social services.

8 In general, Aboriginal gangs lack direct resources and the capabilities to move illegal substances across international borders. They function simply to facilitate local

transport, distribution, and sales. The Aboriginal gangs are therefore dependant on these more established criminal organizations, which are part of an international criminal network, to obtain their supply and to organize their activities.

9   Despite their low-ranking role within these orders, when in 1997 the Canadian government introduced its new anti-gang legislation (Bill C-95), it was on the members of the Winnipeg-based Manitoba Warriors, rather than the Hells Angels, that the courts would test its legislative force. This amendment to the criminal code defined for the first time "criminal organization" and "criminal organization offense" (Stuart 2000, 97). According to the Winnipeg Police Service Annual Report for 1998, under the auspices of a police cocaine sweep operation entitled "Project Northern Snow," on 4 November 1998, a combined force of over 150 officers executed arrest warrants on fifty Manitoba Warriors and associates. The force laid more than 260 related charges. This was the largest sweep under the new Bill C-95 in Canada and the first time that charges under the new law were laid in Manitoba. The following year, the Canadian government spent three million dollars building a high-tech courthouse in which to try thirty-three adolescent members of this Native gang who had been charged with drug offences. If found guilty under C-95, those accused were liable to receive sentences of fourteen years in prison. The Winnipeg Police were able to meet the minimal requirements of the legislation, showing that the accused had participated in or substantially contributed to the activities of a criminal organization. They did so largely with the information they had compiled in their "gang database"—an archive of information that officers gather in their diurnal interactions with the youth they stop and question. One of the defense attorneys noted at the sentencing trial that street-level drug dealers involved were impoverished at the time of arrest, none having more than one hundred dollars on him. There was, moreover, no application to seize the proceeds of crime—of which there appeared to be nothing of worth (Roberts 2000).

10 Unless otherwise notated, all quotes by and references to Brian Contois are derived from a series of interviews conducted with myself (8, 11, 15, and 19 September 2006) and from statements he made over the course of the Pro-youth workshops he provided and which I attended in 2006.

11 Quotes from Ervin Chartrand unless otherwise noted are from personal interviews conducted 30 October and 9 December 2006.

12 Low socio-economic status is often linked with poor health. Low education and socio-economic status are also linked with particular health behaviours. Poor nutrition, low levels of activity, smoking, drinking, and high levels of stress combine to produce poor overall health among the youth who are susceptible to gang involvement. This combination of factors is likely to be linked with depression, long term activity restriction, and chronic diseases. The history of alcohol abuse in Native communities as a legacy of colonialism is common knowledge and is well documented. Drug and alcohol addictions, nonetheless, are diseases that continue to ravage the Aboriginal population. All of the research participants in this study conceded that they had been under the age of thirteen when they began to experiment with drugs and alcohol: "I remember there was always parties at my auntie's place growing up. And my auntie would always have these gang member boyfriends around. I remember when I was five, she was drinking with one of her boyfriends and he offered me a shot of beer. I kind of looked at her and she said, 'Go ahead and see if you can handle it.' So I took it from him and had my first taste of beer" (Buddle, SCO, and MKO 2006, 32).

In most cases, it was an older family member who introduced the youth to intoxicants. Children routinely exposed to drug and alcohol abuse come to except intoxication as normative.

13 Circle of Courage is a prevention, intervention, and stabilization strategy for Aboriginal male gang members aged twelve to seventeen. It is funded mainly through federal grants from the National Crime Prevention Program. COC was created and is administered by the Winnipeg Aboriginal family service organization Ka Ni Kanichihk. The organization's founder and director, Leslie Spillet, and the COC program lead, Lionel Houston, are scrambling to find new funds to operate the program. The funding for COC and four other gang diversion projects extended only to March 2011 and was not renewable. Meanwhile, in 2010 the city and province co-purchased a police helicopter, announced new funds to augment the already sizeable Police Gang Unit budget, and hired additional staff to form a new cadet corp. Provincial talks to build a new prison are also under way. It is clear that saving public funds is not what motivates these criminal justice investments, for it costs only $9,000 to put a youth through the COC program for a year as opposed to $90,000 a year to incarcerate him. The security and corrections industries have profited immensely from the federal government's short-term "tough on crime" re-election strategy, which segregates so-called "criminals" from "decent" people and employs pliable para-military trainees as opposed to life-experienced Native organization personnel.

Works Cited

Alvarez, L. 2007. "From Zoot Suits to Hip Hop: Towards a Relational Chicana/o Studies." *Latino Studies* 5: 53–75.

Barron, S.W. 1997. "Canadian Male Street Skinheads: Street Gang or Street Terrorists?" *Canadian Review of Sociology and Anthropology* 34 (2): 125–45.

Boga, T.R. 1994. "Turf Wars: Street Gangs, Local Governments and the Battle for Public Space." *Harvard Civil Liberty Law Review* 29 (2): 477–503.

Bourdieu, P. 1990. *The Logic of Practice*. Translated by Richard Nice. Cambridge: Polity Press.

Bourgois, P. 1995. *In Search of Respect: Selling Crack in El Barrio*. Cambridge: Cambridge University Press.

Bronfenbrenner, U. 1979. *The Ecology of Human Development*. Cambridge, MA: Harvard University Press.

Buddle, K. 2004a. "Media, Markets and Powwows: Matrices of Aboriginal Cultural Mediation in Canada." *Cultural Dynamics* 16 (1): 29–69.

———. 2004b. "White Words, Read Worlds: Authoring Aboriginality through English Language Media." *The International Journal of Canadian Studies* 30: 121–58.

———. 2005. "Aboriginal Cultural Capital Creation and Radio Production in Urban Ontario." *Canadian Journal of Communications* 30 (1): 7–40.

———. 2007. "Bullets for B-Roll: Shooting Native Films and Street Gangs in Western Canadian Cities." *E-misphérica: Performance and Politics in the Americas* 4 (2). http://www.hemi.nyu.edu/journal/4.2/eng/en42_pg_crowe.html.

———. 2008. "Transistor Resistors: Native Women's Radio and the Social Organization of Political Space in Manitoba." In *Global and Indigenous Media: Cultures, Practices, and Politics*, edited by P. Wilson and M. Stewart, 128–44. London: Duke University Press.

Buddle, K., and Southern Chiefs Organization and Manitoba Keewatinowi Okimakanak. 2006. "Aboriginal Gangs in Manitoba: A Preliminary Report." Unpublished research report conducted in collaboration with the Southern Chiefs' Organization and Manitoba Keewatinowi Okimakanak.

Campbell, A. 1990. "Female Participation in Gangs." In *Gangs in America*, edited by Ronald Huff, 163–82. Newbury Park, CA: Sage.

Canadian Centre for Justice Statistics. 2005. "Crime Statistics in Canada, 2004." *Juristat* 25 (5).

Chartrand, Ervin. 2006. *Patrick Ross*. National Film Board of Canada. First Stories: Manitoba.

Chesney-Lind, M., R.G. Shelden, and K.A. Joe. 1996. "Girls, Delinquency, and Gang Membership." In *Gangs in America*, second edition, edited by C.R. Huff, 185–204. Thousand Oaks, CA: Sage.

Cloward, R.A., and L.E. Ohlin. 1960. *Delinquency and Opportunity: A Theory of Delinquent Gangs*. New York: Free Press.

Comaroff, J., and J. Comaroff. 2006. "Figuring Crime: Quantifacts and the Production of the Un/Real." *Public Culture* 18 (1): 209–46.

Compton, J. 1997. "Real Aboriginal Warriors Are Not in Gangs: Contois Can Overcome Setback." Portage and Main editorial section. *Winnipeg Free Press*, 1 March: A11.

Constant, L. 2006. "Manitoba Keewatinowi Okimakanak Report on Aboriginal Gang and Drug Activity." Unpublished report prepared for Manitoba Keewatinowi Okimakanak, Manitoba.

Contois, B. N.d. "Whitecloud Consulting: Giving Advice to Organizations Seeking to Create Safer, Happier, and Healthier Communities, Families, and Individuals." Unpublished.

Coughlin, B., and S. Venkatesh. 2003. "The Urban Street Gang after 1970." *Annual Review of Sociology* 29: 41–64.

Covey H.C., S. Menard, and R.J. Franzese. 1992. *Juvenile Gangs*. Springfield, IL: Thomas.

Curry, G.D., and S.H. Decker. 1998. *Confronting Gangs: Crime and Community*. Los Angeles, CA: Roxbury.

Curtis, R. 1998. "The Improbable Transformation of Inner-City Neighborhoods: Crime, Violence, Drugs, and Youth in the 1990s." *Journal of Criminal Law and Criminology* 88 (4): 1233–76.

Dohla, L. 2003. "Aboriginal Gangs in Prairie Provinces in 'Crisis Proportions.'" *First Nations Drum*. http://firstnationsdrum.com/2003/04/aboriginal-gangs-in-prairie-provinces-in-crisis-proportions/.

Dutton, M. 1999. Street Scenes of Subalterity: China, Globalization and Rights. Social Text 60: 63-86.

Fleisher, M.S. 1995. *Beggars and Thieves: Lives of Urban Street Criminals*. Madison: University of Wisconsin Press.

———. 1998. *Dead End Kids: Gang Girls and the Boys They Know*. Madison: University of Wisconsin Press.

Fontaine, N. 2006. "Surviving Colonization: Anishinaabe Ikwe and Gang Participation." In *Criminalizing Women: Gender and (In)justice in Neo-Liberal Times*, edited by G. Balfour and E. Comack, 113–30. Halifax: Fernwood Publishing.

Hagedorn, J.M. 1988. *People and Folks: Gangs, Crime and the Underclass in a Rustbelt City*. Chicago: Lake View.

———. 1998. "Gang Violence in the Postindustrial Era." In *Youth Violence*, edited by M. Tonry and M.H. Moore, 364–420. Chicago: University of Chicago Press.

Klein, M. 1995. *The American Street Gang*. New York: Oxford University Press.

Kornhauser, R.R. 1978. *Social Sources of Delinquency*. Chicago: University of Chicago Press.

Lindsay, R. 2000. "Former Manitoba Warrior President Talks to Youth: Joining a Gang a Piece of Cake; Leaving another Story." *Kenora Enterprise*, 19 March: 11.

Mendenhall, B., and T. Armstrong. 2004. *Native American Youth in Gangs: Acculturation and Identity*. Report for the Center for Delinquency and Crime Policy Studies, CSUS.

Merton, R.K. 1949. *Social Theory and Social Structure*. Glencoe, IL: Free Press.

Miller, W.B. 1975. *Violence by Youth Gangs and Youth Groups as a Crime Problem in Major American Cities*. Washington, DC: U.S. Department of Justice.

Moore, J.W. 1978. *Homeboys*. Philadelphia: Temple University Press.

———. 1991. *Going Down to the Barrio: Homeboys and Homegirls in Change*. Philadelphia: Temple University Press.

Nimmo, M. 2001. *The "Invisible" Gang Members: A Report on Female Gang Association in Winnipeg*. Winnipeg: Canadian Centre for Policy Alternatives.

Owen, Bruce. 2006. "Former Car Thief Aims to Help Kids Leave Gang Life." *Winnipeg Free Press*, 4 November, A4.

Ro, R. 1996. *Gangsta: Merchandizing the Rhymes of Violence*. New York: St. Martin's.

Roberts, D. 2000. "Manitoba Gang Members' Trial Moving at a Snail Pace." *First Nations Drum*. http://firstnationsdrum.com/2000/12/manitoba-gang-mem bers-trial-moving-at-a-snail-pace/.

Royal Canadian Mounted Police (RCMP). 2006. *Feature Focus: Youth Gangs and Guns*. RCMP Environmental Scan. http://www.rcmp-grc.gc.ca/pubs/yg-ja/ gangs-bandes-eng.pdf.

Sánchez-Jankowski M.S. 1991. *Islands in the Street: Gangs and American Urban Society*. Berkeley: University of California Press.

Sassen, S. 2002. "Introduction: Locating Cities on Global Circuits." In *Global Networks, Linked Cities*, edited by S. Sassen, 1–36. New York: Routledge.

Short, J. 1996. "Personal, Gang, and Community Careers." In *Gangs in America*, second edition, edited by C.R. Huff, 3–11. Thousand Oaks, CA: Sage.

Silver, J. 2006. *Fast Facts: Aboriginal People, Jobs and the Provincial Budget*. Winnipeg: Canadian Centre for Policy Alternatives.

Silver, J., with J. Hay and P. Gorgen. 2006. *Aboriginal Involvement in Community Development: The Case of Winnipeg's Spence Neighborhood*. Winnipeg: Canadian Centre for Policy Alternatives.

Spergel, I.A. 1992. "Youth Gangs: An Essay Review." *Social Services Review* 66 (1): 121–40.

———. 1995. *The Youth Gang Problem: A Community Approach*. New York: Oxford University Press.

Stuart, D. 2000. "Time to Recodify Criminal Law and Rise Above Law and Order Expediency: Lessons from the Manitoba Warriors Prosecution." *Manitoba Law Journal* 28 (1): 89–112.

Sullivan, M. 1988. *Getting Paid*. Ithaca: Cornell University Press.

Thrasher, F. 1963 [1927]. *The Gang*. Chicago: University of Chicago Press.
Venkatesh, S. 2000. *American Project: The Rise and Fall of a Modern Ghetto*. Cambridge: Harvard University Press.
Venkatesh, S., and S. Levitt.2000. "'Are We a Family or a Business?': History and Disjuncture in the Urban American Street Gang." *Theory and Society* 29: 427–62.
Vigil, J.D. 1988. *Barrio Gangs: Street Life and Identity in Southern California*. Austin: University of Texas Press.
———. 1996. "Street Baptism: Chicano Gang Initiation." *Human Organization*. 55 (2): 149–53.
———. 2002. *A Rainbow of Gangs: Street Cultures in the Mega-City*. Austin: University of Texas Press.
———. 2003. "Urban Violence and Street Gangs." *Annual Review of Anthropology* 32: 225–42.
Wilson, W.J. 1987. *The Truly Disadvantaged*. Chicago: University of Chicago Press.
Winnipeg Free Press. 2010. "Aboriginal Group Objects to Website Ad Promoting Racism." Online edition, 4 March. http://www.winnipegfreepress.com/breaking news/Aboriginal-group-objects-to-website-ad-promoting-racism-86427167 .html.
Wolfgang, M.E., and F. Ferracuti. 1967. *The Subculture of Violence*. London: Tavistock.
Zatz, M.S., and E.L. Portillo. 2000. "Voices from the Barrio: Chicano/a Gang Families and Communities." *Criminology* 38 (2): 369–401.

11

"Why Is My People Sleeping?"

First Nations Hip Hop between the Rez and the City

Marianne Ignace

This essay is the continuation of a journey of discovery I began a few years ago in several overlapping and intersecting roles—as mother of First Nations children who are becoming young adults, as a member of a Secwepemc reserve community in the Interior of British Columbia, and as anthropologist whose "field" is the domain of my own community and home. As Ron Ignace and I wrote in an earlier essay that dealt largely with the changing face of Secwepemc traditional resource use, "Our home, family, and lives are not separated from 'the field,' where we conduct research. Instead, our work pushes us to consciously consider, incorporate, and write about our lives, and the lives of relatives, elders, and friends" (M. Ignace and R. Ignace 2004). This essay takes us into the present of a new generation's perception and interpretations of Secwepemc culture and First Nations identity. The lessons about the ways in which First Nations youth seek and express their emerging sense of individual and collective self have reaffirmed the anthropological task of looking for expressions of culture in ever new and unexpected places, and through unexpected voices. Much of this journey has been autobiographical, or perhaps socio-biographical, in that it was shaped by events and processes in my community, which are, in turn, inseparably connected to global dimensions of knowledge, power, and media.

In 2005, my son George Ignace and I published our initial reflections on the connections between First Nations youth expression of cultural and social identity in an essay titled "Tagging, Rapping, and the Voices of the Ancestors: Expressing Aboriginal Identity between the Small City and the Rez" (M. Ignace and G. Ignace 2005). This paper adds new insights and continues the dialogue, focusing on both graffiti art and hip-hop music as forms of expression.

In recent years, numerous ethnographers have shown the increasing ways in which hip-hop graffiti art and music as contemporary phenomena of globalized yet local cultural markets have been appropriated by young people from multiple ethnic backgrounds on different continents. These studies show how artists weave the functions and messages of hip-hop music as art of resistance into very localized messages shaped by their particular histories, meanings, languages and experiences (see, e.g., Zemke-White 2006; Sarkar 2006; LeBlanc 2006). As a segment of Canadian society more often than not denied a voice, yet profoundly living the effects of colonization, physical, and social trauma, Aboriginal youth in Canada have become consumers of hip-hop culture in its various manifestations. In the physical and virtual spaces between the rural First Nations reserve and the city, and between Indigenous connections to the past and global contexts of marginalization, urbanization, and environmental destruction, our youth also creatively reshape hip-hop culture to express who they are. Listening to these emerging expressions of self and connectedness provides us with windows on the ways in which Aboriginal youth live, experience, and reflect on themselves and the ways in which they are forging new identities. As I will show, these expressions of identity speak of social marginalization, loss, and trauma. As we have entered the twenty-first century, they also reflect on cultural and environmental loss, and on communities affected by drugs, death, and violence.

Contemporary anthropology celebrates cultural hybridity as its subject and multivocality as the subject's way of speaking; however, Aboriginal communities and Nations must still face up to the essentialized legal norms of Indian-ness perpetuated in the Canadian Indian Act. They also have to deny their own hybridity, multivocality, and globally connected destinies in the ongoing test of Aboriginal rights in the courts. While these legal challenges are slow to die, I see this chapter as a way to explore and validate the increasingly complex and connected cultural manifestations of Aboriginal youth, which affirm rather than deny their sense of Aboriginality. As I will show, the representations of Aboriginal youth experience in visual art and rap songs provide dynamic arenas for reflection about identity and belonging, connection to place and community. They are two forms of narrative that tell stories about belonging, connection, place, and experience by challenging hegemonic pre-existing notions of the nature and form of expression associated with these themes. They are intertextual messages (Kristeva 1980) of dialogue between the artists' own lived experiences of the rez and the city, between Aboriginal culture and globalized pop culture, marginalization, and race, and with the images of Aboriginality out there. Aboriginal youth's visual art and rap use are interconnected kinds of *storytelling* (Cruikshank 1998; 2005), where stories creatively employ images of the past, interwoven with commentary on the present and intertextual messages from other contexts, to engage in moral commentary. As such, they give us visions for the future.

I also view this chapter as an experiment in interpretive interactionism, to "grasp, understand and interpret correctly the perspectives and experiences of others" (Denzin 2001).[1] In this case, the "others" are not outsiders to my community, but I am separated from them by generation. Listening to the voices of youth, hearing their explanations of what they expressed through different artistic media, requires interaction and dialogue, or "dialogical intertextuality" (Collins 1990), which allows us to feel the experiences of others' lives, experiences and standpoints—a concept accepted by social scientists but which, as human beings, we all too often forget in our cross-generational dealings.

The Place and the Context

Our community, Skeetchestn, is one of sixteen[2] reserve communities in the Secwepemc (Shuswap) Nation in the south-central Interior of British Columbia. Like the other southern Secwepemc communities, we are less than an hour's drive away from Kamloops, a small city of some 80,000. A sprawling small city, Kamloops has seen an intense increase in housing development during the last two decades, as new suburban neighbourhoods and residential communities expand into its rural surroundings. Youth and adults from the surrounding First Nations reserve communities have ongoing connections with Kamloops by accessing services not available on the reserves, including schooling, shopping, medical care, entertainment, and government bureaucracies. Each morning, the high school bus transports more than a dozen youth from Skeetchestn to Kamloops, returning in the late afternoon. Every family travels to Kamloops more than once a week to access the diverse service providers, to shop, to find entertainment, to "hang out" in the malls or downtown, or to visit friends and relatives in the city.[3] The "other side" or northeast side of the North Thompson River at its confluence with the South Thompson River is the site of the Kamloops Indian Reserve, a large, spread-out reserve at the junction of urban and rural life. The area around the former Indian Residential School on the reserve, now named Chief Louis Centre, is also the site of numerous Aboriginal service organizations for the Secwepemc Nation and the region. Due to long-standing ties of kinship and marriage, Tk'em-lupsemc (Kamloops Band) Secwepemc people have many personal and social interactions with people from Skeetchestn and other surrounding reserves, which take place both on and off the Kamloops reserve.

In addition to the physical connection with the nearby small city and reserve, all generations on the local reserves are hooked up to the wider world through media communications, including television, DVDs, music, and, increasingly, through the Internet, and are avid consumers of modern pop culture, including music, video, fashion, and fast foods. Although the physical connection with large cities like Vancouver is fairly infrequent for many youth, the virtual connection to modern consumer culture has penetrated all aspects of life on the rez.

Yet, despite these pervasive outside influences, the rural rez Skeetchestn also remains a close-knit community of interrelated members, where ties of kinship determine social interactions and attitudes, and where traditional seasonal subsistence activities continue to form an integral part of the life of many community members, including youth. Nearly all youth participate in their families' spring trout harvest at Hi-hium Lake and go spearfishing and net-fishing for salmon in the Thompson and Fraser Rivers. Most male youth also accompany their fathers and uncles to go deer and moose hunting to supply meat for their families. A few of them have undergone the Secwepemc male coming-of-age ceremony of making their first kill and distributing it to elders in the community; a few youth have completed their *étsxem*, or spirit-guardian quest (see Ignace 1999, 184ff). On weekends and at the time of funerals, many youth participate in bone-game or lehal tournaments, and in the summer they participate in powwows and other gatherings that feature traditional drumming, dancing, sweats, and other Indigenous ceremonies.

The participation in traditional ceremonial events most strongly comes out at the time of funerals, when the young people of the community play important roles by hunting to provide for the bereaved and relatives who gather for the wake, tending to the fire that marks the deceased's journey to the other world, helping with cooking, cleaning, and other chores, and keeping the mourning family company during the long hours of the wake. In times like this, "everyone steps in and everyone knows what to do" without having to be reminded (M. Ignace and G. Ignace 2005; M. Ignace and R. Ignace 2004). It is from times of grief also, that my own sense of dialogical textuality developed, leading to new ways of entering and empathizing the experiences of another generation.

Finding Culture in Graffiti: The Process

In 2001, subsequent to a well-received show of Secwepemc photography I co-curated at the Kamloops Art Gallery (Ignace, Ignace and Etienne 1999),[4] I was approached by the Kamloops Art Gallery to facilitate an exhibit of First Nations art and photography. This request came as part of a Social Sciences and Humanities Research Council C.U.R.A. grant on the "Cultural Future of Small Citites" and involved Kamloops Art Gallery, the University College of the Cariboo (now Thompson Rivers University), and, through this specific project, the Simon Fraser University First Nations program in Kamloops, where I teach. As the time for defining the content for the art gallery show approached, a series of devastating events shattered the lives of our family and our community: On 30 December 2002, our twenty-one-year-old son was brutally murdered in Kamloops; two months later, a young man aged sixteen who was best friend, cousin, nephew, or grandson to everyone in the community committed suicide on the reserve. Another month later, a male elder who was one of the pillars of our community passed away. As we were trying to cope with our grief, we noticed the teenagers in our community expressing their thoughts in graffiti "tags" and in hip-hop lyrics. In consultation with a group of young people from the local reserve communities, the First Nations communities of Skeetchestn and Tk'emlups, the Kamloops Art Gallery, and the students' high school art teacher, and some of us as parents, we developed the idea to have these Secwepemc youth express themselves, their world, feelings, and identity in visual art. A group of six young artists from Skeetchestn and Kamloops participated, and in April 2005 showed their work at the Kamloops Art Gallery.

The works they produced speak to the young people's complex layers of existence, and to their reflections on self, community, environmental issues, and globalization, as well as life and death, social problems, and their connections to hip-hop culture. For those who participated in this exhibit, showed their work, and discussed their work at a symposium sponsored by the CURA project, the process of creation and interpretation represented a way to reflect, to be seen, and to be heard and understood.

Much of the art, especially of the male participants, was heavily influenced by graffiti art. Phillips (1999) has shown how graffiti art in ethnic urban areas of Los Angeles intricately provides messages of "disenfranchised" groups, linked to history, race, and political change. Other authors have pointed to the changing and emerging ways in which graffiti art, as connected with urban hip-hop culture,[5] arose as a symbol of marginalized urban gang culture, but has transcended that connection in new and emergent ways among multi-ethnic minorities, including Indigenous peoples. As an ethnographer learning about the lives and art of others—specifically, urban blacks in Los Angeles—Phillips has also reflected on the ways in which her study of hip-hop graffiti shaped her own understanding of society and culture: "Graffiti has provided me a special window into people's lives. This window has allowed me to see the positive in what is usually viewed as negative, to find morality in what is often considered depravity, and to discover a creativity and depth of history that makes me grateful to live in the time and place that I do" (1999, 351).

Graffiti (pl. of graffito, "scratched or scribbled messages") are defined as drawings or inscriptions made on public walls or other surfaces. What Phillips calls *community graffiti* are tags, or insignia, on public spaces in the community, often intricately interwoven with drawings and spray-painted surfaces. Their significance rests on the artistic and aesthetic distortion of letters and shapes to produce messages, similar to a secret code, indecipherable to outsiders, yet familiar to insiders in both a decoding sense and an affective sense. Especially in the popular image sustained by the dominant (Euro–North American) culture, this kind of graffiti has more often than not been associated with vandalism and the defacement of public walls through the random "scribbling" of spray-painted messages, thus requiring public works teams to sanitize the criminal defacement of public spaces.

> While "bombing"—the secret and hurried inscribing of spray-painted messages and images in public places—is connected to the social and artistic connotations of graffiti art, elaborate "graphing" of authorized public spaces through the detailed multiple layering of intricate scripts and images has gained popularity as an art form rather than "crime art." The essence of graffiti, of course, is the *unauthorized* and thus defiant nature of its production, which resists and opposes bourgeois culture. (M. Ignace and G. Ignace 2005: 21)

With their connotations of "vandalism art" and "guerilla art," community graffiti give voices to the lives of individuals as members of social groups who otherwise feel marginalized and without voice. It provides ways of leaving visual tracks of the group's experience, interests, and perceptions in the public landscape, in defiance of and revolt against public norms but also as an invitation to read their messages. These visual tracks or coded messages, however, are all too often shrugged off by mainstream society but serve as ways of communication with members of the group or subculture (Ferrell 1993, 51), and, I would add, as a challenge to outsiders to decode, decipher and come to understand.[6]

Figure 1 Graffiti on the author's horse barn at Skeetchestn Reserve. Photo: Marianne Ignace 2004.

In the world of academic discourses on the history, meanings and aesthetics of graffiti art, various art historians, archaeologists, and folklorists have pointed to the connection between contemporary graffiti art denoting in semi-coded messages that "so-and-so was here" and the ancient cave arts of ancient peoples (e.g., Guthrie 2006; Reisner and Wechsler 1974; Phillips 1999). Within the pre-contact traditions of the Secwepemc and other Plateau Aboriginal peoples, rock paintings throughout the Indigenous landscape were associated with either spirit guardian quests (potentially Guthrie's graffiti-producing teens!) or other experiences of visits, or encounters with people or animals in far away yet familiar places (Teit 1900, 1909; York, Daly, and Arnett 1993). Symbolic images of people, animals, and natural phenomena, rendered in a shorthand artistic style that requires insider skill to decipher the message left by the sojourner, remind the current generation of the travels, encounters, thoughts, and experiences of long ago ancestors. Indeed George (Geo) Ignace, one of the Secwepemc artists, was intrigued by similarities he perceived between the ancient rock paintings of anonymous ancestors throughout the Secwepemc landscape and his peers' "bombed" messages in the urban landscape or on the reserve: "Yeah, I thought of that, how those old Secwepemc pictographs are kind of like today's graffiti, and how they used to travel around and write their messages on rock walls. Maybe it's like us going to the jungle of the city and tagging. Just like the tags, you have to figure out what they meant by their pictures, and maybe you can never figure it out" (George Ignace, personal communication, 2005). In his view, both graffiti and pictographs represent clues to the travels and experiences of their producers. His ancestors left their marks and messages in the caves and rock faces of natural landscapes of the Interior Plateau, his peers leave them on the urban and suburban walls of the city and the local rez. For outsiders in either time or space, the meaning of the messages is elusive unless the artist is given opportunity to explain them.

Explaining Voices: First Nations' Graffiti Art and Its Meaning

Beyond the interpretations of the young artists' work we had written about previously (M. Ignace and G. Ignace 2005), the 2005 CURA symposium and art show offered insights provided by the artists themselves as they showed and explained their work. Housed in their own space, the "cubicle" of the Kamloops Art Gallery, the show featured some twenty-five pieces of work by six First Nations artists from schools in the Kamloops area, primarily St. Ann's Academy. The works on display used a variety of media—three-dimensional papier mâché and plaster masks, collages of cut-out print materials and drawings, as well as pencil drawings, felt pen drawings, acrylic and water colour paintings, and finally poetry and samplings of original hip-hop music.[7]

A major theme expressed in several of these works is the artists' self-reflection on their Aboriginal identity. The plaster and papier mâché works of Melissa Moses show symbolic images often associated with Plateau Aboriginal peoples, including soaring eagles, and interconnected salmon, water, and humans. Lyle Paul commented on his piece titled *Secwepemc* as follows: "My mom gave me the idea of doing this one day, she said 'do something that means something to you.' And I said, 'Secwepemc,' so I decided to do that word in graffiti, I also did the *sk'elep* [coyote] and the eagle in the background with the moon behind it, and I stood another poem [in graffiti] in the tree trunk, it says,

> 'My pride is being in the First Nation,
> knowing I'm the Creator's creation.
> The gifts mother earth brings,
> the songs sk'elep sings,
> to these I give praise for the morning and
> night haze.'

I ... did that with airbrush and pastels."

In other works, the artist's identity is interwoven with images from the outside world and global connections. Thus, in a collage behind a curtain of strings—"it's kind of to protect my thoughts and stuff inside"—Ayla Joe represents herself as connected not only to the central theme of connectedness to her Interior Salish relatives and extended family but also a Navajo grandfather, surf culture, concerns with racism involving not only Aboriginal peoples but other visible minorities, and perils of drugs encroaching on the community and family.

In Sage Thomas's work, images of Aboriginal grandparents appear side by side with images of Buddha and Sanskrit writings. In another work by the same artist, cut-out photos of Southeast Asian Indigenous peoples are juxtaposed on symbols of Buddhism and pictures of international currencies, again showing unexpected connections between different spaces and cultures.

Geo Ignace's work *Native Issues*, which he calls "my more Indian piece," is a reflection on the transition between the life of his Secwepemc and Cree ancestors, and the impact of the Residential School.

> The transition from this life [pointing to teepees and nature] to this life [hollow-eyed Aboriginal people among the buildings] is in the middle [a stern high-rise that conveys the combined and intertwined image of the Indian Residential School and an urban high-rise], and this is what changed us, and that's the Residential School. And now we gotta live like this [points to the residential-school building/high-rise] if we want to keep prospering. And this [pointing to a light-coloured face floating above the faces of Aboriginal people] is the priest, lookin', but they didn't look hard enough to see the beauty of our lifestyle. So they stayed in their ways, they stayed behind, they didn't dive into this world with us.

His comments also offered further insights of how he views First Nations experience and destiny as connected to Indian Residential Schools, and what it holds for the future. Central to this picture are the downcast hollow eyes of those who experienced Indian Residential Schools, with the ghost-like demons of their trauma drifting by. On the right margin, however, is a cloud-like blank space. As the artist noted, "I was going to put something in there, but then I realized, that's the future, and I don't know what the future is going to hold yet, so I left it blank." In other words, the artist expresses hope for the shape the future will take rather than surrendering to the bleak effects of the past.

Other drawings give us clues about reflections on life and death, which for all of these youth were connected to real and sometimes violent losses

Figure 2 George Ignace's oil pastel drawing Native Issues—an artistic reflection on the Indian Residential School. Reproduced with permission. Photo: Marianne Ignace 2004.

of family and community members. In an earlier work (M. and G. Ignace 2005, 20) we noted about Lyle Paul's pencil drawing *Road to the End*:

> Roads and railways lead to the city, and then contort and crumble in the spaces away from the city. The individual, on a quest towards understanding, not unlike the spirit guardian quests of his ancestors, has the road/railway to the future coming from within him, seeks to find the path to places in all four directions. In a new guise, he has become a "kid with a [spray] can." The road turns into a precipice and destruction is in all directions. A "stop" sign that warns the traveler is contorted and displaced.

Here we have images of tangled, intertwined roads to destiny, and the search of spaces away from the city, leading to expression as spray can artist.

Geo's pencil drawing *Abnormal*, a combination of graffiti inscriptions, cartoon-like figures, and abstract shapes, is filled with haunting images of thoughts about the manifestations of death and afterlife. As he noted in the aftermath of the violent death of his brother, the suicide of his best friend, and the death of an important elder, "It's basically what the whole picture is based around, abnormal. I was abnormally thinking when I drew it. And the transition [from life to death] is abnormal." The top part of the drawing is his reflection on life after death:

This is how I picture afterlife. It's all mental, you're not in a physical form, it's all mental, so anything is the way you want it to be. You don't know what mountains look like in the afterlife, they could be trees. That's what it's all about. I believe there is no heaven and hell, it's both. It's all who you chill with. And I don't know what's next, that's why this [space] at the top is blank. The bottom half of the drawing represents drugs and people trapped in different lifestyles and not living like themselves. They're all trapped, livin' like something that they aren't and basically, this is the grave-yard, this is where all these people end up. And this is my view on death: it's either from homicide, suicide or time.

And thus, in the central part of the picture are the images and graffiti tags of those who died: Skooks (his brother), Evan (his friend and cousin), and "Sam Bones" (the elder) connected to the artist's suspended sense of abnormal, and speculation about what that life after death is like.

Figure 3 George Ignace's pencil drawing "Abnormal" (2003), a reflection on life, death and after-life. Used with permission. Photo: Marianne Ignace 2004.

Reflections on Nature, Culture, and Urbanization

A further common theme in these art works is the young people's reflection on nature, Aboriginal culture, and growing urbanization connected to environmental destruction. One of Sage Thomas's water colour paintings shows the fragile existence of a few withering flowers in the foreground against the backdrop of an urban skyline. In Geo Ignace's work, reflections on nature and urbanization figure prominently: "Most of my artwork, it's about the battle between the natural way of life and the urban way of life, the faster way of getting stuff done, I was trying to portray chemicals and poisons of the city, this is basically the battle between mother nature and urbanization."

In Geo's words, life on the reserve (Skeetchestn) is increasingly affected and haunted by the physical encroachment of the city and the dangers of environmental destruction through pollution, war, and destruction in other parts of the world as seen on television and movie images. Physical and virtual spaces intermingle but combine to create a sense of loss, mourning, and ghettoization. In his commentary on his acrylic pencil drawing, *Inner City Bandits—Kids with Cans*, he notes, "During my lifetime [he was 17 at the time of this statement] what I've seen, is, I've seen urbanization gradually building up wherever I go. I've seen cities growing up. It's all about how natural disaster and humans are about to become the death of themselves, like with the bombs. That's why it's *Inner City Bandits—Kids with Cans*. Yeah, basically, this is where I see the rez going, in some odd years."

Inner City Bandits—Kids with Cans represents gripping and graphic images of the threats to the "green" life posed by exploding planes—without doubt, images caused by the 9/11 attacks—as well as urban gangsters and, again, high-rise buildings. Among the cartoon characters are graffiti inscriptions like "sunk," "whoa," and "abnormal." The culmination of his thoughts on the effects, however, is displayed in the top left-hand corner, the black and white space for the future of kids on the rez, depicted as "kids with cans": Like their ancestors in *Native Issues*, who were shaped by the abuses and trauma of Residential Schools, the rez kids of the future are hollow-eyed, or even have "X-ed out" eyes, signifying death.

Hip-Hop Culture, Black Ghetto and Native Kids with Cans

As we see in many of the youths' visual art works discussed above, the emergence of First Nations graffiti artists as "kids with cans" is closely connected with the growing consciousness of environmental destruction and change, the experience of growing urban encroachment onto reserves,

Figure 4 Mural at St. Ann's Academy by George Ignace, Melissa Moses, Lyle Paul, Sage Thomas and Lucinda Paul, 2003. This mural has since been painted over. Photo: Marianne Ignace 2003.

and the cognizance of global threats of war and violence. Likewise, in several of Lyle Paul's works, kids with cans from the reserve express themselves as graffiti artists with aerosol cans. The connection between the black ghetto of hip-hop music and the kids on the reserve is vividly portrayed in a large mural at St. Ann's Academy, painted by the group of artists: Here as in real life, the river separates the person from the reserve, whose message is "whoa!" On the other side of the river, a black hip-hop artist among urban high-rises, connected to the reserve by a graph, rises like smoke from the city that reads "accept abnormal skills."

Over the course of the project, as the artists grew from age fifteen or sixteen to seventeen or eighteen, some of the artistic productions changed: Murals that initially depicted the "kids with cans" activities of "bombing" public places changed to more intricate graphs on paper and canvases. Indeed, a large mural that showed "kids with cans" at work was painted over with new graphics. Throughout this period, some of the visual artists and additional friends began to turn to hip-hop music as new and additional way of expressing themselves. The lyrics of their hip-hop music productions—recorded in the author's basement on home computer equipment, with a keyboard and voice microphones, continued and extended the themes expressed in the visual art and deal with questions of identity, alienation, and urbanization, often told as complex voice images and layered stories. Not coincidentally, the initial insignia of the group of young recording artists was CWK, signifying the backwards tag "kids with cans," displayed on many public spaces in the reserve community. As one of the aunts of the hip-hop artists exclaimed, "What does that mean, does it mean Country Western Kids?" Thus, "Country Western Kids" became the name of the group, later to be replaced by "Sundown Stylistics/Low Budget Studio," featuring George ("Geo") Ignace, Jesse ("Beamo") Seymour, Torbin ("Alias") Alec, and several friends. Like most of their peers, they had been inspired as consumers by American hip-hop artists like Tupac, Wyclef Jean, Styles, Jay-Z, Eminem, and others. In their lyrics, they connected what they listened to with the realities of their lives in the reserve community.

"Why is my people sleeping?" First Nations' Experience in Hip-Hop Music

As in graffiti art, hip-hop or rap music includes further associations of dress style, use of the English language, body language, and gestures, which are all part of hip-hop culture. Taken together, hip-hop culture has become a favoured medium of expression among youth on Aboriginal reserves/reservations across North America (M. Ignace and G. Ignace 2005), but beyond that, of Indigenous and migrant/immigrant groups in urban Quebec, Africa, Latin America, and other continents. These youth, in expressing race relations and social and economic realities, forge hybrid identities for themselves, transcending their own groups (see e.g., Zemke-White 2006; LeBlanc 2006; Sarkar 2006).

Graffiti art, as we have seen, gives visual expression to Aboriginal voices of marginalization, while providing spaces for creative and critical reflection and for the synthesizing of multiple layers of experience. Rap or hip-hop music, through its lyrics and musical loops, is the auditory complement of this. Tricia Rose (1994) defined hip-hop or rap music as "a form of rhymed story telling accompanied by highly rhythmic, electronically based music ... Rap music has articulated the pleasures and problems of black urban life in contemporary America" (Rose 1994, 2). Zemke-White (2006, 11) adds that "styles have changed and now rap often is accompanied by specially performed musical beds which hearken to sampling by melodic or textual reference to another song."

From a youth perspective, rap represents the "evolution of native culture: ... Hip-hop music seems to have quite a successful avenue with the younger generation of Native people (that's us!). As the younger generation, we often get the comments 'why do you like hip-hop music so much? It's not your music! You should go back to your own music!' So why are so many Native youth belting out the hip-hop?"(Daniels 2001).

Rex Smallboy of the Canadian hip-hop group Warparty notes that hip-hop provides a medium of expressing "everything from love, reserve life, jealousy, hate, success, emceeing, alcohol and drug abuse, suicide, and our people's history." He adds, "It seems to me that hip-hop provides a medium that youth relate to and can incorporate their own ideas into, in order to tell their stories. Hip-hop as a medium (or genre) has become cultural to us as Native youth. Even though hip-hop didn't originate with Native people, it has become very accepted and integral to Native youth getting our message out" (Daniels 2001).

In researching rap music among Maori youth in Aotearoa (New Zealand), Kirsten Zemke-White (2006) found that Aotearoa rap is used to assert and construct local identities, exploring race, culture, and history. The Polynesian youth of Aotearoa feel a spiritual connection to rap and hip hop, hearing something of themselves in it, and they "have taken to it like it was already theirs" (Zemke-White 2006, 4). Casting the meaning and function of Maori hip hop within a Maori frame of thought and culture, she notes, "I offer that rap has been a *turangawaewae* [place to stand] for the *rangatahi* [youth] and they have injected this fertile African American popular music genre with their own culture and ideology" (ibid.).

Like visual art, hip hop has provided the young artists with ways of telling stories about reserve life, personal worries and experiences, violence, or reflections on existence. As "Alias" and a young female hip-hop artist (personal communication) noted, music has become a lifeline of expression, helping them to stay the course and resist surrendering to the growing epidemic of hard drugs and violence on reserves that has come to affect youth. Moreover, First Nations hip-hop music in the Skeetchestn/ Kamloops area and elsewhere in Aboriginal Canada provides a network of creativity and sharing among artists in the basement recording studio, but it also involves the heroics of performance and communicating with the peer audience at local "gigs" in parks, at youth conferences, and other venues.

As with graffiti "tags," the messages can be elusive, consisting of quickly juxtaposed verbal images that reveal while concealing at the same time. Below are some examples from hip-hop songs produced by members of the Sundown Stylistics in Geo's studio at Skeetchestn Indian Reserve in 2005–06.[8]

Figure 5 Jesse "Beamo" Seymour and George "Geo" Ignace performing at a First Nations Graduation Ceremony in Kamloops. Photo: Marianne Ignace 2005.

Like the examples of visual art discussed above, the hip-hop songs give expression to loss and alienation from the traditions of the past, as well as urbanization and coping with the growing epidemic of drug and alcohol abuse on reserves. They give sometimes sad, and sometimes funny messages that derive from these multiple impacts:

What's Happening, What's Happening?[9]

Please someone, tell me what's happening, what's happening?

Do you know what it's like to lose your closest of bros,

And do you know what it's like to have kids but don't know,

Do you know what you trust had to go,

Everything that you love was just crushed,

Y'had to cope,

You cope with alcohol, pills, and you're doped,

So now you know what it's like with no hope,

But you grow, and you might see what life is
like,

It's a mystical, an unpredictable life,

Without or with the bro,

I'm going to stick it for life,

This is my honour, my power,

My way and my life,

So I'll be asking for your guidance

When I'm lost in the strife.

In a way parallel to *Native Issues* (above) and other pieces of visual art, the lyrics of these songs represent verbal imagery about the current state and future of First Nations societies:

Why Is My People Sleeping?

This part goes out to all my people out there,
everybody,

This one goes out to the Nation, the Nation,

I ask why is my people sleepin',

Why is we quiet, why is my people crazy, why
aren't we trying,

Why ain't my people thinkin',

I hear a crime,

So why is a woman weepin',

Not colliding,

Why do we keep on drinking,

Fuck with ...

It is the day I'm finally speaking,

Listen up.

It's the way my change of thinking,

I ain't gonna lie,

We're divided, not united, so we'll wake.

Finally, in fusing experiences of living on the land with commentary alluding to urban landscapes, and expressed in the rhymes of rap-song, the artist tells a story of contemporary hunting experience:

> See me ridin' in,
> I just feel like chillin', just chillin',
> Sittin' in my truck ridin'...
> Cruisin' into DMC now, and shit,
> Huntin' around and shit,
> Here we go, here we go
> At moments dreamin' my life
> Holdin' it, foldin' it, click
> Two 22's, on the hunt, huntin' who
> A three-point buck, free choice,
> Duck,
> Gut and then what,
> Skin is deep, here's the meat,
> Barbecued, and the ribs is sweet ...
> Cliffs to see,
> Cliffs and trees, the deer I see ...

In cryptic images, this song tells a story about place—DMC is "Deadman's Creek," the name imposed on the Skeetchestn Reserve by white people. It juxtaposes notions of hip-hop culture, like "chillin' with my friends" with hunting experiences that combine the traditional notions of dreaming about animals, spotting deer, gutting and skinning animals with the handling and imagery of guns, which in turn include intertextual references to guns, shoot-outs, and gang warfare in Black American rap songs, but transforming them into the presence of native hunting activities.

A provocative and stirring example of a song that weaves together images from hip-hop language with contemporary Aboriginal experience on the rez and in the city is the following song, "She Don't Know What to Do," by Geo. In gripping verbal images it tells the story of a young woman's slide into drug use, prostitution, hopelessness, and despair, all precedented by the sad history of previous injustices and circumstances. Based on a composite of his own autobiographic experience, and knowledge of the trauma of young Aboriginal people as it affects countless Indigenous women and communities in Canada and elsewhere in the world, it weaves together urban rap figures of speech and intertextual references ("mean muggin'," "trippin' on Ex [ecstasy],") with narrative from local contexts and experience. It plays on the contradictions between female native person as respected and revered "goddess" and the reality of addiction, poverty, and helplessness, ending in a moral message asking for change.

She Don't Know What to Do

Yeah, mike check, check one, check two,
Yeah, be good, be good, ready to go.

So I seen her trippin' on Ex,
She was a goddess,
A victim to the world,
To the Rez, to the projects, had tattoos,
Had a good sense of knowledge,
Yet she still drank and she sniffed nail polish.
She was kicked out at 15,
Turned to the streets,
Hoed to buy clothes,
Hookin' to eat,
So I stopped 'n I thought,
Why does she think the way she thinks?
And most of all, why does she drink the way
she drinks?
She snorted lines,
She was a foster kid,
My bro told me that she was lost in the head,
She was beautiful, got straight A's
Far as I know she was always mean muggin',
Ha, lookin' all rude,
She was a dime lost in her mind,
She was confused,
A victim to the times,
With nothin' to do.
Now she is 20,
And she's just glad to be alive,
Has 2 kids, a girl and a little guy.

She don't know what to do,
She don't know where to go,
She don't know where to run,

She don't wanna go home,
She don't know what to do,
She don't know where to go,
She don't know where to run,
And she don't wanna go home.

She still does drugs,
Now she is back in the streets,
On her back in a Jeep,
In the back of a Jeep,
Tryin' to earn up the cash
From the fronts from last week,
Tryin' to earn up the cash
From the crack from last week,
No food in the kitchen,
The kids are just bitchin',
She has problems, but nobody won't listen,
She is wishin' for the easy way out,
She is tryin' to change,
Fishin' for the easiest clout,
Fryin' her brain—cocaine, crack, gone in her
veins,
No gang, smack gone in her brain.
Kids ballin' every night,
Dyin' for change,
She hears the callin' of the pipe,
It's cryin' her name,
Another Queen turned feen,
With broken-up dreams.
Another teen raised mean,
Choken-up dreams,
She was 25, buried alive up in the woods,
Left her kids behind with their minds bein' so
misunderstood,
This is life, this is life,
It's fucked up, man. This is mix tape, capital

G, Geo aka The Voice.

Things gotta change,

Things gotta change, shit yeah!

In conclusion, then, both graffiti art and hip-hop music produced by contemporary Aboriginal youth represent honest and immensely thoughtful and perceptive reflections on contemporary existence, trauma, concerns, and experiences—experiences we all know about from statistics through the news, as anthropologists, from ethnographic observation, or as members of First Nations community, from our own or our family members' lived experience. In 1996, the Report of the Royal Commission on Aboriginal Peoples identified the situation faced by Aboriginal youth in contemporary and future Canadian society.

> [Aboriginal young people] are the current generation paying the price of cultural genocide, racism and poverty, suffering the effects of hundreds of years of colonialist public policies. The problems that most Aboriginal communities endure are of such depth and scope that they have created remarkably similar situations and responses among Aboriginal youth everywhere. It is a though an earthquake has ruptured their world from one end to another, opening a deep rift that separates them from their past, their history and their culture. They have seen parents and peers fall into this chasm, into patterns of despair, listlessness and self-destruction. They fear for themselves and their future as they stand at the edge. (Canada, RCAP 1996, 149)

Graffiti and hip-hop music of Indigenous youth give expression to these patterns of despair, listlessness, and self-destruction, and to the chasm that separates Aboriginal youth from the past of their ancestors. By telling them as visual or aural stories in the sense I referred to storytelling early in this chapter, they give voice to young Aboriginal people, allowing for creative representation, messaging, commentary visioning of their world, and dialogue with others for the "sharing of coded stories" (hooks 1992). In her discussion of Aotearoa rap, Zemke-White aptly suggests that "rap is inherently configured to express place, names, wh nau, community, historical anger, and racial pride, making it an ideal mechanism for cultural criticism and ethnic affirmations" (2006, 277).

As we have seen, similar to Aotearoa rap, the themes addressed by Aboriginal youth in both visual art and rap song discussed above include and reflect on intertextual references to Aboriginal traditions, the injustices of colonial history and the present conditions—often matters of life, death, and violence—that affect Aboriginal peoples on the rez, no longer insular but closely affected by the city. The examples of graffiti art and rap songs also reflect on environmental destruction and the ghettoized future of kids caught in the space between the city and the rez as "Inner City Bandits" and "Kids with Cans," and thus provide the viewer with moral commentary on how youth experience is affected by global and local environmental destruction. Beyond using Indigenous iconography and messages, these examples of graffiti and rap music, similar to what is produced in other parts of the Indigenous world thrive on visual and verbal imagery, and on the rhythms and rhymes of hip-hop culture[10] as associated with African American ghetto. Intertextual references that weave together textual allusions to American Rap, pop, and hip-hop culture with iconography of past and present Aboriginal culture provide fertile arenas for reflection on the past and the creation of new stories in the present.

By telling us about their experiences in their own voices and from their own perspective, Aboriginal youth also tell us how they see the future of their peoples shaping up, and how they connect to the past of their peoples, thus finding new spaces for their indigeneity, albeit in different shapes and forms than their own parents may expect. As belle hooks has stipulated (1990, 5), the intellectual engagement with popular culture—in this case at the intersection of art, Aboriginal community, and identity—provides a space for critical exchange. It is up to us to read and understand what they say and how they say it, and to listen, because therein lies the future.

Notes

I thank George "Geo" Ignace, Torbin "Alias" Alec, Jesse "Beamo" Seymour, Shawna, Ayla Joe, Lyle Paul, and Dennis "Yams" Michelle for sharing their art, songs, and thoughts. I also thank my husband, Ron Ignace, and the participants of the symposium on Aboriginal peoples in the cities at the 2006 CASCA conference in Montreal for their input and suggestions.

1 I thank Meeka Morgan for pointing out, and putting into practice, the relevance of these concepts to contemporary First Nations research (see Morgan 2005).

2 A seventeenth reserve community, Tskw'aylacw or Pavilion, is part Secwepemc and part Lillooet or st'at'imc.

3 Kamloops has an urban Aboriginal population of several thousand, comprising First Nations people from throughout the Interior and many other Aboriginal Nations across Canada, as well as a constituency of Metis people. For historical and socio-economic reasons, much of Kamloops' urban Aboriginal population is concentrated on the North Shore.

4 The show "Re Tsuwet.s re Secwepemc—Shuswap Photography Then and Now" was co-curated by Marianne Ignace and Sarah Jules. It featured photographs that show the history and decolonization of Secwepemc photography (see Ignace, Ignace, and Etienne 1999).

5 The term "hip-hop culture" refers to the "offbeat" youth culture characterized by its attachment to rap/hip-hop music, style of clothing, language or dialect, gesture, affiliation of style, and taste stemming from the roots of the hip-hop movement.

6 An immense popular and academic interest around graffiti art exists in North America and even more so in Europe, where a World Congress on Graffiti art was held in Vienna in 1997. Web searches reveal nearly 100,000 hits of websites associated with graffiti. For academic works on graffiti, see Wimsatt (1994) and Reisner and Wechsler (1974).

7 The First Nations youth art show was part of a larger show titled *Urban Insights* (Kamloops Art Gallery, May–June 2005), one of the cumulative projects of the SSHRC CURA grant held by the Kamloops Art Gallery and Thompson Rivers University.

8 These songs are part of a growing number of self-produced CDs sold by the young hip-hop artists among local youth of the area.

9 Lyrics from Geo's songs and Sundown Stylistics used with permission.

10 While the linguistic analysis of the rap songs is not the objective of this article, what should be noted is the importance of rhyme in rap music. Rhyme as a poetic device, however, is absent from the production of rhythmic language in the Indigenous languages of Western North America, which feature such stylistic devices as alliteration, onomatopoeia, and chanted rhythmic speech. Even more so than in other parts of Canada, Secwepemctsin and other local Aboriginal languages are critically endangered and have almost ceased to function in daily conversation. Some songs by Geo and the Sundown Stylistics include a few Secwepemc noun words but are otherwise far more influenced by verbal imagery and idioms from black rap music.

Works Cited

Collins, Patricia H. 1990. *Black Feminist Thought: Knowledge, Consciousness, and the Politics of Empowerment.* New York: Routledge, Chapman, and Hall.

Cruikshank, Julie. 1998. *The Social Life of Stories.* Vancouver: University of British Columbia Press.

———. 2005. *Do Glaciers Listen? Local Knowledge, Colonial Encounters, and Social Imagination.* Vancouver: University of British Columbia Press

Daniels, Carmen. 2001. "The Evolution of Culture, Part 1." AYN (Aboriginal Youth Network) Desk. Retrieved December 9, 2007.

Denzin, Norman K. 2001. *Interpretive Interactionism.* Second edition. Applied Social Research Methods Series, volume 16. Thousand Oaks, London, New Dehli: Sage Publications.

Ferrell, Jeff. 1993. *Crimes of Style; Urban Graffiti and the Politics of Criminality.* New York: Garland Publishing.

Guthrie, R. Dale. 2006. *The Nature of Paleolithic Art.* Chicago: University of Chicago Press.

hooks, bell. 1990. Postmodern Blackness. *Postmodern Culture* 1 (1).

———. 1992. *Black Looks [:] Race and Representation.* Boston: South End Press.

Ignace, Marianne. 1999. "Spirit Guardian Questing in the Nineties: A Mother's Thoughts." In *Coyote U: Stories and Teachings from the Secwepemc Education Institute*, edited by P. Murphy, G. Nicholas, and M. Ignace, 184–88. Penticton: Theytus Press.

———. 2005. *The Voices of First Nations Youth as Reflected in Art.* Small Cities CURA Project: Film, 20 min. 4 sec. Filmed and edited by Marianne Ignace.

Ignace, Marianne, and Ron Ignace. 2004. "The Secwepemc: Traditional Resource Use and Rights to Land." In *Native Peoples: The Canadian Experience*, third edition, edited by R. Bruce Morrison and C. Roderick Wilson, 377–99. Toronto: Oxford University Press.

Ignace, Marianne, and George Ignace. 2005. "Tagging, Rapping and the Voices of the Ancestors: Expressing Aboriginal Identity between the Small City and the Rez." In Will Garrett-Petts, ed., *The Small Cities Book*. Vancouver: New Star Books.

Ignace, Marianne, Ronald Ignace and Gerald Etienne. 1999. *Re Tsuwet.s re Secwepemc: The Things We Do*. Catalogue to accompany the Exhibit of Secwepemc Photography, Then and Now, In Commemoration of the Tenth Anniversary of the Partnership between Secwepemc Cultural Education Society and Simon Fraser University. Kamloops Art Gallery 1999. 20 pp.

Kristeva, Julia. 1980. *Desire in Language: A Semiotic Approach to Literature and Art*. New York: Columbia University Press.

LeBlanc, Marie Nathalie. 2006. "Power and Identity Construction: Youth and Hip-Hop Facing Local Issues of Globalization and Popular Culture." Paper presented at the CASCA Conference, 9–14 May, Concordia University, Montreal.

Morgan, Meeka. 2005. "Making Connections with Secwepemc Family through Storytelling: A Journey in Transformative Rebuilding." Unpublished M.A. thesis, Department of Sociology and Anthropology, Simon Fraser University.

Phillips, Susan. 1999. *Wallbangin': Graffiti and Gangs in L.A.* Chicago: University of Chicago Press.

Reisner, Robert, and Lorraine Wechsler. 1974. *Encyclopedia of Graffiti*. New York: Macmillan.

Rose, Tricia. 1994. *Black Noise: Rap Music and Black Culture in Contemporary America*. Middletown, CT: Wesleyan Press, 1994.

Royal Commission on Aboriginal Peoples. 1996. *Perspectives and Realities*. Volume 4 of the Report of the Royal Commission on Aboriginal Peoples. Ottawa: Minister of Supply and Services Canada.

Sarkar, Mela. 2006. "'Pour Connecter avec le Peeps:' Quebequicité and the Quebec Hip-Hop Community." Paper presented at the CASCA Conference, 9–14 May, Concordia University, Montreal.

Teit, James A. 1900. *The Lillooet Indians*. Memoirs, American Museum of Natural History 9 (5). Publications of the Jesup North Pacific Expedition, Vol. 11, Part V. Leiden and NewYork. Reprinted by AMS Press, New York, 1975.

———. 1909. *The Shuswap Indians*. Edited by Franz Boas. Memoirs of the American Museum of Natural History 4 (7); Publications of the Jesup North Pacific Expedition, 2 (7). Leiden and New York. Reprinted by AMS Press, New York, 1975.

Wimsatt, William Upski. 1994. *Bomb the Suburbs: Graffiti, Freight-hopping, Race and the Search for Hip-Hop's Moral Center*. Chicago: The Subway and Elevated Press.

York, Annie, Richard Daly, and Chris Arnett. 1993. *They Write Their Dreams on the Rock Forever: Rock Writings in the Stein River Valley of British Columbia*. Vancouver: Talonbooks.

Zemke-White, Kirsten. 2000. *Rap Music in Aotearoa: A Sociological and Musicological Analysis*. Ph.D. thesis, Department of Sociology, University of Auckland, NZ. http://hdl.handle.net/2292/97.

12
Plains Indian Ways to Inter-Tribal Cultural Healing in Vancouver

Lindy-Lou Flynn

I n 1989, I began to document and analyze the cultural and ceremonial institutions that Aboriginal peoples across Canada have recently developed or revived in response to their shared historical experience of colonialist domination. Primarily, I have focused on methods by which this response (a response that I have termed an "inter-tribal healing and empowerment movement") has been mobilized in the cities, where great numbers of Native people make their homes today.[1] Since 1991, I have conducted an ethnography-based study of the cultural discourse and institutions (which, in part, may be understood as adaptive strategies) developed by Native people who reside in Vancouver, British Columbia, and its neighbouring environs.[2]

For many anthropologists, Northwest Coast territory is synonymous with Franz Boas and potlatches. For most Canadians, as well as for some Aboriginal people themselves, the City of Vancouver is imagined to comprise a Native population of predominantly Northwest Coast people. Over the past few decades, however, Vancouver and its outlying suburbs have increasingly become home for Aboriginal peoples not only from local Northwest Coast islands and villages but from distant culture areas including the Subarctic, Plateau, Eastern Woodlands, and, significantly, the Plains. In this paper, I discuss how and why Plains Indian, or Plains-style, cultural ways, such as sweat lodge ceremonies and powwows, have recently diffused to Vancouver and assertively been activated, primarily by Plains Cree and Lakota cultural leaders, as social and ceremonial cross-cutting institutions in the inter-tribal context of this large coastal city.[3]

Historical Overview: Child Apprehensions and the Banning of Ceremonies

After the BNA or British North American Act of 1867 arbitrarily created a country called "Canada," the federal government quickly introduced the Indian Act of 1876, a legal tool through which they could control Indian lands and resources, schooling, band governments, membership, and a surfeit of other agenda (Purich 1986). Regarding the Indian Act and education, the following statement was made by Prime Minister John A. Macdonald in Canada's House of Commons on 9 May 1883, when his government was considering adopting the American model for "industrial schools":

> When the school is on the reserve, the child lives with its parents, who are savages; he is surrounded by savages and though he may learn to read and write, his habits, and training and mode of thought are Indian. He is simply a savage who can read and write. It has been strongly pressed upon myself, as head of the Department [of Indian Affairs], that Indian children should be withdrawn as much as possible from the parental influence, and the only way to do that would be to put them in central training industrial schools where they will acquire the habits and modes of thought of white men.... That is the system which is largely adopted in the United States.... That is the scheme which I will lay before the House rather later in the week. (House of Commons Debates 1883)

And so the wheels were set in motion for implementing state policies that would incarcerate Indian children for over a hundred years. For generations, thousands of children were legally kidnapped, taken to residential schools sometimes as far away as another province, and kept there for periods of up to ten years. Excesses by authorities ran the gamut through physical, emotional, psychological, and sexual abuse (see Haig-Brown 1988; Flynn 1993; Fournier & Crey 1997; Miller 1996; Milloy 1999). Anthropologist Derek G. Smith has likened residential schools to prisons, using the theories of Michel Foucault (1979). In particular, Smith points out that residential schools kept Indian persons under constant surveillance, referring to Foucault's idea of the ever-pervasive panopticon:

> The conviction that Indians are children, either individually, or collectively as a "race," rationalizes [for the colonizer] the need for them to be "civilized" on the one hand, and also the need for this civilization to be viewed as a problem of guidance, training, direction, "schooling"—a problem of pedagogy, and of being *disciplined* in the sense meant by Foucault (1979). Residential schools are a very powerful instrument of intense surveillance

of a population, and a very powerful instrument for transforming it, of *disciplining* it to be other than it now is. It is indeed an "aggressive" form of intercultural domination ... justified as being for the essential good of the people being dominated as well as for the good of the state, made respectable and acceptable by placing the task of "civilizing aggressively" in the hands of religious agents who are thereby *de facto* collaborators of the state.... My conviction is that the missionaries did as they did because *this was their commission from the state* in the "policy of aggressive civilization." (Smith 1992, 12–14; italics in original)

As the threat of child apprehension to residential schools was slowly winding down in the 1950s, the federal and provincial governments' child welfare system quickly rose up to take its place, accelerating an already firmly established trajectory of terror on the family structure and cultural continuity of Native people in Canada:

> Patrick Johnston, a researcher for the Canadian Council on Social Development, has dubbed the accelerated removal of children beginning in 1959 the "Sixties Scoop," but the wholesale abduction of aboriginal children has persisted long past that decade. By the late 1970s, one in four status Indian children could expect to be separated from his or her parents for all or part of childhood. If non-status and Metis children, on whom statistics were not maintained, are included, the statistics show that one in three, or in some provinces every other aboriginal child, spent part of his or her childhood as a legal ward of the state. In British Columbia, even today, one of three legal wards is a First Nations child. (Fournier and Crey 1997, 88)

Many oppressive amendments have been made to the Indian Act since its inception in 1876, including the criminalization of the Northwest Coast potlatch in 1884 and the Plains Indian sun dance in 1895. An amendment in 1914 outlawed the wearing of any Aboriginal "costume" and further restricted dances and gatherings. Even with some of the more tyrannical laws being quashed after 1951, such as the banning of ceremonies, this act continues to oversee First Nations peoples from cradle to grave. My fieldwork consultants are all survivors of these Indian Act laws and much more. They bring this "baggage of abuse" with them into the contemporary world, and it is this trauma of cultural disruption and dysfunction from which they are attempting to recover, as is evident in the narratives and theoretical discussions below.

Life Stories/Ethnography

In the summer of 1991, I conducted an ethnographic project on the phenomenon of powwows in British Columbia.[4] Almost immediately after beginning my research, I was instructed by Native people in Vancouver that if I wanted to know about Plains ways, I had to see Wally Awasis, Plains Cree, originally from Thunderchild Reserve, Saskatchewan. Wally and his brothers, Kenny, Dale, and Duncan, had formed an influential drum group in Vancouver in 1985 called Arrows To Freedom. The Awasis brothers had become powerful role models, and their drum group had become a vehicle for cultural and spiritual healing. The Awasis family is typical of other Native families in Canada. Out of twelve children, five were apprehended for one residential school, three were taken to a foster home and a separate residential school, while others have met precarious deaths through accident, illness, or alcoholism. Through government interference, this nuclear family was separated into several groups, some family members having no contact with others for ten to fifteen years or more.

Like other residential school "students," Wally Awasis and his siblings had been told repeatedly at school that Indian people and their cultural ways were disgusting and uncivilized. As Wally relates it, the All Saints Indian Residential School in Prince Albert, Saskatchewan, which he attended from 1962 to 1969 with four siblings, including Kenny, left him with a shattered self-esteem, no sense of dignity, and little knowledge of his Plains Cree Indian culture or even of his family. After release, like so many others, Wally spiralled through a cycle of gangs, alcoholism, drug addictions, and prison sentences. His despair brought him finally to drug addiction and severe alcoholism, and he was living on Vancouver's skid row by 1984. The next year, Wally's beloved sister Geraldine, who had been incarcerated in residential school with him, died in Vancouver of cirrhosis of the liver. She was twenty-nine years old. Grief-stricken, Wally made a crucial decision. Rather than hang himself, which was his first considered option, he voluntarily entered the Round Lake Native Treatment Centre near Vernon, B.C., similar to Poundmaker's Lodge in Alberta. Wally Awasis first described his life-transforming experiences at Round Lake to me in 1991. Although he has told me these stories many times since then, I use his first interviews here, as they are the most highly detailed.

> And so I went to Round Lake, and I went there with the idea that I was going to take it *really* serious. And I did. But within those two months that I was there, they taught me ... about being Native, about being proud of

my culture, about saging, about sweetgrass ceremonies, sweat lodge. I learned then that all those ... things that people were telling me in boarding school was false. 'Cause I met a real nice gentleman—his name is Alden Pompana [Dakota Sioux elder], and Alden is my spiritual leader now ... because he saved my life. He taught me about Native Indian spirituality: about the Pipe; about Sundancing; about dancing, drumming, singing; about the heartbeat of the Indian Nation coming from the heart. That feeling you get when you hear that drumbeat is like that time you were in your mother's womb. And all those things: the Indian church, why it was built round and low to the ground—the sweat lodge—why you crawled into it, to humble yourself to the Creator, and why it was built round, just like your mother's womb. I mean that's what it represents is going back into your mother, and being reborn when you come back out.

You could lie down in there; you could sit up, or do the warrior's stance when you're in there.[5] Whatever you want to do when you sweat in there is just like being in your mother's womb. Whichever way you felt comfortable, that's how you prayed. You don't have to sit there with your hands together in a kneeling position. And you could talk about anything you want. And it was in the dark. Totally dark. There was no light in there. And they poured water on the rocks. You know the steam that comes out of it is like your mother's blood, the warmth of your mother's blood. And you feel like, what he said to me was, "You're in a safe place. You're back just like you're back in your mother's womb, and it's not too late to change. Right from this moment on is a new beginning, and every day is a new beginning. Just leave the past behind. Just start all over again. Unload it all here. Let the Creator take it away from you in these tobacco bags." You know ... we make tobacco offerings in these bags and they put them inside a sweat lodge. He says, "Let them go up there. Say whatever you have to say and we'll take those bags down and we'll burn them, and all your prayers will be in these tobacco bags and they'll go up to the Creator because as fast as the smoke rises, your prayers are being heard by the Creator. They're not necessarily being answered that fast, but they're being heard by the Creator. And remember that when you go out into the water (right after you come out of a sweat, you go into the water), you wash all that away."

And to *me*, that made more sense than me burning in hell for my sins. There was a way out. There *was* a way out, y'know. You *can* ask for forgiveness, and no matter who you hurt, or how much you hurt people, or whatever you have in your life, you can forgive yourself. You can forgive *them*, you know, the things that people done to you. And you can work and live with that. And you don't *need* to suffer in prison because of it, the way a lot of our people are now in prisons because, they're in there—they're victims of circumstances. They're not in there because they're mean people or anything like that or they're just criminals. A lot of them are in there because they have no other way of expressing their anger or the bitterness they feel within themselves, or their low self-esteem, and they don't *know* how to get out of it, because nobody's been able to teach them how they can turn themselves around by going back to their culture. And I really believe that culture is healing now.[6]

When Wally returned to Vancouver from treatment, his brothers, Duncan and Dale, put themselves into Round Lake, too. Those three sober brothers then, valiantly, in my estimation, humbly learned some powwow songs from tapes and from elders, and formed the Arrows To Freedom Drum group in an attempt to stay sober, and to pass on the teachings from Round Lake to Urban Indian people who were suffering in the same way as they had been. Kenny is said to have "sobered up at the drum." In other words, Kenny literally stopped drinking the moment he sat down and began drumming and singing with his brothers. All four brothers have been clean and sober since that time.

Because Northwest Coast people, Wally says, practised their hereditary ceremonies in private on their home reserves, the only places that Native people of any culture, including Northwest Coast, could get together in 1985 in Vancouver were the skid-row Indian bars. Wally and his brothers set out to change that. In the space of only a few months, these determined grassroots warriors brought their drum and newly learned powwow songs to a local community centre called Cedar Cottage Neighbourhood House for a small weekly family night created originally by Laverne Williams (Lil'Wat Nation educator). Wally explained to me the obviously desperate need of Indian people for something uplifting and Aboriginal in Vancouver at that time:

> But when I went in there the following year, we were getting two hundred people every Monday night, coming from Anacortes, Washington; Bellingham; coming from Musqueam, Squamish, Mission[7]—all these people wanting to listen to this drumming and singing, and ... a lot of young people, and what we were gearing towards doing there was trying to get the kids, the Indian kids, to deter them, to have someplace to go that's fun, so they didn't have to hang around skid row, to get them away from prostitution, drug abuse, alcoholism, all that stuff, and in the meantime they'd be learning about their culture, respecting themselves, and doing something about their lives, and taking better control and direction of their lives, offering them something that nobody else had ever given them. And it worked! And it attracted them!

Since 1985, the four Awasis brothers have established in and around Vancouver (individually or in conjunction) several drum groups and myriad related ceremonials (such as sweat lodge ceremonies), events (such as powwows and Native Family Nights), cultural programs and workshops (through school boards, friendship centres, and other outlets), and alcohol and drug treatment programs (such as their Alcoholics Anonymous–based Red Road Warriors Support Group) in order to create a sense of community and empowerment for Urban Indians. The work of this family has been seminal and has substantially altered the range of Aboriginal activities available in Vancouver (see Flynn 2004, 456–57).

Some Theoretical Perspectives

One theoretical approach to understanding the texts, actions, and successes of the people with whom I work is based in symbolic anthropology. For my purposes, the idea of symbolic healing as suggested by psychological anthropologist, James B. Waldram, is foremost. Waldram has spent many years interviewing Native men in prairie prisons who have learned about Plains Ways such as drumming, singing, and sweat lodge ceremonies while incarcerated. In fact, the name "Arrows To Freedom," which Wally Awasis chose for his drum group in Vancouver, came from the name of a Native newspaper at Drumheller Penitentiary in Alberta, where Wally did time in 1977. Inspired by the thoughts of prisoners published in this ATF news bulletin, Wally gave tobacco to the Native Brotherhood in prison and asked permission to use the name for a drum group if he ever got sober on the outside. They agreed. It wasn't until 1985 that his transformation occurred. Drumheller Penitentiary was also the place where Wally got a brief taste of drumming and singing, and as he later claimed, kept it in his mind. Writes Waldram:

> Symbolic healing .... is culturally based and, in effect, healer-centred. According to Dow, "the experiences of healers and healed are generalized with culture-specific symbols" (1986, 56), and "the first requirement for symbolic healing is that the culture establishes a general model of the mythic world believed in by healers and potential patients" (1986, 60). Such a model presupposes that both patients and healers share more or less the same culture and world view in order for there to be a successful therapeutic outcome, a principle accepted by other authors as well.... It would be contradictory to suggest that symbolic healing could exist in situations where the cultures, and more specifically the symbols, metaphors, and "mythic world" are not shared between the healer and the patient. (Waldram 1997, 76–77)

Leaders such as the Awasis brothers have been taught and then activated the "symbols, metaphors, and mythic world" inherent in their own Plains ways in order to establish a common ground among the diverse Native cultural groups who are living in Vancouver, and it is precisely this common ground that promotes an inter-tribal healing.

One of the most important symbols of healing for Native people in Vancouver is the drum. Writes Delphine Red Shirt (Oglala Sioux), "In our culture there are no voids. There is a place for everyone, 'Hel iyotaka ye,' in the feminine voice, someone would say, 'Sit down there.' We leave no empty places, especially around the drum. If there is an empty place at the drum, you take up the drumstick and sit down and join in the singing. 'Hel op'a ye,' someone would say. 'Join in. Take part in it.' We are like that—we leave no empty spaces, especially around the drum" (1998, 108).

The drum, in Vancouver as elsewhere in Indian Country, then, is a crucial symbol of healing, empowerment, and the formation of community. Anthropologist Michael Asch has written on the importance of drumming, singing, and dancing as a ritual providing "a profound confirmation of potential community strength and resilience" (1988, 94), and I submit that his argument certainly applies to Vancouver. If I were forced to choose one symbol that characterizes the recovery, power, strength, and unification of inter-tribal Native people in that city, it would be the Plains Indian ground drum—the single most important cross-cutting institution being the drum group, and as an extension of it, the Plains powwow. Red Shirt tells us that the drum leaves no empty places, and Indian Country within the City of Vancouver is no exception. In an overwhelming, sometimes foreign and frightening environment, when an Aboriginal person first moves to the city, the drum at least assures, reassures, makes sure—that a person is not *out of* "place," that a person *has* a place, that a person *knows* his/her place—a place within his/her own people. Whether "sitting at a drum" or beside one, being in a place wherein drummers are drumming and dancers are dancing, or simply knowing and becoming *a part of* the extended families and friends who lead and share drum groups, the drum, in the context of Vancouver, compels Urban Indians to feel comforted and safe. It reminds them of home. It makes Vancouver their home. It establishes or reinforces their identity as Native. Utimately, the drum helps to heal and to empower them. As one long-time Arrows To Freedom drummer and singer, John Quewezance (a Saulteaux foster home survivor, originally from Keesekoose Reserve, Saskatchewan), told me in 1995, "It's something that's mine that's very pure, very strong, and it's healing. It heals, too. It heals the hurts from generations way back."[8] Other than the drum, spiritual symbols such as sweat lodge, sacred pipe, tobacco, eagle feathers, sage, and sweetgrass are also critical in Plains world view.

Briefly then, Vancouver is transformed into inter-tribal Indian Country through the social action of Plains Indian drum groups and spiritual leaders. In this way, sacred space and sacred time are created, through those drum groups and spiritual leaders, in the context of the city. Because the city, in contrast to the reserve, is seen by *some* Native people as a profane space suspended in profane time, the creation of sacred time and sacred space is vital to the spiritual well-being and cultural healing of Urban Indians.[9]

A Discussion of Plains Ways as Cross-Cutting Institutions

There are a plethora of reasons why Plains-style ceremonies work so well as cross-cutting institutions in a city, while Northwest Coast potlatching (or Iroquoian Longhouse ceremonies in the Eastern Woodlands), for example, do not, and in fact, *cannot* be used as cross-cutting institutions due to the nature of hereditary/clan ownership of ceremonies and songs. I argue that complex rules concerning protocol, ownership, and other factors gave rise over the recent past to the introduction and acceptance of Plains culture in a city context. Important here are the differences in world view between the egalitarian Plains-based travelling hunting-and-gathering cultures and the sedentary aristocratic clan systems of peoples such as Northwest Coast and Iroquoians.[10] Part of that egalitarianism, I submit, is that Plains peoples were willing (and able) to share many of their ceremonies with outsiders, allowing for a cross-cultural healing movement to be initiated. As suggested above, this cross-cultural sharing was not possible for some other cultures such as Northwest Coast, as their hereditary chieftainships and family-owned songs, dances, and ceremonies would not/cannot allow for the inclusion of large numbers of outsiders. High numbers of outsiders would need to be incorporated into a hereditary system, and this incorporation could potentially generate traumatic social consequences for insiders. Due literally (one might say) to "structural difficulties," therefore, it would have been impossible for Northwest Coast (or Iroquoian) peoples to offer their cultural ways as cross-cutting institutions in a city such as Vancouver (or Toronto), in which there reside members of dozens of different Native nations.

My contention, then, is that Plains ways have been purposely activated, especially over the past twenty to thirty years (depending on location), in order to precipitate a Canada-wide Aboriginal healing and empowerment movement (which was concentrated, until recently, in the south, and west of Quebec).[11] This inter-tribal movement, in my view, was created by, and continues to emanate from, Native grassroots leaders (mostly Plains Cree, Lakota, Saulteaux, Ojibwe, and Blackfoot) who live and work out of urban areas such as Vancouver, Toronto, Edmonton, Calgary, Saskatoon, and Winnipeg. These leaders are constantly in touch with elders who live primarily on reserves and who act as their teachers, mentors, and spiritual guides.

Admittedly, there is a certain amount of conflict between Plains peoples who live in cities and those who remain on reserve concerning which ceremonies should be shared with outsiders and which should not. Such conflict is continually being dealt with through negotiation, prayer, and protocol.

A Brief Comment on Theories of Cultural Ecology

Anthropologist Robin Ridington has taught that an underlying principle inherent in theories of cultural ecology (Steward 1955, for example) is the idea that the environment presents both "natural opportunities" and "natural limitations" for any given culture. As Ridington has often claimed, "You can't build a pyramid on an ice floe."[12] This encompasses my argument on why Plains ways have been so easily transported and utilized as cross-cutting institutions, especially, for my purposes, in Vancouver (Northwest Coast territory) but in other culture areas, as well. Plains peoples are no longer reliant on buffalo, were never reliant on agriculture, and cars, vans, and trucks have replaced horses—so they can travel wherever they like. They can put up a powwow, sweat lodge ceremony, or a Sun Dance anywhere they choose to do so (as long as that choice is in accordance with proper spiritual protocol). Their central symbol, the large Plains ground drum, travels with them wherever they go. A good example of how another spiritual phenomenon was able to manifest itself across the Plains partly as a result of travel (in this case, the sudden accessibility of railways to Native people) is the Ghost Dance, led by the prophet, Wovoka (see Mooney 1974 [orig. 1896]). Similar to the contemporary Aboriginal healing movement, the Ghost Dance was also needed and wanted at a particular historical moment in Indian Time and it too diffused to other communities where people wanted, needed, and were ready for it (see also Wallace on revitalization movements).

Plains ways, then, are much more easily transported than are the ways (including tangible and intangible symbols, material artifacts, and so on) of some other cultures. Plains peoples are accustomed to packing up and moving on, and when they do so they take their portable symbols and ceremonies with them, and they share them with members of other cultures. A certain generosity of spirit comes into play here, too. Ultimately, Plains peoples share *selected* ceremonies *by choice*. I want to clarify here that not all Plains ceremonies are shared with others. Many are not. There are Plains songs and dances that are family or individually owned and performed only on home reserves, but in my experience, popular perception mistakenly assumes that activities such as public pow-wows are the *only* ceremonies celebrated by Plains peoples.

Another vital point is that while inter-tribal or Plains-based ways of adapting to a city are, indeed, strategies for cultural survival and renewal, they have not become the *exclusive* ways or beliefs held by all urban Aboriginal people. Many Native people in Vancouver, for example, go back and forth between two or more "ways." They have become, then, bi- or tri-cultural. A great number of Northwest Coast people now participate in Plains-style drumming and singing, sweat lodge ceremonies, and powwows. Some have become well-known dancers or drummers on the powwow circuit; however, these same people may speak their own languages, be active in Northwest Coast potlatching, and in some cases may also be leaders and/or participants in strictly Northwest Coast organizations such as the Indian Shaker Church.

Plains ways have become the primary cross-cutting institution in Indian Country across much of North America, especially in cities, but a significant part of the current Aboriginal empowerment movement/process promotes the idea of learning about, and also participating in, the ways of one's culture of origin. In 1991, Wally Awasis explained to me what he told Squamish Nation elders when they called him to their Longhouse at Burrard Reserve (North Vancouver) asking him to explain why he had brought his large Plains Cree drum and ceremonies to their territory (Vancouver):

> So I took my group down there and I spoke to the elders. And they really liked what I had to say. And I told them that we came here because we're lost in the city. We're Urban Indians but we've lost our culture, and since I've come from Round Lake, I've learned that the Indian Way is the better way for Our People, and there was nothing being provided in the cities for our young people. A lot of them were involved in alcohol and drug abuse and prostitution, you know, having sugar daddies and all that stuff downtown, and being taken advantage of. And I said, "I'm not trying to say that this is a better way, that this drum that I have here is better than what you have here," I said, "but what I'm saying is that if this attracts them, then they need a start somewhere, and if this can attract them, then we can also teach them that 'you know, you have your own Way, you have your own culture,' and we always stress to these young people," I said, "to go back and learn your own culture, but this will give you a better appreciation of your culture—it's a start."

The widespread promotion and acceptance of Plains ways has recently inspired Northwest Coast people to celebrate more of their own traditional ceremonies in Vancouver rather than to hold them only on their home reserves. In August of 1999, local community leader Evens Stewart (Nis'ga) explained to me good-naturedly that he was so tired of Plains powwow family nights at the "Indian Centre" that he and some others, including Henry Robertson, Sr. (Kitlope-Kemano master carver), installed their own weekly Northwest Coast Night there in 1999.[13]

Summarizing, I submit that the acceptance of Plains Ways inter-tribally has persuaded other cultures to adapt their own traditions to an ever-expanding Urban Indian population. To take no social action toward cultural adaptation to the city, as non-Plains culture groups will readily acknowledge, means that they risk losing their own people, especially their youth, to a sometimes complete immersion in Plains-style ways. I have often suggested that in a sense Plains Indians actually encouraged Northwest Coast people to adapt their own cultural ways to the city. That said, it is important to note that Plains and Northwest Coast leaders have worked respectfully with one another for decades in the Vancouver area and continue to do so, as discussed below.

The Legacy

In addition to his other endeavours, Wally Awasis was employed as a full-time "Native Child Care Worker and Cultural Teacher" from 1987 to 1999 at Grandview *Uuquinak'uuh* Elementary School on Vancouver's East Side. *Uuquinak'uuh* means "grand view" or "beautiful view" in Nuu-Chah-Nulth (corrective of "Nootka"). This position gave Wally the opportunity of inspiring hundreds of Urban Indian children. He taught them to drum, sing, and dance. He taught them how to put on cultural performances, powwows and Native events both at Grandview School and on nearby reserves and for other Lower Mainland schools. Assisted by Kenny Awasis, he introduced them to sacred ceremonies.

The powwows and Native family nights that were either initiated or greatly expanded since 1985 by Arrows To Freedom in Vancouver have become core traditions in that city. Dozens of powwows now occur in and around Vancouver on a year-round basis, and Kenny Awasis has been joined by others who are conducting sweat lodge ceremonies on local reserves. Powwows can be lavish affairs featuring competition drumming and dancing, with guests from other provinces and the United States, or they can be small local events held in poverty-immersed areas such as Hastings and Main, Canada's poorest street address. There is not one kind of powwow or family night in Vancouver, but many, depending on circumstances. The focus of all of them, however, remains as Arrows To Freedom initially envisioned: identity, spirituality, recovery, and renewal.

These many activities, as well as the work Wally Awasis accomplished at Grandview School over so many years, have also kept countless Native adults and children from being absorbed into the notorious Downtown East Side skid-row area (also referred to in Vancouver as "ten square blocks of hell").

During an interview with Wally in July of 2006, he reminded me that Vancouver does not have any significant or large organized Aboriginal gangs as do many prairie cities. Wally believes that this is partly due to the fact that Arrows To Freedom created a conscious strategy of offering Urban Indians a better way of achieving a sense of identity and status than through a street life predicated on criminal associations and addictions.

This "Indian Way," Wally told me, provides the authentic self-esteem emanating from the pride and positive identification inherent in their own Aboriginal cultures, a philosophy or "Indian theory" constructed and constantly reiterated by Wally, his brothers, and other cultural and spiritual teachers and elders. Wally is convinced that this strategy can be implemented anywhere there are clean and sober Native leaders willing to act as role models, to share traditional teachings, and to organize events and ceremonies for their own disheartened and at-risk Native people.[14] This "front line" approach, as previously discussed in this paper, was taught to Wally at Round Lake Treatment Centre in 1985 and exemplifies the essence of "culture as healing."

In 2004, Wally Awasis graduated with a bachelor of education degree through the well-known and respected Native Indian Teacher Education Program (NITEP) at the University of British Columbia, Vancouver. One year later, he returned to his home reserve at Thunderchild First Nation to teach at the Piyesiw Awasis (Thunderchild) Community School. Wally was promoted to the position of school principal in 2008. He had also been greatly honoured by his own community shortly after his return when he was appointed to a four-year term as Thunderchild First Nation Annual Pow-Wow Committee Coordinator.

Duncan Awasis has served as the Piyesiw Awasis School's cultural advisor and elder, but he has also worked for many years conducting sweat lodge ceremonies and counselling Native prisoners at Prince Albert Penitentiary in Saskatchewan. Since 1985, Duncan has acted as both a ceremonialist and an alcohol and drug abuse counsellor in Native communities all across Western Canada.

Dale Awasis earned a bachelor of education degree in the 1980s at the University of Saskatchewan, and graduated with a master of arts degree in leadership and administration from Gonzaga University at Spokane, Washington State, in 2007. He has simultaneously taught school board curricula and Cree culture and language on reserves all over western

Canada, most recently at Kisipatnahk ("on the hill") School near Hobbema, Alberta, for the Louis Bull Tribe. Also in 2007, Dale Awasis was elected chief of Thunderchild First Nation for a three-year term. In January 2010, he travelled to the United Nations in Geneva, Switzerland, where he spoke on Indigenous rights.

Kenny Awasis continues to organize countless cultural and spiritual events and programs for individuals and organizations, including school boards, in and around Vancouver. In addition to ATF, Kenny has been drumming and singing for many years in Vancouver with the Thunderchild Drum, led by his first cousin, drum-keeper Raymond G. Thunderchild ("Bigfoot"). Raymond's superb singing voice is well known and admired on the powwow circuit. More information about the life history of Ray Thunderchild and about Plains Indian ways, particularly as celebrated and employed as healing strategies on the Northwest Coast, is presented in the book *Spirit of Powwow* by Kay Johnston and Gloria Nahanee (2003). The Squamish Nation, just across the Lion's Gate Bridge from Vancouver, hosted annual powwows from the 1940s to 1958 when they faded out. Squamish Nation leader Gloria Nahanee graciously acknowledges that thirty years later, "Wally Awasis, from the Arrows to Freedom Drum, encouraged me to revive the Squamish Nation Powwow. His support and advice were precious to me. Ray Thunderchild's dedication to the Powwow Trail, and his support and advice have helped me through the difficult and the happy times as we worked to bring back the powwow to my Squamish Nation" (Johnston and Nahanee 2003, 4).

Over the past twenty-five years all four Awasis brothers have earned the privilege of conducting a plethora of traditional Plains Cree spiritual ceremonies, and are increasingly invited to do so across Canada and into the United States. The ATF Drum still travels with Wally and is activated whenever he chooses to do so.

The highly respected Dakota Sioux elder and ceremonial leader, Alden Pompana, originally from Sioux Valley, Manitoba, now conducts his ongoing and much appreciated cultural healing work out of the City of Prince George, B.C., but travels extensively.

Conclusion

Plains Indian Ways continue to breathe life into Native people in the intertribal heart of Vancouver, healing "the hurts from generations way back"[15] and inspiring pride in being Aboriginal to a new amalgamation of Urban Indians, many of whom were guided at some point in their lives by the Awasis family.

Figure 1 Duncan Awasis, Kenny Awasis. Front (L–R): Alden Pompana, Dale Awasis, Wally Awasis. Founders of Arrows To Freedom Drum and Dance Society with their spiritual advisor, Alden Pompana, at a Plains Cree "Spirit Welcoming Ceremony" for Wapastim Acaak Awasis, baby son of Wally Awasis and Victoria Stevens, 13 November 1998, Surrey, B.C. Photo by Lindy-Lou Flynn.

True to their original motto of 1985, Wally, Kenny, Dale, and Duncan Awasis epitomize their philosophy: "Arrows To Freedom: Freedom from Alcohol and Drugs. Sobriety in Action." True to their elders' teachings, they are keeping the circle strong.

Acknowledgements

I am grateful to the countless Native people who have informed my research for over two decades. I also thank anthropologist Allan J. Ryan for the pivotal role he played in my initial powwow ethnography project in 1991 in southwestern British Columbia and Washington State. Research for this paper was supported in part by Multiculturalism Canada (the Multiculturalism Directorate of the Secretary of State, 1991); a Graduate Research Award from the University of Western Ontario, 1992; a Social Sciences and Humanities Research Council of Canada (SSHRCC) grant, "Cultural and Linguistic Correlates of Reserve English among Mohawk and Ojibwe Speakers in Southwestern Ontario" (Regna Darnell and Lisa P. Valentine, project supervisors) 1992/93; the Explorations Division of the Canada Council, Ottawa, 1993/94; by SSHRCC Doctoral Fellowships at the University of Alberta, 1995–1999; a University of Alberta Department of Anthropology/Faculty of Graduate Studies Research Grant, 1999; and by Province of Alberta Graduate Fellowships, 1999–2001.

Notes

1 Many scholars apply the term "pan-Indian" to any event or phenomenon that involves a mixing or sharing of different Native nations and their cultural ways, structures, institutions, or symbols. I find this term problematic and prefer to talk about such things as "inter-tribal," a term used by Native people themselves to describe, for example, a special powwow dance that calls forth people of all nations to come forward and join each other in a particular type of social dance. I submit that the term "inter-tribal" is more accurate and respectful than the ubiquitous "pan-Indian," a descriptor that creates the false and misleading notion that Native people are somehow rendered "all alike" should they decide to share or mix certain beliefs, symbols, ways, or places as situational adaptive strategies.

2 This paper is a revised and updated version of a presentation I gave at the British Museum in London, England, in February 2003 for Pow-Wow: Performance and Nationhood in Native North America/An Ethnography Conference, organized by Dr. Jonathan King and Dr. Richard Storrie.

3 I use the expressions "Indian" and "Urban Indian" because they are employed so consistently by the Native people with whom I work. In a range of scenarios, it is considered quite pretentious to be dropping the terms "First Nations" or "Aboriginal," especially on the East Side of Vancouver. One of the drum groups I have documented called itself Indian Time, and sayings such as Indian Tacos, Indian Candy (dried sweet salmon), Indian Country, Indian Healings, Indian Medicine, and the Indian Way are used with great pride by my consultants, as is the common expression "Urban Indian." A popular e-mail and text messaging shortcut recently developed by Native people to describe themselves online is NDN. This acronym is included in a recent Aboriginal publication out of Winnipeg, Manitoba, titled *Urban NDN*. For many younger Native people, the terms Urban Indian and NDN are not only acceptable but empowering. For older Native people, these expressions can be comfortable and familiar. Aside from generational criteria, urban phraseology is also determined by factors such as place of birth or length of stay in the city and by regional or tribal differences. There is much more to consider on this topic, but those discussions are beyond the scope and intent of this paper. Ultimately, however, I am of the mind that when my fieldwork consultants stop speaking and writing the terms "Indian" and "Urban Indian," I will follow suit.

4 In 1991, I was contracted through the Museum of Anthropology (MOA) at the University of British Columbia in Vancouver, and by Multiculturalism Canada/Ottawa, to research the phenomenon of powwows in British Columbia. See Works Cited for further information. This project has developed into long-term fieldwork that has informed both my Ph.D. dissertation on Urban Indians in Vancouver and a book manuscript nearing completion on Arrows To Freedom and the Awasis family.

5 Wally Awasis has explained to me that the "warrior's stance" refers to when a person (usually a man) goes down on one knee (usually the right knee), bending his right arm and holding his right clenched fist up to the sky, over the fire in a sweat lodge but also displayed in other private and public contexts and situations (symbolic of victory for Plains Indian warriors).

6 All quotes from Wallace James (Wally) Awasis were recorded by the author during fieldwork that took place 4 September 1991, East Side, Vancouver, B.C., unless otherwise noted.

7 Locations are: Anacortes, Washington State; Bellingham, Washington State; Musqueam Reserve, Vancouver; Squamish Nation Reserve, North Vancouver; and Mission, B.C., in the Fraser Valley.
8 Fieldwork Interview with Albert John (Johnny "Q") Quewezance, recorded by the author 1 August 1995, East Side, Vancouver, B.C.
9 See the works of Victor Turner for his discussions on the sacred and the profane.
10 See classic works by Franz Boas, Edward Sapir, and Philip Drucker for Northwest Coast; Clark Wissler, Robert H. Lowie, and John C. Ewers for the Plains; and Lewis Henry Morgan for the Iroquois.
11 In 1976, Wendy Wickwire published a compelling paper in the *Canadian Journal for Traditional Music* titled "Traditional Musical Culture at the Native Canadian Centre in Toronto." This paper is a discussion on the influx of Aboriginal people to Toronto, focusing on southern Ojibwe. It is one of the earliest scholarly discussions I have found on the diffusion of Plains-style drumming and singing to a Canadian city outside the Plains culture area (in this case via Detroit). This paper is a seminal work on Urban Indians and on Native cultural healing in Canada.
12 Personal Communication with Robin Ridington, 1991, University of British Columbia, Department of Anthropology and Sociology.
13 Fieldwork Interview with Evens Stewart recorded by the author 20 August 1999, East Side, Vancouver, B.C.
14 Fieldwork interview with Wally Awasis July 2006, Edmonton, Alberta.
15 Fieldwork interview with Albert John (Johnny "Q") Quewezance, recorded by the author 1 August 1995, East Side, Vancouver, B.C.

Works Cited

Asch, Michael. 1988. Kinship and the Drum Dance in a Northern Dene Community. Originally published in 1969; 1988 version is updated. Canada: Boreal Institute for Northern Studies. Academic Printing & Publishing.
Dow, J. 1986. "Universal Aspects of Symbolic Healing: A Theoretical Synthesis." *American Anthropologist* 88: 56–69.
Flynn, Lindy-Lou. 1991. "The Role of Pow-Wows in the Construction and Perception of Native Identity in Southwestern British Columbia." Fieldwork archives and final report to Multiculturalism Canada (Multicultural Directorate of the Secretary of State) and Museum of Anthropology (MOA), University of British Columbia, Vancouver.
———. 1993. "'To Break the Conspiracy of Silence': A Healing and Empowerment of Native Peoples across Canada." Unpublished master's thesis. Department of Anthropology, University of Western Ontario, London, Ontario.
———. 2004. "Wally Awasis: Adaptation and Transformation in Vancouver." In *Native Peoples: The Canadian Experience,* third edition, edited by R. Bruce Morrison and C. Roderick Wilson, 456–57. Don Mills, ON: Oxford University Press.
Fournier, Suzanne, and Ernie Crey. 1997. *Stolen from Our Embrace. The Abduction of First Nations Children and the Restoration of Aboriginal Communities.* Vancouver: Douglas & McIntyre.
Foucault, Michel. 1979. *Discipline and Punish. The Birth of the Prison.* New York: Random House.
Haig-Brown, Celia. 1988. *Resistance and Renewal. Surviving the Indian Residential School.* Vancouver: Tillacum Library.

Johnston, Kay, and Gloria Nahanee (illustrations by Susanne Lansonius). 2003. *Spirit of Powwow*. Surrey, BC: Hancock House Publishers.

Macdonald, Prime Minister John A. 1883. House of Commons Debates, 46 Vict. 1883, vol. 14 at 1107–08.

Miller, J.R. 1996. *Shingwauk's Vision: A History of Native Residential Schools.* Toronto: University of Toronto Press.

Milloy, John. 1999. *A National Crime. The Canadian Government and the Residential School System, 1879 to 1986.* Winnipeg: University of Manitoba Press.

Mooney, James. 1974. *The Ghost Dance Religion and Wounded Knee.* New York: Dover Publications. Originally published in 1896 by the Government Print Office, Washington.

Purich, Donald. 1986. *Our Land. Native Rights in Canada.* Toronto: James Lorimer & Company.

Red Shirt, Delphine. 1998. *Bead on an Anthill. A Lakota Childhood.* Lincoln and London: University of Nebraska Press.

Smith, Derek G. 1992. "'Governmentality,' Indian Residential Schools, and the Canadian Policy of 'Aggressive Civilization' in the Late Nineteenth Century Northwest Territories." Paper presented at the Canadian Anthropology Society/ societé d'anthropologie canadienne (CASCA) 19th Annual Meetings at Montréal, Québec.

Steward, Julian. 1955. *Theories of Culture Change.* Urbana: University of Illinois Press.

Waldram, James B. 1997. *The Way of the Pipe: Aboriginal Spirituality and Symbolic Healing in Canadian Prisons.* Peterborough, ON: Broadview Press.

Wallace, Anthony F.C. 1956. "Revitalization Movements." *American Anthropologist* 58: 264–81.

Wickwire, Wendy. 1976. "Traditional Musical Culture at the Native Canadian Centre in Toronto." *Canadian Journal for Traditional Music* 4. http://cjtm .icaap.org/content/4/v4art10.html.

Contributors

Lynda Brown was born in Nunavut, and her family originates from Pangnirtung and Scotland. She lived mainly in Alberta and Ontario while growing up. Upon graduating from Trent University with an Honours B.A. in Native studies and psychology, she moved to Ottawa. Lynda volunteers her time, focusing on Inuit women, children and affordable housing. Lynda is a traditional throat singer and drummer, and shares her cultural knowledge through demonstrations and workshops.

Kathleen Buddle is an associate professor of anthropology at the University of Manitoba. Her research addresses First Nations media activism in Canada; cultural performance and politics in urban Aboriginal localities; Native street gangs, the manufacturing of prairie lawlessness and disciplining of the bodies of criminal others; and the authorizing of new social categories by Native women's organizations as they struggle to shift public debates about Native families onto more productive terrain.

Regna Darnell is Distinguished University Professor of Anthropology and First Nations Studies at the University of Western Ontario and holds a cross-appointment in ecosystem health in the Schulich School of Medicine and Dentistry. She has published widely in First Nations languages and cultures, especially Anishinaabeg and Plains Cree.

Sadie Donovan is a Ph.D. student of Anglo-Celtic settler ancestry. She is completing her degree at Simon Fraser University in British Columbia and is interested in research pertaining to the equitable education of Aboriginal youth.

Lindy-Lou Flynn is a cultural anthropologist who has conducted fieldwork in Aboriginal communities for over twenty years, primarily in western Canada. Her focus is on the healing and empowerment movement initiated by Native people in their ongoing recovery from colonialism. She is a full-time instructor of anthropology and Native studies at Keyano College in Fort McMurray, Alberta.

Marianne Boelscher Ignace teaches at Simon Fraser University. Her interests include the politics and negotiation of meaning in indigenous-language discourse and knowledge systems, including ecological knowledge. She has carried out long-term collaborative ethnographic and linguistic research with the Secwepemc and Haida peoples, which has resulted in various monographs, journal articles, and book contributions.

Heather A. Howard teaches at Michigan State University and is affiliated faculty with the Centre for Aboriginal Initiatives at the University of Toronto. Her research examines the politics of knowledge production and practice in community-based health education, social service delivery, and indigenous historiographies of urban space. She is the co-editor of *Feminist Fields: Ethnographic Insights* (1999) and *Keeping the Campfires Going: Native Women's Activism in Urban Areas* (2009).

Heidi Langille, with roots in Nunatsiavut (Northern Labrador), has been a "life-long Urban Inuk." She has travelled across the North in different capacities, meeting new people and learning from them. Heidi volunteers her time, with a focus on children and affordable housing. She has given many presentations and interactive demonstrations on Inuit culture, heritage, values, and beliefs, including traditional throat singing.

Darrel Manitowabi is an assistant professor of Native studies at the University of Sudbury College, Laurentian University. He is a citizen of the Wikwemikong Unceded First Nation and currently resides on the Whitefish River First Nation. Manitowabi's research interests include indigenous well-being, indigenous anthropology, Anishinabe Kendasawin (Ojibwa knowledge), and indigenous–state relations.

Jaimy L. Miller is from Edmonton, Alberta, and is a descendent of the Papaschase Band. She completed her M.A. in anthropology in 2006 and her master of public administration in 2010. She is currently working in the field of Aboriginal relations in Edmonton.

David Newhouse is Onondaga from the Six Nations of the Grand River near Brantford, Ontario. He is chair of the Department of Indigenous Studies at Trent and an associate professor in the Business Administration Program. His research interests focus on the development of modern Aboriginal society. He visits Starbucks as often as possible.

Donna Patrick is a professor in the School of Canadian Studies and the Department of Sociology and Anthropology at Carleton University, Ottawa. Her current research focuses on urban Inuit and more specifically on Inuit literacies and community-based activities, which connect Inuit in Ottawa to the arctic. Other interests include indigenous rights and language rights, and language endangerment discourse, including the political, social, and cultural aspects of language use among indigenous peoples in Canada.

Craig Proulx is an associate professor in the Department of Anthropology at St. Thomas University in Fredericton, New Brunswick. His research focuses on Aboriginal peoples in Canada (urban and rural), legal anthropology, anthropology of sport, anthropology of media, and critical discourse analysis. His book *Reclaiming Aboriginal Justice, Identity and Community* is based on fieldwork with the Community Council Project in Toronto.

Julie Tomiak is a Ph.D. candidate in Canadian Studies, with a specialization in political economy, at Carleton University. Her research focuses on the changing relationships between indigeneity, space, public policy, and rights. Her dissertation examines how neoliberal state rescaling and indigenous struggles for self-determination intersect in Ottawa and Winnipeg.

Mihaela Ecaterina Vieru is a Ph.D. candidate in the program of Canadian Studies, with a specialization in political economy, at Carleton University, Ottawa. She has an M.A. degree in Canadian studies from Carleton University (2006). Her research interests focus on ethnicity, multiculturalism, integration, citizenship, and national security in Canadian and international contexts.

Index

Books in the Aboriginal Studies Series
Published by Wilfrid Laurier University Press

Blockades and Resistance: Studies in Actions of Peace and the Temagami Blockades of 1988–89 / Bruce W. Hodgins, Ute Lischke, and David T. McNab, editors / 2003 / xi + 276 pp. / map, illustrations / ISBN 0-88920-381-4

Indian Country: Essays on Contemporary Native Culture / Gail Guthrie Valaskakis / 2005 / x + 293 pp. / photos / ISBN 0-88920-479-9

Walking a Tightrope: Aboriginal People and Their Representations / Ute Lischke and David T. McNab, editors / 2005 / xix + 377 pp. / photos / ISBN 978-0-88920-484-3

The Long Journey of a Forgotten People: Métis Identities and Family Histories / Ute Lischke and David T. McNab, editors / 2007 / viii + 386 pp. / maps, photos / ISBN 978-0-88920-523-9

Words of the Huron / John L. Steckley / 2007 / xvii + 259 pp. / ISBN 978-0-88920-516-1

Essential Song: Three Decades of Northern Cree Music / Lynn Whidden / 2007 / xvi + 176 pp. / photos, musical examples, audio CD / ISBN 978-0-88920-459-1

From the Iron House: Imprisonment in First Nations Writing / Deena Rymhs / 2008 / ix + 147 pp. / ISBN 978-1-55458-021-7

Lines Drawn upon the Water: First Nations and the Great Lakes Borders and Borderlands / Karl S. Hele, editor / 2008 / xxiii + 351 pp. / illustrations, maps / ISBN 978-1-55458-004-0

Troubling Tricksters: Revisioning Critical Conversations / Linda M. Morra and Deanna Reder, editors / 2009 / xii + 336 pp. / illustrations / ISBN 978-1-55458-181-8

Aboriginal Peoples in Canadian Cities: Transformations and Continuities / Heather A. Howard and Craig Proulx, editors / 2011 / viii + 256 pp. / colour and b/w photos / ISBN 978-1-55458-260-0